Social Security

STUDIES IN GOVERNMENT
AND PUBLIC POLICY

SOCIAL

SECURITY

History and

Politics from the

New Deal to

the Privatization

Debate

Daniel Béland

University Press of Kansas

© 2005 by the University Press of Kansas
All rights reserved

Published by the University Press of
Kansas (Lawrence, Kansas 66045), which
was organized by the Kansas Board of
Regents and is operated and funded by
Emporia State University, Fort Hays State
University, Kansas State University,
Pittsburg State University, the University
of Kansas, and Wichita State University

Library of Congress Cataloging-in-
Publication Data

Béland, Daniel.
  Social security : history and politics
from the new deal to the privatization
debate / Daniel Beland.
        p. cm.
  Includes bibliographical references
and index.
    ISBN 0-7006-1404-4 (cloth : alk. paper)
    ISBN 978-0-7006-1404-2 (cloth : alk.
paper)
    ISBN 0-7006-1522-9 (paper : alk. paper)
    ISBN 978-0-7006-1522-3 (paper : alk.
paper)
  1. Social security—United States.   I.
Title.
  HD7125.B23 2005
  368.4'3'00973—dc22
                    2005010055

British Library Cataloguing-in-Publication
Data is available.

Printed in the United States of America

10 9 8 7 6 5 4 3

The paper used in this publication meets
the minimum requirements of the
American National Standard for
Permanence of Paper for Printed Library
Materials Z39.48–1992.

CONTENTS

More than seventy years after President Franklin Delano Roosevelt pushed for the enactment of a federal old age insurance program, the future of Social Security has become a major source of concern for citizens and politicians alike. Yet, during the first mandate of President George W. Bush, the so-called "war on terror" and the debate over access to prescription drugs for Medicare recipients overshadowed this major issue. However, the last weeks of the 2004 presidential campaign witnessed a significant comeback of Social Security reform on the federal political scene. During the third presidential debate, President Bush reaffirmed the idea that a portion of the payroll tax should be channeled into personal savings accounts. Democratic candidate John Kerry opposed this idea, arguing that it would put the future of Social Security at risk. After his reelection, President Bush launched a campaign in favor of Social Security privatization. There is a strong ideological commitment in the White House regarding this issue, and partial privatization could have helped President Bush build a meaningful legacy in domestic policy. Unfortunately for the president, the institutional and political obstacles to comprehensive reform remained formidable, and Social Security is still known as the "third rail of American politics." In such a context, President Bush's campaign went nowhere. But this outcome did not eliminate the widely shared concerns about the future of Social Security.

I wrote this book in order to shed light on the past, present, and future of Social Security reform. In that regard, I believe that knowledge of the international and comparative literature on social policy is crucial to understanding what is at stake in the current Social Security debate. Such a new comparative insight should help the reader better understand what is specific about the politics of Social Security in the United States. I also think that history is another useful way to put the current debate over Social Security reform in perspective. Social Security is the product of more than six decades of history, and knowledge about how this program has changed over time as a political issue could help citizens and scholars to make sense of the apparently technical discussions about Social Security retrenchment and restructuring.

I also decided to write this book to contribute to broader theoretical debates about policymaking and welfare state development. The starting point of my reflection on social policy is historical institutionalism, an approach I discovered when I was a graduate student. Although I have long embraced this approach, I believe that the study of ideas should supplement the traditional analysis of political institutions and policy legacies. The approach sketched in Chapter 1 of this book could prove useful to the analysis of Social Security politics and, more generally, of policymaking and welfare state development, in the United States and abroad.

Another crucial debate I tackle in this book is the one on the influence of race and gender on American social policy. I feel that these two factors must become permanent elements of the mainstream literature on social policy analysis in the United States. Yet the assumption that race and gender matter should not lead to the idea that these two factors always exert a direct political influence across policy areas. Major variations exist from one program to another, and this book underlines what is specific about the political relationship among gender, race, and Social Security history. Although I show that there is no direct evidence that race strongly impacted the development of Social Security, I also acknowledge the direct influence of race in other policy areas and in American politics at large. Finally, I show how gender, as opposed to race, had a traceable impact on Social Security development in the United States.

This book is written in such a way that both academics and informed readers should get something from it. Academics will find a critical discussion of the existing literature on American social policy as well as theoretical insights about welfare state development and the role of ideas and institutions in policymaking. Informed readers will find a concise exploration of the manner in which the politics of Social Security evolved over time. This exploration is not overly technical, and I have tried to avoid jargon as much as possible. Furthermore, the book presents the history of the program in a chronological way. Too many social science books are difficult to read because the exposition of the empirical material reflects abstract theoretical considerations that obscure the story being told. I hope that I avoided this pitfall and that the readers will find the integration of the theoretical and the historical aspects of the book compelling. I wrote this book with a broad audience in mind.

I conducted a significant portion of the research for this book in the context of a Ph.D. dissertation, which was later published in France as *Une sécurité libérale?* in 2001. Instead of translating that work into English, I decided to write a new book that would address broader theoretical and historical issues. Because I worked on this project for almost a decade, many people helped me along the road. First, I would like to thank the original members of my Ph.D. committee: Robert Castel, Anne-Marie-Guillemard, John Myles, Pierre Rosanvallon (chair), and Bruno Théret. I owe a special debt to John Myles, who encouraged me to write this book in the first place. John is a model for young scholars who seek serious academic work while keeping their minds open.

I am also greatly indebted to Edward Berkowitz and Jill Quadagno. As reviewers for the University Press of Kansas, they provided insightful comments on my manuscript. Thank you to Larry DeWitt, chief historian of the Social Security Administration, who took the time to provide detailed comments on the first draft of the book. DeWitt also gave me a copy of his unpublished paper on race and Social Security, which I found very stimulating. I would also like to thank my editor, Fred Woodward, and the wonderful team at the University Press of Kansas. Fred is an experienced editor, and I benefited from his advice when preparing the final draft of this work.

Other people helped me along the road. Among them, David Moss, who provided comments on one of the chapters; Jacob Hacker, who helped me clarify many of the theoretical issues; Stephen Skowronek, who introduced me to historical institutionalism; and Kent Weaver, who knows so much about pension reform and who helped me as much as he could despite his busy life. Along the way, I was also helped by the following scholars: Andrew Achenbaum, Lucy apRoberts, Karen Anderson, Robert Ball, Brian Balogh, Fred Block, Sarah Brooks, Herb Emery, Christoffer Green-Pedersen, Peter Hall, Estelle James, Steve Kay, Eric Laursen, André Lecours, Patrik Marier, Casey Mulligan, Andrew Rich, Ronen Shapira, Toshimitsu Shinkawa, Theda Skocpol, Steve Teles, Larry Thompson, François Vergniolle de Chantal, Alex Waddan, Bill Wilson, and John Williamson. At the University of Calgary, my colleagues—especially Art Frank, Tom Langford, and Bob Stebbins—provided advice and encouragement.

Many institutions supported this project over the years. First, the Social Sciences and Humanities Research Council of Canada, the Canada-U.S. Fulbright Program, and the Social Sciences Division of the University of Chicago provided financial support for the initial research stage of my dissertation. Second, I had the privilege of holding visiting appointments at the following institutions: Harvard University (Malcolm Wiener Center for Social Policy, Kennedy School of Government), University of Chicago (Social Sciences Division), George Washington University (History Department), and the National Academy of Social Insurance. Finally, the University of Calgary provided me with a stable academic position and a timely sabbatical leave in the fall of 2004. I am grateful to these institutions and the people who make them great.

My wife, Angela, read every single sentence of this book more than once, and her advice proved extremely useful. More important, she provided the moral and emotional support I needed, in good and bad times. Although my parents never attended college, they have always respected my choice to become an academic. Thank you so much to them and to the rest of my family!

Note on the Paperback Edition

For this paperback edition, I edited the book from cover to cover, adding a few new references and editing or inserting sentences when necessary. Although this is not a "revised edition" in the strict sense of the term, I enacted significant editorial changes in order to increase the book's coherence and the readability. In Chapter 6, I updated some of the information about President Bush's 2005 Social Security campaign, which is further discussed in the new afterword.

Calgary, Canada

AALL	American Association for Labor Legislation
AAOAS	American Association for Old-Age Security
AARP	American Association of Retired Persons
AB	Aid to the Blind
ADC	Aid to Dependent Children
AFDC	Aid to Families with Dependent Children
AFGE	American Federation of Government Employees
AFL	American Federation of Labor
AMA	American Medical Association
APTD	Aid to the Permanently and Totally Disabled
CES	Committee on Economic Security
CIO	Congress of Industrial Organizations
COLA	Cost of Living Adjustment
CWM	[House] Committee on Ways and Means
EPIC	End Poverty in California
ERISA	Employee Retirement Income Security Act
FC	[Senate] Finance Committee
GDP	gross domestic product
IRA	Individual Retirement Account
NAACP	National Association for the Advancement of Colored People
NCSC	National Council of Senior Citizens
NDC	notional defined contribution
NFFE	National Federation of Federal Employees
NFIB	National Federation of Independent Business
NRPB	National Resources Planning Board
OAA	Old-Age Assistance
OASDI	Old Age Survivor and Disability Insurance
OASI	Old Age and Survivor Insurance
OBRA	Omnibus Budget Reconciliation Act
PAYGO	pay-as-you-go
PBGC	Pension Benefit Guaranty Corporation

SSA   Social Security Administration
SSB   Social Security Board
SSI   Supplemental Security Income
UAW   United Automobile Workers
UMW   United Mine Workers

In the world of modern welfare states, American social policy is often described as "exceptional." Social Security, however, is the exception within the exception. Although the American welfare state is a fragmented system in which "residual" public policies tend to supplement—and compensate for the lacunae of—private benefits,[1] Social Security stands as a quasi-universal and comprehensive social insurance scheme. Even though personal savings and private benefits play a significant role in the field of old age security, the federal social insurance program created in 1935 still represents the most central element of America's retirement system.

Covering the vast majority of American workers,[2] the popular Social Security program is widely perceived as the "third rail of American politics" (touch it and you die). Yet, as in most advanced industrial countries, a debate over the future of Social Security has been raging in the United States since the late 1970s.[3] Although the American demographic situation is more favorable than the one prevailing in many of those other advanced industrial countries, conservatives have long argued that pay-as-you-go (PAYGO) pension systems such as Social Security are financially unsustainable and that a restructuring of that program is necessary. Depicting Social Security as unfair toward young workers and future generations, conservatives assert that Social Security should become a fully funded system in which workers would contribute to personal savings accounts. Labeled as Social Security privatization, such a shift from defined-benefit to defined-contribution pensions would constitute a radical change in the structure of the program. Despite the fact that the "double payment" problem—workers must pay for current pensions while putting money aside in individual accounts for their own pensions—would complicate the implementation of full Social Security privatization, a *partial* shift to individual accounts is possible, and in recent years, countries such as Sweden have opted for that model.[4]

Underlining the long-standing popularity of the program and the risks associated with Social Security privatization, many experts and politicians firmly oppose this proposed policy alternative. For them, Social Security is a great program that protects the large majority of the workforce *and* reduces poverty among the elderly. Furthermore, defenders of Social Security argue that it offers defined-benefit pensions that better protect individuals against economic insecurity than defined-contribution savings schemes, depicted as vulnerable to ill-advised investment choices and stock market downturns. From their perspective, carving personal savings accounts out of the existing program could prove especially detrimental to women, African Americans, and other minorities who are more dependent on Social Security for their retirement support than are middle-class white males. Proponents also argue that higher administrative costs inherent to individual accounts could penalize workers, especially those with low incomes.[5]

Using this debate as a starting point, this book has four main, closely related, objectives. First, it reconstructs the political history of Social Security in order to show how this program has changed as an issue over time, and it sheds light on the current debate over Social Security privatization. Second, it offers new comparative insights about this history that could improve our understanding of the current debate. Third, it formulates an original theoretical framework that underlines the relationship between ideas and institutions in policymaking. Finally, the book draws on this theoretical framework to discuss the potential impact of gender and race in Social Security development.

History and the Debate over Social Security Privatization

A stimulating way to understand current policy debates is to take a long-term historical perspective and look at how a specific program emerged and developed over time. As scholars such as Paul Pierson have demonstrated, timing and historical sequence impact policy outcomes. Social programs create specific economic logics and political constituencies that have an effect on future reform attempts.[6] Furthermore, the structure of these programs affects the way in which reform is conducted. Finally, path dependence shapes policy ideas as well as institutions and programs. Knowing the arguments that were used to justify the enactment and the expansion of Social Security contributes to our understanding of the contemporary debate over privatization as policymakers borrow from a relatively stable ideological repertoire in order to promote specific policy alternatives. As I show, the rhetoric advanced to support Social Security privatization today is strikingly similar to the one used in the past to legitimize federal social insurance. Because the American ideological repertoire is centered on individualism and self-reliance, there is little room for discourse about social solidarity in the field of social policy reform.

Comparative Insight

Most books dealing with Social Security history in the United States contain little reference to the experience of foreign nations in the field of pension reform.[7] Although exceptional in many regards, the American situation is commensurable to the one prevailing in other advanced industrial countries, and studies have shown that one can gain crucial insight from comparative research on welfare state development.[8] The comparative data discussed throughout this book underline both the common international features and the peculiarities of American Social Security history. On the one hand, Social Security is a pay-as-you-go program grounded in the same institutional logic as other public pension schemes. On the other hand, the exclusion of labor and business officials from the management of Social Security and the individualistic discourse used to legitimize the program constitute original traits that contrast with the situation prevailing in other advanced industrial countries such as Canada, France, Germany, Sweden, and the United Kingdom. This book draws upon the existing comparative literature on social policy in order to place Social Security history in a broad international context.

Ideas and Institutions

Since the beginning of the 1980s, historical institutionalism has emerged as one of the more influential theoretical perspectives in social sciences and public policy studies. Imagined as an alternative—and sometimes as a supplement—to approaches focusing on economic development, class inequality, and cultural values, historical institutionalism is grounded in the assumption that political institutions and previously enacted public policies structure the political behavior of bureaucrats, elected officials, and interest groups during the policymaking process. Although insightful, this approach tends to relegate policy ideas to the back of the theoretical burner when dealing with welfare state politics. This underestimation of the policy impact of ideas is detrimental to our understanding of social policy reform and, especially, Social Security politics. Here, I develop a theoretical framework about the role of ideas that improves the explanatory power of historical institutionalism while helping students of public policy grasp how and when ideas matter in social policy reform. Tied to existing policy legacies, perceived social problems mesh with policy alternatives grounded in specific paradigms. During the 1930s, for example, a paradigm rooted in fiscal conservatism guided the elaboration of the federal old age insurance program. When stressing the "need to reform" and promoting new policy alternatives, politicians and reformers frame the issues while drawing on the common ideological repertoire available in their society. For example, references to personal responsibility and self-reliance are often called on to justify social programs in American society. The ability to successfully construct policy issues within traditional ideological frames is a major aspect of the political process, before, during, and after the legislative moment.

This history of Social Security is thus structured by theoretical insight about the relationship between ideas and institutions in Social Security development. This close articulation between theory and history has two consequences. On the one hand, by recognizing that institutionalist arguments are relevant to the analysis of Social Security reform, my analysis shows how a more direct and systematic discussion concerning ideational processes can shed an interesting light on the program's fate. On the other hand, reconstructing the long-term history of a major program like Social Security is an excellent way to show the insightfulness of the amended historical institutionalist approach put forward in Chapter 1.

Race and Gender in Social Security History

Since the late 1970s, the academic debates about Social Security and, more generally, American welfare state development have increasingly focused on two issues neglected in traditional academic debates: race and gender.[9] Although distinct, these two issues refer to the impact of prejudice against specific segments of the population that have long been subject to discrimination. Moreover, these issues are directly related to the role of ideas and institutions in policymaking, because arguments about race and gender deal with the way beliefs shape policy outcomes and the way formal institutions condition the mobilization of political actors involved in the struggles over prejudice and discrimination. Drawing on the growing literature on race and gender in the United States (which will be discussed at the end of Chapter 1), the following chapters discuss the potential impact of these two factors on Social Security reform. This is especially crucial because traditional histories of Social Security seldom cover these factors in a comprehensive manner.

Regarding these two related issues, the main argument of this book is that gender is more important than race in understanding the political history of Social Security. Gendered forces can be seen to have impacted major Social Security provisions. For example, the spousal benefits enacted in 1939 were grounded in traditional assumptions about gender and family roles. Although changes have been enacted since the 1970s to remove discriminatory elements of the Social Security Act, the current structure of Social Security family benefits is an undeniable legacy of the 1939 reform and the gendered ideas that were dominant at the time. In contrast, there is no direct evidence that racial prejudice and the related mobilization of southern Democrats shaped key features of the Social Security program. Of course, this does not mean that race is *never* a significant factor in welfare state development: substantial variations exist from one policy area to another, and as will be shown, there is evidence that race has had a more direct impact on welfare reform than on Social Security politics. Nevertheless, the argument put forward here is that race has not carried much weight in Social Security history and that overall, Social Security has remained largely isolated from racist efforts aimed at excluding African Americans from civil rights and economic security. What has been labeled as the effect of racism in Social Security politics frequently refers to business power, which fluctuates over time. Paradoxically, the current debate over Social Security privatization features race in a prominent manner: both camps make *reference* to race in order to justify either the preservation or the restructuring of the program. Like gender, race has now become a significant aspect of the debate over Social Security's future. This fact illustrates the enduring weight of identity politics in contemporary American society.

Plan of the Book

Although this book is grounded in a systematic analysis of both primary and secondary sources, the emphasis is on specific theoretical issues and comparative insights. Because timing and historical sequence matter, the program's history is reconstructed in a mostly chronological way. Theoretical discussions are integrated with the historical narrative, and their scope is limited to increase the clarity and the conciseness of the text.

Chapter 1 formulates the theoretical assumptions structuring the empirical analysis that follows. Drawing on the distinction between societal and institutional accounts, the chapter begins with a critical survey of historical institutionalism, a useful approach to the politics of social policy reform. Yet the chapter shows that an understanding of policy change must integrate a more systematic analysis of the role of ideas in policymaking. This critical remark leads to an extended discussion concerning the potential influence of ideas on social policy development. The final section underlines the specificity of Social Security politics before discussing the literature on gender and race in a section that shows how the study of these two factors is compatible with the general institutionalist approach formulated here. Readers who have little interest in theories of policymaking and welfare state politics may choose to begin reading at Chapter 2 and return to Chapter 1 later, if necessary.

Chapter 2 looks back to the debate over pension policy in the three decades preceding the enactment of the Social Security Act in 1935.

The chapter discusses the impact of political institutions and policy legacies on social reforms debated during the Progressive Era and the 1920s. Then it shows that, although pension reform emerged relatively late on the national reform agenda, the actual timing of these debates would stimulate the development of old age security after 1929. By the time the Great Depression struck the nation, pension reform had become a central policy issue that state and federal politicians could readily promote as a response to the depression. An example of the impact of policy paradigms on historical sequence is the fact that the social insurance paradigm associated with the American Association for Labor Legislation delayed the appearance of a large pension movement in the United States.

Chapter 3 analyzes the enactment of the 1935 Social Security Act. What is fascinating about this omnibus legislation is that it created a measure that had seldom been discussed before 1934: old age insurance. As I argue, the conjunction of five specific factors explains the emergence of this unexpected federal measure: (1) the dramatic impact of the Great Depression, which created the apparent need to expand the scope of federal social policy; (2) the advent of the Townsend Plan, which helped maintain pension reform on the federal legislative agenda; (3) President Roosevelt's well-documented obsession to develop a social insurance scheme as an alternative to both social assistance and the fiscally unsound Townsend Plan; (4) on the policy legacy side, the limited development of private pension benefits as well as the absence of old age insurance at the state level; and (5) the relative disinterest in old age insurance among the policy elite, which allowed the president and the Committee on Economic Security (CES) considerable autonomy in shaping the legislative agenda in that specific policy area. Paradoxically, the social insurance paradigm tied to President Roosevelt transformed ideas and techniques stemming from the private sector into political tools aimed at securing the survival of the federal old age insurance program in a potentially hostile political environment.

Despite the autonomy of the presidency in formulating the basic goals and features of Social Security, Congress did reduce coverage through the exclusion of specific occupational groups in which African Americans were overrepresented. Yet there is no direct evidence that racial prejudice—through the possible influence of southern Democrats—explains the significant reduction in coverage enacted in Congress: saying that a measure disproportionately affected African Americans does not necessarily mean that discrimination and prejudice were at its origin. Most people excluded from Social Security during the legislative process were white, and administrative concerns, not pressures from southern Democrats, were the explicit origin of the—temporary—exclusion of agrarian and domestic workers from Social Security.

Chapter 4 studies the development of Social Security from the late 1930s to the early 1970s. The 1939 amendments, grounded in traditional gender roles, shifted the program's logic toward PAYGO financing and income redistribution. Yet, in order to preserve the paradoxical compromise embedded in the 1939 legislation, political actors never acknowledged the scope of this paradigmatic shift. After World War II, Social Security Administration officials took an active role in shaping the reform agenda through their domination over social policy expertise. Nevertheless, despite the role of bureaucratic forces traditionally stressed in research about postwar expansion, five other factors are probably as crucial as bureaucratic mobilization in explaining why Social Security expanded to become the largest program of the federal social policy system: (1) the development of private pensions, which contained potential business opposition to the program in the context of "pension integration;" (2) the nature of American political institutions that make bold reform, outside of rare episodes of sudden change, unlikely; (3) favorable actuarial and demographic conditions that made benefit increases possible without massive and immediate tax hikes; (4) the enactment of the 1950 amendments, which favored the emergence of larger constituencies militating against path-shifting reforms such as a "flat pension"; and (5) the postwar liberal consensus and the advent of New Republicanism under President Eisenhower, which marginalized radical opposition to Social Security, even within the Republican Party. Facilitated by interest group mobilization and "credit-claiming" strategies in Congress, these developments culminated during the Nixon administration with changes in actuarial assumptions and with increased electoral competition between the Democratic Congress and the Republican presidency that, in turn, fueled the program's sudden expansion.

Chapter 5 discusses the politics of Social Security reform from the mid-1970s to the mid-1980s. During that period, the United States became one of the first advanced industrial countries to implement significant cutbacks in its public pension system. At a time when countries such as Canada and France were still debating the need to expand public pension provisions, the United States witnessed a shift from the politics of expansion to the politics of cost containment and retrenchment. As a response to the advent of a short-term "fiscal crisis" in Social Security, federal officials attempted to reduce benefits and increase revenues while avoiding a massive electoral backlash against themselves. This chapter covers the genesis of the 1977 and 1983 amendments to the Social Security Act and show that these legislative reforms were enacted in a context during which the need to reform the program seemed obvious, at least from a financial standpoint. Yet this "need" never translated into significant policy shifts, and Social Security survived the era of "fiscal crisis" despite some notable reduction in benefits.

Notwithstanding the absence of short-term fiscal crisis during the 1990s, exceptional stock market performances and conservative mobilization gradually pushed the issue of Social Security privatization onto the federal policy agenda. In that context, conservative experts and political actors interested in restructuring that federal program in the sense of a new financial paradigm exploited various aspects of the American ideological repertoire in order to convince individuals, as well as interest groups, that Social Security privatization was the only and/or best option available to guarantee the economic security of future retirees in a manner consistent with "American values" and the financial logic of contemporary capitalism.

As Chapter 6 shows, the term *privatization,* as applied to Social Security, is potentially misleading because most restructuring proposals debated today do not imply an abolition of the payroll tax or the government's central role in retirement policy. In fact, the chapter demonstrates that the issue of Social Security privatization has been paradoxically framed as an attempt to "save Social Security" by transforming its very nature. Demographic pessimism and a discourse centered on personal and collective gain have been used to undermine the institutional legacy of the New Deal and to restructure Social Security in a manner coherent with economic individualism and the financial logic of capitalism. Ironically, the individualistic rhetoric previously used to depict Social Security as a truly American program has been mobilized against it in the name of personal savings and financial gain. This shows that the very same frame can justify conflicting policy alternatives and that individualistic representations are still dominant within the American ideological repertoire.

Finally, the afterword offers a comparative perspective on President Bush's failed 2005 campaign to privatize Social Security. Drawing mainly on the British experience, this comparative discussion offers further insight about the relationship between ideas and institutions in Social Security politics.

CHAPTER ONE

Ideas, Institutions, and Social Security

Since the 1970s, social scientists have put forward theories to explain the origins and the transformation of modern social policies. These theories of welfare state development, generally grounded in a comparative perspective, were prefigured by influential studies published during and immediately after World War II.[1] Yet, according to John Myles and Jill Quadagno, "it was only in the mid-1970s, following more than two decades of accelerated expansion, that both the sheer scale of, and striking diversity among, the welfare states of the industrialized nations made them the focus of concentrated attention as a defining feature of so-called modernity."[2] This chapter briefly reviews the main theoretical approaches.

Instead of simply borrowing from existing theories,[3] the main aim of this chapter is to put forward a consistent historical institutionalist approach to policymaking that takes into account the interplay among policy ideas, political institutions, and economic change. Drawing on these theoretical insights, the final section underlines the institutional and ideological specificity of Social Security politics before discussing the role of race and gender, two factors that, according to recent historical accounts, may have shaped the program's development. Within this book's exploration of how Social Security has changed over time as a political and ideological issue, the general arguments formulated in this theoretical chapter should help the reader to better understand the changing faces of Social Security history since the New Deal.

Societal Perspectives

It is now common to separate theories of social policy development into two main camps. The first—societal approaches—emphasizes economic and cultural factors that are believed to be largely autonomous from political institutions. The other—institutional approaches—emphasizes the impact of political structures and existing policy legacies on social policy development.[4] Although efforts have been made to bridge the gap between these two camps,[5] significant differences still exist between them. This section is a critical presentation of three well-established societal approaches that underlines their most significant shortcomings.

Societal approaches, although diverse, fall into three main categories according to the main factor they emphasize: economic development, cultural values, and political mobilization. These three main societal perspectives all point to some relevant explanatory factors, but they fail to shed a satisfactory light on social policy development. A more complex and integrated theoretical framework is needed to take these factors into account while acknowledging the crucial structuring role of political institutions and policy legacies.

Although the industrialism, or economic development, perspective on social policy can be traced back to the late nineteenth century,[6] it became an articulated model only decades later, notably in the work of authors such as Harold Wilensky as well as Clark Kerr, John T. Dunlop, Frederick Harbison, and Charles A. Myers.[7] According to these authors, the process of industrialization undermines traditional forms of social support based on kinship and intergenerational solidarity. This decline of family support and the advent of a "wage society," in which unemployment becomes an enduring source of economic insecurity, exacerbates the demands for social spending. In the context of a fragmented urban society, government must restructure and increase its social and economic interventions in order to reproduce the labor force while achieving social cohesion and political consensus. From this theoretical perspective, economic and demographic changes related to industrialization constitute the root cause of modern social policy. In his widely discussed book, *The Welfare State and Equality,* for example, Wilensky argued that population aging related to industrialization was the most essential factor in the origin of modern social policy development. Broad economic, demographic, and social transformations create the need for a more active government, and cross-national variations in social spending are the product of uneven levels of economic development. Grounded in evolutionist and economist assumptions, the industrialism approach downplays the autonomous role of political institutions and mobilization. For authors such as Wilensky and Kerr, Dunlop, Harbison, and Myers, a nation's level of economic development determines policy outcomes, that is, a predicted increase in public spending.

At the most abstract level, industrialism provides essential insights concerning the general economic and demographic conditions necessary to create the need for bold social reforms. Indeed, the idea that industrialization, economic growth, and demographic aging affect welfare expansion is rarely questioned in the comparative literature on social policy.[8] Yet the industrialism perspective is unable to explain significant variations across nations in terms of policy design and social spending. For example, an analysis of the relationship between economic and demographic trends, on the one hand, and social spending levels, on the other hand, does not help scholars understand why the United States, unlike other advanced industrial societies, has not created universal health insurance. This model also fails to explain differences within the same nation. For example, how can it be explained that Social Security is at the foundation of the American pension system given that the federal government plays only a residual role in the field of health insurance? Because authors such as Kerr and Wilensky pay relatively little attention to political conflicts and mobilizations, their approach offers nothing more than a general understanding of the broad economic and social trends that form the necessary background conditions for social policy development in modern industrial societies.

If the industrialist approach seems problematic, the culturalist perspective formulated by authors such as David Levine, Roy Lubove, and Seymour Martin Lipset is even less adapted to explaining cross-national

and intranational variations in social policy outcomes. For these authors, a historically constructed set of "national values," consisting of
expectations and assumptions about economic and social realities,
explains cross-national variations in social spending and policy design.[9]
The central thesis of the culturalist approach is that "nations perceive
reality in their own ways and act according to those perceptions' relation to their own history."[10] In other words, shared normative beliefs
shape the political life of a country while reducing the number of options available to policymakers. Large-scale, shared identities and values
structure political behavior and policy outcomes.[11] Such a set of shared
values can be measured through surveys and historical analysis. For
example, in his book, *The Continental Divide,* Lipset formulated this type
of analysis in order to explain major policy differences between Canada
and the United States.[12] Studying the social insurance movement during the Progressive Era, historian Roy Lubove also focused on shared
values, arguing that the weight of voluntarism and old liberalism explained the failure of most social insurance proposals before the New
Deal. Like Lipset and Levine, he considered values as the main sociological factor at play: political decisions reflect national beliefs that facilitate—or create obstacles against—social policy development.

Like industrialism, the cultural approach offers explanations that are
too vague and static to explain cross-national and intranational differences in policy outcomes. As stated by Skocpol, "Arguments about
national values are too holistic and essentialist to give us explanatory
leverage we need to account for variations in the fate of different social
policies, or for changes over time in the fate of similar proposals."[13] Moreover, reformers and political actors from competing camps frequently
refer to the same basic values to criticize or justify a specific policy proposal.[14] Concerning the impact of public opinion in these policy debates,
one could also argue that "public views of social policy both shape and
are shaped by the framework of social provision that exists in a nation.
Yet national values explanations almost always assume that public policies are a result of popular understandings, rather than the other way
around."[15] This means not that policy ideas and ideological representations have no impact on social policy development but that their role is
more complex than what proponents of the culturalist perspective would
argue. The theoretical framework formulated later in this chapter aims at

offering a more insightful perspective on the role of policy ideas and ideological representations while moving beyond essentialist and overly simplistic arguments about "national values."

During the late 1970s and early 1980s, the class, or political, mobilization perspective emerged at the center of the theoretical debate on welfare state development. Grounded in neo-Marxist assumptions about the impact of class inequality and mobilization on policymaking, this perspective has taken at least two specific forms: the social democratic model (Walter Korpi and Gøsta Esping-Andersen) and the corporate liberalism model (William Domhoff and Jill Quadagno). According to the former model, Scandinavian welfare states offer more generous and universal benefits than their European and North American counterparts because of the exceptional influence of the labor movement in Scandinavian countries. More generally, Korpi and Esping-Andersen have argued that social policy outcomes are mostly determined by the struggle between labor and capital. In this context, there is a strong correlation between labor's strength (unionization rate; cultural and political unity of the movement) and social policy's degree of comprehensiveness. In countries where the labor movement is weak and highly divided, social policy tends to be less comprehensive.[16] The corporate liberalism model, put forward in order to explain the comparatively modest nature of American social policy, focuses on business interests instead of labor mobilization. Assuming that the latter is generally limited, advocates of this model concentrate on the hidden or explicit influence of progressive industrialists who participate in the configuration and the enactment of social reforms.[17] From Domhoff's perspective, for example, social policy in the United States was shaped by the interests of a specific faction of the capitalist class that played a central role during the New Deal.[18]

The most significant shortcoming of the class mobilization perspective is that authors drawing on it frequently assume a necessary correspondence between class mobilization and political power. On the contrary, the fact is that the demands of class-based groups such as labor and business may be shaped by the institutional and policy context within which they mobilize, and thus there is no necessary correspondence between socioeconomic demands and policy outcomes. "Institutions refract, distort, and reconstruct societal forces even as they respond to them, and established policies may endure even after the original conditions that gave rise to them no longer hold sway."[19] Even though the class mobilization perspective rightly underlines the essential role of sociopolitical struggles in social policy development, its failure to recognize the structuring impact of formal institutions and existing policy legacies reduces its capacity to explain cross- and intranational differences in social policy outcomes.[20] This remark naturally leads to a brief discussion on historical institutionalism, a theoretical perspective that stresses the way state capacities and formal political institutions impact policymaking.

Historical Institutionalism

Since the 1980s, historical institutionalism has been a powerful alternative to the societal approaches discussed above. In the area of social policy, such authors as Ellen Immergut, Ann Orloff, and Theda Skocpol have criticized societal assumptions by exploring the impact of political institutions and policy legacies on social policy development.[21] At first, historical institutionalism was aimed at "bringing the state back in." The primary step in this process is the recognition of state autonomy and the analysis of state capacities:

> States conceived as organizations claiming control over territories and people may formulate and pursue goals that are not simply reflective of the demands or interest of social groups, classes or society. This is what is usually meant by "state autonomy." Unless such independent goal formulation occurs, there is little need to talk about states as important actors. Pursuing matters further, one may then explore the "capacities" of states to implement official goals, especially over the actual or potential opposition of powerful social groups or in the face of recalcitrant socioeconomic circumstances.[22]

In order to show that "independent goal formation occurs," Skocpol and her collaborators first published several articles about the New Deal and the elaboration of the 1935 Social Security Act in the United States. Considering the "recalcitrant socioeconomic circumstances" of the

1930s, those interested in studying state autonomy and state capacities perceived the enactment of the Social Security Act as a relevant case study. The fact that several culturalist and neo-Marxist studies focused on state formation and social classes during the New Deal provided institutionalist scholars with an opportunity to put forward an alternate vision of the relationship between state and society.[23] Against the corporate liberalism model, institutionalist authors showed that key laws enacted during the New Deal were not mere reflections of "the interests of the capitalist class:" bureaucrats and elected politicians enjoyed a significant degree of political autonomy vis-à-vis interest groups and social movements. Governmental officials could not be considered mere servants of a social class but autonomous political actors. They had interests and strategies of their own as well as the ability to pursue them without relying exclusively on a dominant social class.[24] Against culturalist claims, institutionalist authors argued that the reference to broad national values could not explain specific political decisions. Culturalist arguments just seemed too vague to prove useful in the analysis of concrete political and policymaking processes.[25]

During the second half of the 1980s, scholars such as Skocpol and Orloff transformed historical institutionalism into a more complex framework centered less on state autonomy per se than on the structuring impact of formal administrative and political institutions on policymaking. This evolution toward a more integrated, polity-centered model was well described in Skocpol's *Protecting Soldiers and Mothers.* According to Skocpol, "This approach views the polity as the primary locus of action, yet understands political activities, whether carried out by politicians or by social groups, as conditioned by the institutional configurations of governments and political party systems."[26] Beyond the idea of state autonomy, Skocpol formulated a broader institutionalist model that focused on four different factors:

> (1) the establishment and transformation of state and party organization . . . ; (2) the effects of political institutions and procedures on the identities, goals, and capacities of social groups . . . ; (3) the "fit"—or lack thereof—between goals and capacities of various politically active groups, and the historically changing points of access

and leverage allowed by a nation's political institutions; and (4) the way in which previously established social policies affect subsequent politics.[27]

During the 1990s, many social scientists adopted a similar historical and institutional perspective on social policy reform. For example, the impact of party systems on policy outcomes was discussed in Antonia Maioni's book on the political history of public health insurance in Canada and the United States. For Maioni, the Canadian political system, as opposed to the American one, favored the emergence of a strong social democratic third party during the postwar era. This party pressured mainstream political parties to enact progressive social reforms such as national health insurance.[28]

Beyond party politics, courts can play a central role in shaping economic and social interests. For the United States, such scholars as Victoria Hattam and William Forbath actually demonstrated that the antilabor attitude of the federal Supreme Court at the turn of the twentieth century directly shaped labor's political strategies. Facing strong opposition from the courts when embracing an ambitious social and political agenda, most American unions finally welcomed "pure and simple trade unionism," that is, an emphasis on collective bargaining at the expense of political mobilization in favor of broad social programs and economic regulations.[29] The ideas developed by Forbath, Hattam, and Maioni are at odds with the societal assumptions of the class mobilization approach discussed earlier. For these institutionalist scholars, political institutions such as courts and party systems structure the political battlefield while influencing the way interest groups put forward their political strategies.

In order to better understand how political institutions shape labor and interest group behavior, historical institutionalists also described how institutions permit interests to shape policy through specific "veto points." Concerning the politics of health care reform, for example, Immergut demonstrated that the structure of the Swiss federal system explains why Swiss physicians enjoy greater political influence than their colleagues in France and Sweden. Despite the fact that physicians from these countries were equally well organized, the decentralized polity and referendum procedures of Switzerland gave Swiss doctors greater opportunities to veto health insurance and other policies that harmed their interests.[30] Thus, "political institutions shape (but do not determine) political conflict by providing interest groups with varying opportunities to veto policy."[31]

Finally, institutionalist scholars turned to the concept of policy feedback to describe the enduring impact of previously enacted policies on policymaking. This concept really makes institutionalism "historical" because it shows how policymakers have to take into account vested interests created by well-established programs. From this perspective, existing policies shape the perceptions and the strategies of the political actors. When they enact new legislation, they have to take into account the institutionalized policy legacy of decisions made years or decades earlier. Present-day politicians have to live with the decisions of their predecessors.[32]

Paul Pierson is probably the institutionalist author who has the most systematic views on the role of policy feedback in welfare state politics. In his work on the "new politics of the welfare state," he has described how retrenchment was a risky business for politicians who faced the "armies of beneficiaries" that emerged in the aftermath of postwar social policy expansion. According to Pierson, social programs create vested interests that favor the reproduction of the current institutional logics; social policy development is essentially a path-dependent process. Inspired by the work of the economist Douglas C. North, Pierson has argued that significant path-breaking processes seldom occur because politicians never take the risk to alienate themselves from powerful constituencies "attached" to the social programs implemented decades before. Instead, they adopt blame-avoidance strategies that usually perpetuate the institutional status quo. These strategies reflect institutional constraints stemming from previously enacted policies.[33]

The concept of policy feedback draws attention to the frequently decisive importance of timing and sequence in social policy development. Social scientists have long recognized that the order in which countries undergo broad socioeconomic or political transformations makes a significant difference in the nature of those changes.[34] In the field of social policy reform, one should recognize the truly historical nature of policy development: "*Often it is the sequence and timing of an event or decision that is the most crucial determinant of policy outcomes. If*

factor A comes before factor B, the effect may be very different than if
B precedes A, even though the same basic factors are involved. Simi-
larly, the effect of particular events or decisions within one institutional or policy context may be fundamentally different than their
effect in another context."[35] From this perspective, the specific path of
social policy development can shape future policy outcomes.

In recent years, some scholars have argued that general claims concerning policy feedback and historical sequence also apply to *private*
social provisions, which impact the politics of social policy reform in
various ways. As discussed above, institutionalist scholars reject the neo-
Marxist idea that powerful economic interests determine policy outcomes in a direct way. From an institutional perspective, party systems
and political institutions mediate and transform these economic interests. Without rejecting this institutional assumption, Jacob Hacker has
rightly argued that economic interests impact the "rules of the game"
during the policymaking process.[36] In this context, it is possible to extend the concept of policy feedback to the private sector in order to
understand how well-established, structured, private "vested interests"
create new constraints and opportunities for policymakers.[37] Under the
Truman administration, for example, labor unions never fully supported
the president's attempt to create a national health insurance system
because of the hopes created by the rapid development of private health
insurance. In the context of postwar economic prosperity, the confidence of the population and most of the political class in the virtues of
the private sector apparently reduced the need for such a statist model.[38]
More important, the growing private insurance business created new,
institutionalized constraints for policymakers as private companies and
beneficiaries organized to protect their interests in the political arena.
This logic was largely reinforced by "checks and balances" and the
absence of party discipline in Congress. In this context, these interest
groups could individually pressure elected officials to block the enactment of threatening health insurance bills.

Without denying the autonomy of political actors, political "rules of
the game" also reflect feedback effects emanating from a private sector
that is largely structured by existing regulations and tax policy. Related
to these public policies as well as to long-term economic transformations, the development of private benefits impacts policymaking in a

way that can either reinforce or undermine existing policy paths. As opposed to the industrialism perspective discussed above, the careful study of private benefits and economic change helps institutionalist scholars better understand cross-national—and intranational—variations in policy outcomes. This is especially true in the United States, where private benefits have played a significant role in providing workers with economic security.

Implicitly, this discussion about policy feedback from private benefits underlines the crucial role of "business power" in social policy. In a recent contribution, Hacker and Pierson argued that business influence is not constant over time and that variations in business power have characterized American history. Furthermore, public policies largely shape the vested interests of employers, who adapt to changes in the policy environment. Formal political institutions also structure business mobilization capacities. Following Hacker and Pierson, in this book I take institutionalized business power into account while highlighting its variation over time and across institutional settings.[39] These general remarks about business power also apply to the labor movement, whose capacity to impact policy outcomes is largely shaped by existing institutional settings.[40]

This model about business and labor power, as well as the concepts of veto point, policy feedback, and historical sequence, are powerful intellectual tools that help students of politics understand the institutional obstacles and "windows of opportunity" that shape political actors' behavior. Overall, historical institutionalism contributes to our understanding of the "rules of the game" that impact policymaking.

Bringing Policy Ideas In

Despite the recent and most welcomed recognition of the relationship between path dependence and private benefits, historical institutionalism as it stands is not a totally satisfactory approach to policymaking.[41] According to Elizabeth Clemens and James Cook, for example, historical institutionalism has created new theoretical puzzles: "Insofar as institutional arguments maintain that variation and change are minimized, those same arguments are ill-suited to the explanation of change."[42] Because historical institutionalist researchers tend to down-play the role of policy ideas, mainstream historical institutionalism is excellent for explaining how institutions create obstacles and opportunities for reform, but it cannot shine a satisfactory light on the content of reforms that bring policy change.[43] In order to understand better the origin and the meaning of policy choices, I would like to bring policy ideas to the center of this theoretical framework.[44]

Certainly, policy ideas have not been totally excluded from historical institutionalist research on social policy. Among the theoretical tools associated with historical institutionalism, the concept of social learning, which is closely related to policy feedback, is the one that favors the most direct reference to the political impact of policy ideas. According to Hugh Heclo, "Policymaking is a form of collective puzzlement on society's behalf; it entails both deciding and knowing." In this context, "policy invariably builds on policy, either in moving forward with what has been inherited, or amending it, or repudiating it."[45] For Heclo, the assessment of previously enacted measures and their socioeconomic consequences impacts policy decisions. More precisely, the concept of social learning contains three main elements:

> The first is the presence of intellectual machinations as components of the policy process. . . . The second element is the reaction to previous policy: a process of learning may be said to occur when policy makers respond to the failures of a past policy, draw lessons from that experience and incorporate these into the making of new policy. Finally, the model reserves a central place for experts specializing in specific policy areas and working in relative autonomy from politicians and social pressures.[46]

Unfortunately, the traditional concept of social learning does not capture the constant struggle between ideological models and policy understandings that make political actors draw different lessons from previously enacted policies. In order to understand how political actors learn from specific policy episodes, it is necessary to reconstruct their normative and technical assumptions.[47]

Beyond social learning, institutionalist scholars working on social policy have done relatively little to integrate the analysis of policy ideas into their *theoretical* framework. Although these authors frequently take policy ideas into account in their empirical studies, they do not provide scholars with a comprehensive theoretical model that can improve our understanding of the political struggles over policy ideas. A look at Theda Skocpol's famous *Protecting Soldiers and Mothers* illustrates this claim. Even though the author discusses the idea of a matriarchal welfare state, her theoretical model leaves little room for a systematic analysis of policy ideas in the institutional context of the American polity.[48] The same remark applies to Pierson's account on the new politics of the welfare state, which tends to reduce the role of ideas to calculus and electoral strategies.[49]

As opposed to those interested in social policy, institutionalist researchers studying economic policy have formally attempted to bring policy ideas into historical institutionalism's theoretical landscape.[50] In *Politics and Jobs,* for example, Margaret Weir explored the way in which "American political institutions have influenced the range of ideas that have been considered in national policy about employment."[51] According to her, two essential features of the American polity shape the politics of ideas: "The first is the relative openness of the federal government to new ideas; the second is the limited capacity of the government to serve as a site for the production of ideas about employment."[52] In her book, she also explored the specific role of actors and institutions involved in the production—and the reproduction—of policy ideas.

Peter Hall's work on economic policy in France and the United Kingdom is another stimulating contribution to the debate about the interaction between policy ideas and institutional politics. For Hall, the traditional notion of social learning says little about the political impact of policy ideas.[53] In order to fill this theoretical gap, he introduced the concept of policy paradigm, which refers to "a framework of ideas and standards that specifies not only the goals of policy and kind of instruments that can be used to attain them, but also the very nature of the problems they are meant to be addressing."[54] Both technical and ideological in content, paradigms constitute the pragmatic worldview of bureaucrats, policy experts, and elected politicians who struggle within institutional structures. Such a worldview impacts learning and strategic processes. Furthermore, paradigm shifts explain radical political transformations labeled as "third order change." These shifts are also related to social learning processes: "Like scientific paradigms, a policy paradigm can be threatened by the appearance of anomalies, namely by developments that are not fully comprehensible, even as puzzles, within the terms of the paradigm."[55] Such an analogy between scientific and policy paradigms is problematic because, as mentioned above, ideological conflicts shape the social learning process itself.[56] Moreover, Hall's model does not really take into account how policy ideas are framed to appeal to the public.[57] Considering the limits of this model, it seems appropriate to put forward a more comprehensive theoretical perspective concerning the relationship among policy ideas, political institutions, and policymaking.

An interesting starting point for the elaboration of a coherent theoretical framework concerning the political impact of policy ideas is John W. Kingdon's agenda-setting theory.[58] Although distinct from historical institutionalism, this theory can provide institutionalist scholars with interesting insights concerning the political role of policy ideas. Drawing on Kingdon's distinction between agendas and alternatives, this section identifies actors and ideational processes present at different stages of the policymaking process.

The concept of agenda refers to "the list of subjects or problems to which governmental officials, and people outside of government closely associated with those officials, are paying some serious attention at any given time."[59] Consequently, agenda setting is the process that narrows the "set of conceivable subjects to the set that actually becomes the focus of attention."[60] Starting from this definition, one needs to take into account the well-known distinction between public and policy agendas. If the concept of public agenda points to the interaction between public opinion and issue salience in the media, policy agenda concerns the problems policymakers themselves perceive as significant at a specific moment in time.[61] Although public and policy agendas are related, one should acknowledge their relative autonomy. The focus of Kingdon's work is on policy agenda, which explains why scholars mostly interested in policymaking processes tend to draw on his work.[62]

Although the term *agenda* refers to a cluster of issues considered as the "pressing problems of the moment," alternatives represent the policy options available to solve these problems.[63] According to Kingdon, agendas and alternatives are the product of the interaction among three autonomous streams through which social and political actors mobilize to support specific issues or policy options.[64] A critical examination of these three elements—problem, policy, and political streams—will lead to a broader discussion about the interaction between policy ideas and political institutions.

The first of these elements is the problem stream. It refers to the selection of issues that are considered as significant social and economic problems. Potentially relevant issues are numerous, but politicians cannot address all of them at once. Many issues die away because attention fades, whereas some problems are of a cyclical nature and tend to correct themselves over time.[65] Because policymakers can only focus on a few vital issues simultaneously, the political construction and selection of the problems on the agenda constitute a crucial phase of the policymaking process. Bureaucrats, elected politicians, and the public generally become aware of socially constructed economic and social problems through statistical indicators, spectacular "focusing events," or feedback effects from previously enacted policies.[66]

The second element of Kingdon's agenda-setting theory is the policy stream, which gathers together policy experts working for academic institutions, governmental agencies, and interest groups. Involved in different "policy communities" related to specific fields of governmental intervention (that is, health care, transportation, Social Security), these actors frame policy ideas and proposals that stew in what Kingdon calls a "policy primeval soup" that contains many ideas floating around that "combine with one another in various ways."[67] Against a rationalistic vision of policymaking starting from the assumption that policy ideas always emerge as responses to well-known problems, he states that some experts or interest groups could support specific policy alternatives in the absence of a clear problem to solve. Moreover, a policy solution designed as a response to a particular problem can actually get attached to another problem if needed.

Yet against the impression that policy ideas have little consistency, I must stress that most alternatives are related to specific policy paradigms that constitute the structured intellectual background of policy decisions. These paradigms serve as "road maps" for experts and policymakers by providing them with a relatively reasoned set of assumptions concerning the functioning of economic, political, and social institutions.[68] Far from being purely cognitive, paradigms are inherently normative: they help policymakers decide how to reform existing programs or to create new ones. In Chapter 3, the analysis of the social insurance paradigm associated with President Franklin D. Roosevelt will show how specific policy assumptions shaped the enactment of Social Security in 1935.

Policy paradigms and policy alternatives are interactive in nature: each exists only in opposition to other policy ideas available in a specific political environment at a precise moment in time. On the one hand, policy entrepreneurs such as think tanks that support new policy alternatives attempt to undermine support for existing programs they wish to amend or replace. On the other hand, if new policy ideas become popular, those committed to established alternatives and paradigms must either integrate the new material into their frameworks or justify their exclusion in an explicit manner. Among other examples discussed in this book, the analysis of President Clinton's 1999 Social Security proposals will provide ground to these claims about the interactive nature of ideational politics. The analysis of the current debate over Social Security privatization will also underline the central role of think tanks in the elaboration of policy paradigms and alternatives.

The third element of Kingdon's agenda-setting theory is the political stream. As mentioned above, experts constantly discuss suitable alternatives within specific policy communities, and their proposals need to be associated with a problem perceived as significant (that is, demographic aging, budget deficits) in order to reach the policy agenda. Yet this is possible only if these proposals receive the direct support of a major political advocate. Consequently, the political side of agenda setting is crucial. Among the factors that set down this third stream are electoral results, pressures from interest groups, and the perceived state of public opinion. The election of a new government or the emergence of a powerful interest group can reshape the policy agenda and help push new policy ideas to the center of the political debate. During these moments of political opportunity, policy entrepreneurs are instrumental in bringing together their own favored solutions with a recognized social or economic problem. Policy entrepreneurs favor the convergence of the three streams necessary to the legislative triumph of their policy ideas.[69] For example, as evidenced in Chapter 3, without the intervention of President Roosevelt it is unlikely that a federal old age insurance program would have been enacted as part of the 1935 Social Security Act.

Policy entrepreneurs and other political actors generally succeed in imposing certain policy ideas partly because such entrepreneurs and actors appeal to the public through the mobilization of political symbols ever present in the shared "ideological repertoire" of their society.[70] Before, during, and after the legislative process, policymakers must justify their political and technical choices. In this context, well-crafted ideological representations "provide actors with symbols and concepts with which to frame solution to policy problems in normatively acceptable terms through transposition and bricolage."[71] Drawing from existing political traditions and widely accepted ideological repertoires, elected politicians legitimize their programs in order to reduce political risks or claim credit for their potentially positive social and economic consequences. Ideological frames "appear typically in the public pronouncements of policy makers and their aides, such as sound bites, campaign speeches, press releases, and other very public statements designed to muster public support for policy proposals."[72]

Ideological framing serves two main political purposes. First, the framing process is a strategic and deliberate activity aimed at generating public support for existing programs or debated policy alternatives. This means that the capacity to communicate ideological frames to the public can help politicians and bureaucrats to justify their choices.[73] Like policy ideas (that is, alternatives and paradigms), frames are also interactive in nature: they anticipate what potential opponents could say to undermine the support for specific policy alternatives. From this perspective, frames have a preventive component, in the sense that those involved in policy debates frequently mobilize them to shield their policy proposals from criticism. Frames can therefore take the form of "strategic misconceptions" that mask the actual functioning— or the negative consequences—of specific public policies.[74] As will be shown in Chapter 4, beginning in the late 1930s, federal bureaucrats and politicians framed Social Security as a purely contributive program grounded in self-reliance; this discourse had the effect of hiding the redistributive nature of this federal program.

Second, and perhaps more important, ideological framing contributes to "the social construction of the need to reform." "In a political environment, the advocates of reform need to employ strategies to overcome the skepticism of others and persuade them of the importance of reform. In other words, they must create a discourse that changes the collective understanding of the welfare state, because doing so 'shapes the path' necessary to enact reform."[75] When supporting path-breaking changes such as Social Security privatization, policy entrepreneurs have to justify the need to reform in order to shake up the existing "policy monopoly" that exacerbates institutional inertia.[76] In Chapter 6, I will show how conservative think tanks have used demographic fears to undermine the support for Social Security and construct the need to reform Social Security in order to create individual savings accounts as part of that federal program.

The ability to frame a policy program in a politically and culturally acceptable *and* desirable manner is a key factor that can help explain why some policy proposals triumph over others and why elected officials decide to "do something" in the first place. Additional factors include support from key political constituencies, technical feasibility in the context of established policy frameworks, and the relative simplicity of the policy ideas themselves—very complex ideas that are difficult to explain to the public and even to elected officials. To favor the enactment and the implementation of their policy proposals, bureaucrats and elected officials must also take into account vested economic and political interests. Indeed, the political field is a structured arena of conflict in which ideas form "weapons of mass persuasion" related to existing social and institutional forces.[77] In such a constraining environment, political actors must master the institutional "rules of the game" while manipulating the symbols available in their society's ideological repertoire. Their behavior reflects ideational and institutional structures that create political obstacles as well as opportunities for reform.[78] As mentioned above, broad economic trends and feedback effects from previously enacted *private* benefits also structure the policy arena.[79] In Chapter 4, the comparison between health insurance and Social Security reform during President Truman's second term will illustrate the claim that private benefits can impact policy outcomes in the public sector.

Understanding the Politics of Social Security

The set of theoretical arguments in this section should help readers better grasp the changing faces of Social Security politics since the 1930s. I first discuss what is specific about Social Security politics in the United States, then two factors ever present in the contemporary debates about American social policy: race and gender. The discussion about race and gender focuses on the literature dealing specifically with the political history of Social Security.

What Is Specific about Social Security?

Although the broad institutionalist outlook developed in this book is relevant for the political and sociological study of all types of social policy, its application must take into account structural variations from one policy area to another. For example, the economic, ideological, and institutional issues related to social assistance programs financed through general revenues are slightly different than those tied to contributive, social insurance programs. Moreover, income maintenance programs such as Social Security are distinct from social services and health benefits, which involve professional constituencies such as doctors and social workers. As opposed to other types of social programs, PAYGO pension programs such as Social Security have at least four distinct characteristics that affect the political battles surrounding them: (1) their intimate connection to demographic change and intergenerational solidarity; (2) their immediate relationship with the transformation of labor markets that affects the status of older workers and private pension coverage; (3) the broad constituencies they create, generally the vast majority of the elderly population; and (4) the long-term nature of pension commitments, which affect one's economic and personal choices over most of the life course.

The first characteristic, the relationship between pension reform and demographic change, requires little explanation. In most Western nations, modern public pension systems emerged after World War II in a particularly favorable demographic context. Because fertility rates were significantly higher after 1945 than during the previous decade, it became possible to offer more generous pensions paid for by a growing and younger workforce. Considering the decline in fertility rates and the increase in life expectancy, however, the future financial equilibrium of PAYGO schemes is now perceived as uncertain. Related to the institutional and financial logic of PAYGO programs that directly transfer resources from workers to retirees, this connection between demographic change and social policy favors the advent of a "politics of assumptions" characterized by ideological constructions about "intergenerational equity" and "demographic time bombs."[80] Although these issues are also present in the debate over the future of public health insurance, PAYGO pension schemes are especially tied to them.

Beyond demographic transformations per se, the second characteristic is that public pension schemes are directly related to the evolution of labor markets, especially the so-called exclusion of older workers. Employers' decisions about private pensions and early retirement schemes impact the financial situation of public pension systems, as massive early retirements may increase the financial burden on these systems.[81] Moreover, the development of private pension schemes can either increase or reduce the support for existing public pension schemes. Whereas the "integration" of public and private defined-benefits schemes tends to reinforce business and labor support for the former, the advent of private savings schemes at odds with the functioning of public policies may undermine the political and economic legitimacy of the latter.[82]

The third key characteristic of modern PAYGO public pension schemes is the vast constituencies they have created. Although the first social insurance schemes created more than a century ago in Germany aimed at protecting poor workers only, most public pension systems have generalized their coverage since World War II. Today, these systems cover the vast majority of the population in most advanced industrial societies. For that reason, annual public pension spending represents a significant proportion of the gross domestic product (GDP) in these societies.[83] Moreover, the fact that the majority of the elderly population now depends on public benefits for their economic security reinforces the legitimacy of—and the political support for—these benefits.

What is common to all modern PAYGO public pension schemes is the fourth characteristic, the long-term nature of the entitlements and the political commitments they generate. Individuals who start a career at the age of twenty-one may contribute for more than forty-five years before receiving a full Social Security pension. The contributory nature of PAYGO schemes and the discourse about "earned rights" surrounding them creates legitimate expectations on the part of beneficiaries, although the total amount of benefits paid to many retirees has often been superior—or inferior—to their total Social Security contributions.[84] The fact that PAYGO systems such as Social Security are grounded in long-term financial commitments reinforces institutional inertia. Because the transition from a PAYGO to a fully funded system involves a "double payment" problem—distributing current benefits while putting money aside in savings accounts—institutional inertia and path dependence are probably more likely in this social policy area than in any other.[85] Furthermore, as evidenced by Andrea Campbell, the development of Social Security has stimulated the political participation of the elderly. This is especially true concerning low-income elderly, who have found an interest in fighting for the preservation and the expansion of Social Security.[86]

In addition to such an army of beneficiaries, public pension systems create vested administrative and managerial interests that frequently fight to expand or preserve the integrity of pension benefits. In European countries such as Belgium, France, and Germany, for example, labor unions participate in the management of public pension schemes, and this specific institutional setting increases their influence of the politics of pension reform. In contrast, no attempt has ever been made in the United States to transform unions into a "social partner" that has a significant administrative stake in the public pension system. As will be shown in Chapter 3, this situation largely stems from the absence of corporatist traditions and institutions in American society.

Perhaps because of this situation, the literature on Social Security history in the United States focuses far more on the role of federal bureaucrats who managed that program than on the role of labor unions. According to political scientist Martha Derthick and others, members of the Social Security Administration (SSA) were among the most crucial actors in the politics of Social Security expansion.[87] It is true that because of the exceptional stability and enduring policy expertise of its expansionist leadership, the SSA has played a significant role in American social policy development (see Chapter 4). In a recent book, for example, historian Edward Berkowitz showed how Social Security commissioner Robert Ball successfully promoted the expansion of Social Security during President Nixon's first mandate.[88] Overall, top-ranked SSA bureaucrats such as Ball used their expertise and political connections to promote the expansion of social security between the late 1930s and the mid-1970s. The actions of these bureaucrats particularly impacted the agenda-setting process as they promoted their expansionist agenda within and even outside government. Yet, the following empirical chapters emphasize the central role of other actors and institutional forces that put this bureaucratic mobilization into perspective. Even though federal civil servants pushed for the development of "their" centralized program, they could not have succeeded in their expansionist project without the support of other actors and, perhaps more important, the institutional logic of path dependence discussed above. From this perspective, the SSA only played a decisive role in Social Security reform between the 1936 presidential campaign and the enactment of the 1950 amendments to the Social Security Act. After the enactment of these amendments, the program became so important to American workers, employers, and federal politicians alike that no "bureaucratic conspiracy" would have proved necessary to preserve and expand Social Security. SSA officials worked within a broad policy community centered on stable congressional committees where decisions were largely driven by credit-claiming strategies.[89] Reflecting enduring economic growth, favorable demographic conditions, and the creation of the massive constituencies (that is, beneficiaries, employers, labor officials) mentioned above, the electoral strategies of members of Congress and presidents certainly represent one of the most essential factors behind the postwar expansion of Social Security. If bureaucrats helped shape the reform agenda, it is Congress that enacted the postwar Social Security reforms.

Yet an analysis of Social Security development in the United States cannot stand without a discussion about the role of federal bureaucrats in the "politics of ideas" surrounding that program. Immediately after the enactment of Social Security, bureaucrats, reformers, and elected officials framed this program as a form of self-reliance mediated by the federal government. This frame, grounded in negative attitudes toward social assistance, drew on the idea of self-reliance ever present in the American ideological repertoire. In a way, this discourse on "earned rights" is both common and highly exceptional. If the idea of "earned rights" exists in other countries, the emphasis on individual entitlements and self-reliance is probably stronger in the United States than in any other advanced industrial country. This reality provides ground to Nancy Frazer and Linda Gordon's claim about the strict ideological opposition between "contract" (insurance) and "charity" (assistance) in American social policy.[90]

President Roosevelt played a significant role in establishing this strict distinction between insurance and assistance, reflecting both his personal experience within the private insurance business and structural, ideological forces tied to the limited fiscal capacity of the federal government before World War II.[91] In contrast with most accounts on Social Security politics, the following chapters will particularly stress the role of presidents in the politics of Social Security reform. Presidents affect both framing and agenda-setting processes in a way that has not yet been systematically considered in the traditional literature on Social Security.[92]

The empirical analysis of Social Security must also take into account institutional and ideological variations between two distinct policy moments: the age of expansion and the age of retrenchment. As demonstrated by Paul Pierson, the politics of social policy expansion is distinct from the politics of retrenchment, which emerged during the late 1970s and early 1980s in many advanced industrial societies.[93] During the postwar era, economic prosperity and demographic factors favored growth in social spending related to the logic of "credit claiming." Referring to the competition between elected officials interested in receiving credit for new social benefits, credit claiming contrasts with "blame avoidance," the attempt to protect oneself against potential public discontent related to retrenchment.[94] As elected officials generally seek for reelection and/or the establishment of a positive legacy, they want to receive credits for "good news" while avoiding blame for "bad news" related to social policy. As existing programs such as Social Security have created bold constituencies, enacting cutbacks is a difficult task for elected officials who face strong electoral risks. Yet, the concept of retrenchment alone, analyzed in Chapter 5, is insufficient to fully grasp the new politics of Social Security reform. As evidenced in Chapter 6, the path-departing reform known as Social Security privatization is not so much about retrenchment (that is, cutbacks and refinancing) as about the deep restructuring of the program in the sense of a new institutional logic rooted in a financial paradigm that became increasingly popular during the 1990s.

Although policy paradigms play a more direct role during the enactment or the restructuring of policies than during their expansion, paying simultaneous attention to policy ideas and political institutions is essential to understanding the politics of expansion as well as the politics of restructuring. As stated by Myles and Quadagno, the factors that may explain social policy expansion can also prove influential in the era of cutbacks and restructuring.[95] Despite the fact that the new politics of the welfare state is distinct from postwar expansion, the theoretical framework about ideas and institutions formulated in the previous section can help scholars better understand both historical moments without obscuring their institutional specificity.

Race, Gender, and the Political History of Social Security

Over the last two decades, scholarship about social policy history in the United States has increasingly focused on race and gender, two issues that had long been neglected in the traditional literature on welfare state politics.[96] Ever present in historical and social science research, this growing interest in race and gender largely stems from a critique of traditional perspectives about social and political order that emerged during the 1960s and 1970s in the context of bold feminist and civil rights mobilizations.[97] Although these issues of race and gender are distinct, they both refer to the impact of prejudice and discrimination against specific segments of the population. Racial and gendered forces can impact political decisions and shape legislative outcomes that, in turn, affect the patterns of social inequality themselves. From this standpoint, race and gender are related to the "politics of ideas," because arguments about the political influence of racial and gendered forces frequently emphasize the way cultural and economic prejudice shapes policy outcomes. Furthermore, scholars such as Robert Lieberman, Suzanne Mettler, and Theda Skocpol have shown that political institutions like federalism affect the manner in which race and gender can impact policy processes.[98] Consequently, the analysis of the relationship among gender, race, and welfare state politics is related to the theoretical issues addressed in the previous sections of this chapter.

In general, scholars interested in the possible impact of race and gender on welfare state development underline the fact that policy ideas and institutional legacies are grounded in profound—and sometimes hidden—forms of social inequality.[99] This is because most students of race and gender understand social policy as a system of social stratification that can either reduce or exacerbate economic and statutory inequalities stemming from family relations and labor market outcomes.[100] This is why students of race and gender frequently debate the work of Esping-Andersen, who formulated a typology of "welfare regimes" that underlines the impact of specific policy arrangements on patterns of social and economic inequality.[101] According to him, universalistic social policies such as the ones associated with the social-democratic welfare regime (Denmark, Sweden) produce more egalitarian outcomes than the liberal welfare regime that relies heavily on residual welfare programs that compensate for market failures (Canada, Japan, United Kingdom, United States) and the conservative regime that relies heavily on social insurance schemes that reflect labor market inequalities while transferring much welfare responsibility to the family (Belgium, France, Germany).[102] Scholars working on race and gender have criticized Esping-Andersen for his lack of attention to these issues, yet studies start from his assumption that social policy is closely tied to social and economic inequality. For example, there is a growing body of literature on the dual nature of the American welfare state and on the fact that the distinction between social assistance and social insurance ever present in the United States reflects and reinforces racial inequality. In his book *Race, Money, and the American Welfare State,* Michael Brown emphasized the dual nature of American social benefits as related to race: "As of 1986, white households received 90.5 percent of all non-means-tested transfers and 63.4 percent of means-tested payments while black households received only 8.2 percent of non-means-tested payments but 32.3 percent of means-tested payments."[103] Arguments about gender and the opposition between social assistance and social insurance underline similar patterns of inequality between men and women: the former receive higher social insurance benefits on average than the latter, and many more women depend on means-tested benefits than men.

This book does not challenge the idea that specific policy arrangements such as the division of labor between social insurance and social
assistance can reflect and even reinforce existing patterns of social
inequality. My interest in reconstructing the political history of Social
Security, not in measuring its impact on economic and social inequality, leads me to focus on *causal* racial and gendered forces that may
have impacted policy outcomes since the New Deal.

In the literature on race and on gender, there is a potential confusion between accounts of the *causes* of policy outcomes and descriptive
accounts about the *effects* of policies on social inequality. The following
quotation from Williams's *The Constraint of Race* illustrates the problematic relationship between political explanations and socioeconomic
effects in the literature on race and gender: "In sum, the Social Security
Act created a two tier system. The superior social insurance programs
applied mainly to whites and men, as they were designed to do. The
inferior relief programs . . . applied mainly to people of color and
women, as they were designed to."[104] The problem with this type of
sweeping generalization is that some authors assume that clear racial
and gendered effects are inevitably the product of racial and gendered
forces. Yet, this is not necessarily the case, and rigorous analysis is
always needed to demonstrate that race and gender shape policy outcomes in a specific policy area. If it is true that the decision to temporarily exclude agrarian and domestic workers disproportionately
affected African Americans, this does not mean that racist motives were
the origin of that decision. In Chapter 3, I will draw on recent scholarship to show that it was not the southern Democrats who were instrumental in excluding agrarian and domestic workers. Instead, fiscal and
administrative concerns constituted the true political origin of the temporary exclusion, a decision that had a disproportionate and potentially
detrimental socioeconomic effect on African-Americans.[105]

Although this book underlines the difference between the political
origins and socioeconomic effects of public policies, it also stresses crucial variations from one policy area to another.[106] For example, if racial
categories were not at the origin of the decision to exclude specific professional categories from Social Security, there is evidence that some
decisions taken in the field of old age assistance originated from south-

ern Democrats eager to protect racial hierarchies in their states. Yet, what is true in the field of social assistance is not necessarily true in the one of old age insurance.[107] In Chapter 3, I will underline these variations from one policy area to another. In Chapter 4, I will stress the fact that Social Security is not grounded in racial bias and that, as Lieberman showed, this program did not discriminate against African Americans, which was not necessarily the case with welfare programs. The contributive nature of Social Security and the gradual extension of coverage during the 1950s transformed that program into a quasi-universal and "color blind" program that enjoys strong popular support across racial lines. Paradoxically, as evidenced in Chapter 6, contemporary proponents of Social Security privatization have referred to racial differences in life expectancy to undermine support for the program among African Americans.

Parallel to the debate about race is that about gender inequality, which has emerged as a crucial issue in the historical literature about social policy in the United States.[108] The literature on gender inequality draws heavily on international scholarship about social citizenship and welfare regimes. The recent American scholarship on gender and social policy history is frequently grounded in the assumption that "the welfare state developed in a manner that was 'gendered:' imbued by particular ideas regarding the proper social organization of sexual difference, such as that men and women were treated differently in the policy-making process, with ascribed gender roles and gender inequality perpetuated."[109] In *Protecting Soldiers and Mothers,* for example, Skocpol argues that the Progressive Era witnessed the emergence of a matriarchal welfare state related to the mobilization of women's groups as well as the Supreme Court's more tolerant attitude toward social policy designed for women and children.[110] Although Skocpol seems to exaggerate the true scope and significance of pre-New Deal matriarchal projects, her study illustrated the impact of gender on American social policy. During the New Deal, Aid to Dependent Children (ADC [later Aid to Families with Dependent Children; AFDC]) would constitute the modest legacy of the matriarchal welfare state, whereas programs such as Social Security would emerge to protect male breadwinners and—indirectly—their families against economic risks. It is commonly argued that the distinction between "contract" (insurance) and "charity" (assistance) in American society reflects a gendered division of labor between men and women.[III]

The key issue concerning the relationship between gender and Social Security is that the *policy design* of specific Social Security provisions reflected traditional gender roles after the creation of the spousal and survivor benefits in 1939, which at first covered only women and children. Such benefits were rooted in the traditional assumption that most women should contribute to society mainly as spouses and mothers. So I argue that although race has not significantly influenced Social Security's development and benefit structure, ideas about traditional gender roles have in part shaped this program. As an element of redistribution hidden behind the rhetoric about personal responsibility that surrounded Social Security, spousal and survivor benefits masked "charity" under the veil of "contract" and "earned rights." Yet, it is worth noting that workingwomen have always been entitled to Social Security benefits on the basis of their own contributions. Because men have been entitled to spousal and survivor benefits since 1950, the relationship between gender roles and the benefit structure has become increasingly implicit. Furthermore, only a limited number of legislative amendments have been necessary to eliminate gender discrimination from the program's structure. Yet, it is true that, following the logic of social insurance, Social Security benefits reflect labor market inequalities, which are gendered—and racialized—in nature.

As the objective of this book is to reconstruct the political history of Social Security, I will only examine the issues of race and gender when there is a credible claim that they could have shaped the development of Social Security in a significant and direct way. My conclusions do not extend to policy areas that fall beyond the scope of this study, although I do underline the variations between policy areas and the possible confusion between political forces shaping policy outcomes and the feedback effects of these outcomes on social and economic inequality. Integrating the study of race and gender into mainstream political analysis is a difficult task, and I hope that my attempt will contribute to the debates about the political significance of race and gender in American social policy history.

Conclusion

Through this chapter I have reviewed the main theoretical perspectives at the center of the current academic debates concerning social policy development. After demonstrating the relevance of historical institutionalism for the study of the politics of social policy, I have put forward arguments concerning the political role of frames and policy ideas. Although historical institutionalists often take policy ideas into account in their empirical studies, I argue that a more inclusive approach is needed to enrich the institutionalist perspective and, more concretely, to better understand the politics of Social Security in the United States. There is no contradiction between the systematic analysis of policy ideas sketched above and historical institutionalism as we know it. In fact, ideational and institutional processes are closely related, and I have shown how they interact in social policy development.

CHAPTER TWO

Setting the Reform Agenda

Between the late nineteenth century and the 1930s, many European nations created generally modest public pension schemes aimed at fighting the economic insecurity and social deprivation that affected a growing elderly population. Designed as a response to social problems related to industrialization, the first public pension schemes differed widely from one country to another; institutional and political differences between countries accounted for many variations in timing and policy design.[1]

The first country to implement modern public pension schemes was Germany, which in the late nineteenth century was a strong bureaucratic state pursuing an authoritarian and antisocialist nation-building strategy. As part of this strategy, in 1889 Bismarck's regime implemented a contributory pension and disability program that targeted mainly blue-collar workers. A decade later, farm workers gained coverage under a separate program, and in 1911 white-collar employees were granted separate old age and disability protection. The establishment of these programs and the advent of the German social insurance system formed part of an attempt to divide the labor movement while increasing wage-workers' loyalty toward the recently created German Empire.[2]

More democratic polities also enacted public pension schemes before World War I. In 1908, after three decades of debates, Great Britain, then Europe's most advanced industrial country, launched a noncontributory, means-tested pension for citizens over age seventy. The delay in the implementation of such a program was partially due to the original opposition of fraternal societies, which formed a powerful interest group that often perceived public pensions as a threat to their very existence.[3] Another interesting national case is Sweden, which enacted a contributory public pension scheme in 1913, when it was far less industrialized than Britain. An agrarian lobby successfully pushed for universal coverage, an arrangement consistent with the perceived economic interests of Swedish farmers.[4]

During the first decades of the twentieth century, the Swedish model based on universal coverage remained marginal, and most European countries chose between two main types of public pension schemes. Restricted social insurance schemes similar to Bismarck's were enacted in Austria (1906), France (1910), the Netherlands (1913), Italy (1919), Portugal (1919), Spain (1919), Belgium (1924), and Hungary (1926). These social insurance schemes covered only some specific professional categories, especially blue-collar workers. Old age assistance programs similar to the 1908 British legislation were implemented in Denmark (1891), France (1905), Iceland (1909), and Norway (1923).[5] Yet the distinction between "insurance" and "assistance" should not hide the fact that before World War II both types of pension schemes offered relatively modest benefits that served more as—limited—antipoverty devices than as genuine income-maintenance measures. Moreover, the legal entitlement age was set significantly above the average life expectancy of the covered populations. A large number of covered individuals thus died before receiving any benefits.[6]

Unlike these European countries or even Canada, which developed a modest federal old age assistance program in 1927, the United States did not implement national public pension programs before the Great Depression. Even so, the debate over pension reform and social insurance during the first three decades of the twentieth century affected later developments by moving the issue of old age security onto the public agenda not long before the Great Depression's radical insecurity hit the country in the absence of a genuine "safety net."

In order to illustrate the institutional and ideological obstacles that social reformers faced during the Progressive Era and the 1920s, I discuss the long-term effect of formal political institutions and policy legacies and argue that, even though pension reform emerged relatively late on the national reform agenda, this timing would actually prove crucial for the development of old age security after 1929. I also stress the impact of policy paradigms and emphasize the influence of federalism and other political institutions on reformers' ideas and strategies.

Institutions, Patronage, and Military Pensions

The American Revolution was a direct attack against the European model of concentrated governmental authority and sovereignty. Even if the 1787 Constitution represented an attempt to increase the power of the newly created federal government, it favored the emergence of a highly fragmented polity. Although some scholars have divided American constitutional development into specific historical moments or regimes,[7] checks and balances and federalism have structured the political life of the Republic for more than two centuries.

The Constitution splits and balances powers among the legislative, executive, and judicial branches of the federal government (Articles I, II, and III). Such checks and balances make widespread, radical political change unlikely in the absence of strong electoral coalitions. Still, this extreme power fragmentation does not necessarily mean that bold social reforms such as the advent of national health insurance are impossible, as some scholars have argued.[8] During rare—and relatively brief—institutional windows of opportunity, major path-breaking policy change can occur. From this perspective, having checks and balances helps create a seemingly discontinuous political history during which brief "critical junctures" alternate with longer periods of relative institutional and legislative stability.[9]

On the other hand, federalism limits the authority of the central government by granting state governments their own authority over specific jurisdictions (Article IV and the Tenth Amendment). As opposed to unitary polities such as France and the United Kingdom, for example, national sovereignty is thus shared among local, state, and federal levels of authority. In the comparative literature on federalism, the American system is also described as an "intrastate model" where

regional discontents are usually channeled through the federal legislative process and rarely through formal bargaining between the states
and the federal government. Because states are equally and explicitly
represented in the Senate, there is no need for the type of formal bargaining that is ever present in interstate federal systems such as the
one that has emerged in Canada since 1867.[10] As opposed to the Canadian system, the American constitutional order also lacks fiscal equal-
ization procedures aimed at reducing inequality between regions and
states. This model favors interstate competition and, in some contexts,
a genuine "race to the bottom."[11]

These institutional characteristics proved well entrenched before
the New Deal, when the decentralized structure of American federalism strongly empowered business interests at the state level, where
political power remained fragmented and open to business influence.
And, because states needed to compete for investments, the logic of
tax competition related to the enduring weight of business power
largely prevailed over the one of economic security and redistribution.[12] Furthermore, institutional decentralization permitted the reproduction of the Jim Crow regime in southern states. As segregation
deprived most African Americans of their civil rights, reformers found
it particularly difficult to impose social reforms in the South, a region
where racism strengthened a well-entrenched economic conservatism
tied to an agrarian mode of production dependent upon cheap labor.
At both the state and the federal levels, most southern politicians
opposed social and economic reforms that could undermine the foundations of the segregationist order and the economic interests of their—
white—constituencies.[13] Like checks and balances, federalism did not
constitute an absolute obstacle to reform during the Progressive Era
and the 1920s. Yet, it frequently complicated the efforts of reformers
and progressive politicians who supported the development of modern
social policies.

Fears concerning centralization and other forms of power concentration have remained a constant characteristic of the American political tradition. For that reason, its ideological repertoire embodies
numerous manifestations of a lack of trust toward government, especially the federal one. From the 1780s to the Civil War, the rationale
against the expansion of the federal government was linked to the ideas

of democracy and self-government. The central government was then
depicted as a wholly aristocratic and unreliable political body, and many
politicians, such as President Andrew Jackson and Vice President John
C. Calhoun, defended states' rights.[14] After the Civil War, which represented the peak of the opposition against the central government,
antifederalist mobilization declined as a potent, substantive political
force. Yet fears of political centralization and big government maintained a prominent stature in the American political discourse. Related
to a defense of voluntarism and self-reliance as an alternative to governmental intervention, the rhetoric against big government indeed remained a central frame in the American political debate until—and
even after—the New Deal.[15]

Beyond these general ideological and institutional trends, however,
the American political system that emerged during the nineteenth century had two characteristics that would create further obstacles to social
reform: the power of the Supreme Court and the corrupting influence
of patronage. Discussing these characteristics is necessary to the understanding of the conditions under which Civil War pensions expanded
during and after the Reconstruction.

The "State of Courts and Parties" and
Military Pensions

During the decades following the Civil War, military pensions gradually became an important source of economic security for a significant
proportion of American elderly citizens. According to Theda Skocpol,
the growth of Civil War pensions must be understood in the context of
the "state of courts and parties" that emerged during the first decades
of the nineteenth century.[16] Not originally envisaged in the Constitution, this "state of courts and parties" was the outcome of two specific
institutional developments: the self-proclamation by the Supreme Court
of its power to declare legislation "unconstitutional" (*Marbury v. Madison*, 1803) and the advent of modern political parties under the Jackson
presidency.[17] During the second half of the nineteenth century, judges
and party officials thus played a crucial role in regulating a political
order in which government had weak bureaucratic capacities. This relative weakness of federal bureaucratic structures, as well as the "spoils
system" (party control over administrative nominations), favored the

development of widespread political patronage. Because political parties controlled much of public administration's staffing and functioning, "the autonomous of the public service" remained limited.[18] In this context, public administration was perceived as partisan and dependent upon powerful political machines; government could hardly be expected to administer and implement redistributive public policies in a fair and seemingly neutral manner.

Paradoxically, the first significant efforts to reform the federal civil service and create a modern merit system occurred after the Civil War, exactly when military pensions emerged as a crucial political issue in the United States.[19] Financed through budget surpluses generated by protectionist tariffs that served the interests of northern industrialists, Civil War pensions were first aimed at protecting disabled war veterans and their families.[20] Yet in the context of the fierce postbellum electoral competition between Democrats and Republicans, eligibility criteria were gradually liberalized. The expansion of military pensions, which was supported by the Grand Army of the Republic and other veterans' organizations, also had a strong advocate in the Republican Party, which mobilized a patriotic discourse to justify the growing coverage and generosity of Civil War pensions. As noted by an early student of military pensions, "The History of Civil War pension legislation is one of continually increasing liberality on the part of Congress."[21] As a consequence of the legislation enacted between the 1860s and the first decade of the twentieth century, approximately 30 percent of the male population aged sixty-five and older was receiving a Civil War pension in 1910.[22] In addition to that, more than 300,000 widows and orphans were receiving Civil War benefits. For that reason, Civil War pensions by far represented the most significant federal spending program at the beginning of the twentieth century.

The uneven territorial distribution of military pension benefits clearly gave an advantage to the East and the Midwest as compared to the South. In 1910, for example, more than 40 percent of the population aged sixty-five and older received Civil War pensions in Midwest states such as Ohio, Kansas, and Indiana.[23] In southern states, Civil War pensioners formed a small minority of the elderly population, and the pension system designed to support Confederate veterans and their families was far less generous than the federal system aimed at supporting those who had successfully defended the Union.[24] Considering that Civil War pensions for the Union veterans were largely financed through budget surpluses generated by high tariffs at odds with the South's perceived economic interests, military pensions represented a highly contentious regional and political issue during and after the Reconstruction.[25] Moreover, the apparent corruption in the system's management seemed to favor those individuals and families with political connections. In this context, this very patriotic scheme became a true symbol of patronage and corruption in the eyes of many Americans.[26]

The Long-Term Political Impact
of Civil War Pensions

During the first two decades of the twentieth century, even social reformers actively supporting the transformation of federal military pensions into a genuine, permanent, and universal old age security program recognized that the system created during and after the Civil War constituted more a warning than a great political example to follow. According to progressive reformer and social insurance advocate Charles Henderson, for example, future policymakers would have to fight the distrust toward public pensions induced by the corrupt management of Civil War pensions: "The extravagance and abuses of this military pension system have probably awakened prejudice against workingmen's pensions."[27] In the same vein, a Columbia University professor and a member of the American Association for Labor Legislation (AALL), Henry Rodger Seager, argued: "Our experience with military pensions has not predisposed us to national pensions of any description."[28] Although some reformers used the "industrial army" metaphor to justify their public pension proposals,[29] Civil War pensions represented an obstacle to genuine social reform in the sense that their expansion illustrated the enduring role of patronage, a phenomenon that came under fierce attack during the Progressive Era. Yet it would be misleading to overemphasize this specific aspect of the Civil War pension legacy. Distrust toward government had existed before the expansion of Civil War pensions, and one could argue that their negative political image only reinforced patterns already present in the American political tradition. Furthermore, there is strong evidence that federalism and business opposition had a far greater impact on the politics of social policy reform during the Progressive Era than the negative reputation of patronage-driven military pensions.[30]

A more significant consequence of Civil War pensions is related to the massive yet unevenly distributed protection they granted. The scope of the program and the relative generosity of benefits sheltered thousands of elderly Americans against economic insecurity. At the turn of the century, Civil War pensions indeed paid comparatively higher benefits than those of most European public pension systems. In the United States, "the average pension in the years 1890–1910 was the equivalent of 30 percent of average annual earnings. By way of contrast, Germany's old age and invalidity pensions never reached 20 percent of average earnings, and Britain's pension under the 1908 law was about 22 percent."[31] Civil War pensions were thus apt to prevent poverty among the elderly population entitled to benefits.

The uneven distribution of benefits, however, did not favor a massive elimination of poverty among the elderly. As opposed to most European public pension schemes of the time, Civil War pensions were in fact paid to members of all socioeconomic categories, including middle-class and affluent citizens. Benefits frequently went to well-off white citizens, and a large number of low-income individuals—many of them immigrants or African Americans—were generally excluded: "*The most singular feature of the American pension system is that it primarily redounds to the advantage of a class least in need of old-age pensions.* This, and not the evidences of fraud in obtaining a pension, is the gravest indictment of the pension system, with its annual expenditure of $160,000,000."[32] This seemingly unfair and paradoxical distributive logic is related to the fact that military pensions were not specifically designed to address the needs of the elderly poor and that their justification was a political one.

Although military pensions contributed to the well-being of a significant portion of the American elderly population, their civic—ideological—foundation was far removed from a general and explicit recognition of the specific needs of that population.[33] According to Michael Dahlin, military pensions actually contributed to the masking of the negative consequences of industrialization and urbanization for the elderly population.[34] After 1912, however, Civil War pension spending declined gradually, as did the number of individuals eligible for benefits.[35] By that time, a number of social reformers were already drawing the public's attention toward socioeconomic problems affecting the elderly population. Through their writings and campaigns, these reformers constructed aging as a significant social problem while stressing the need to reform in order to protect an elderly population now described as frail and vulnerable.[36]

Framing the Need to Reform

In the United States, as in most other industrialized countries, during the first decades of the twentieth century a reformist discourse emerged concerning the social and economic fate of the elderly population.[37] Although some historians have recently argued that industrialization and urbanization did not favor a sudden degradation of the elderly's socioeconomic status, reformers depicted old age as a source of deprivation and insecurity. Old age, which had long been perceived as the cause of "private troubles" such as poor health or solitude, was now gradually constructed as a most vulnerable stage of the life course associated with widespread "social problems" requiring collective, not individual, responses.[38] "Far from being a scientific and technical answer to an objective condition, the social insurance movement was from its inception a broadly conceived response to the problem of the individual's security and responsibility and to the problem of society's security and responsibility."[39] Rooted in a sociological and pragmatic vision frequently at odds with "rugged individualism," arguments concerning old age insecurity and poverty focused on four main issues: (1) the decline of traditional family structures, (2) the growing exclusion of older workers from the labor market, (3) the degrading status of elderly people living in poorhouses, and (4) the massive gaps in the protection associated with "welfare capitalism." Reformers' claims concerning old age insecurity sometimes seem problematic when compared with available historical data, yet from a political perspective, the empirical accuracy of the claims is less important than their impact on the agenda-setting process and the construction of the need to reform.[40] The four issues addressed by reformers point to the old age insecurity "problem stream" as it emerged during the three decades preceding the Great Depression.

Aging, Family Structures, and Economic Exclusion in the Industrial Society

The growing interest in the socioeconomic status of the elderly population was ever present in the work of progressive reformers such as Abraham Epstein, Isaac Rubinow, Henry Seager, and Lee Squier.[41] According to these authors, industrialization and urbanization increased economic insecurity affecting older workers and their families. In his book *Social Insurance,* for example, Seager explored the perceived link between urbanization, the decline of traditional family structures, and the decline of the elderly's socioeconomic status. For him, urbanization clearly undermined children's capacity to support their elderly parents.[42] In small urban apartments, it seemed difficult to have three generations living together under the same roof. This was especially the case for working-class families relying on meager industrial wages for their subsistence. For Charles and Carrie Thwing, the individualistic ethos at the center of urban civilization further undermined intergenerational solidarity.[43] Discussing the transformation of family structures in the industrial era, another reformer argued that the traditional patriarchal model that had long been associated with agrarian communities had served to protect the elderly against insecurity and economic deprivation: "The authority of the patriarch is paramount and lasts longer than his productive powers. When no longer able to lead a plow, he is still looked up for an advice."[44] An implicit recognition of traditional gender roles, this citation points to another central issue present in the reformers' discourse concerning old age insecurity: the economic exclusion of older workers in the industrial society.

In the United States, the image of the prematurely disqualified worker unable to follow the infernal rhythm of modern industrial production indeed became an essential component of the early-twentieth-century discourse concerning old age insecurity.[45] From this point of view, technological progress and scientific management were frequently depicted as a major source of exclusion that shortened older workers' active lives.[46] In his book *The Challenge of the Aged,* Epstein discussed the impact of specialization related to the advent of scientific management:

> In our present industrial establishments, specialization has become the almost universal rule. Production is so standardized that each individual performs only two or three operations in the whole complicated business of producing the finished article. Standardized production not only eliminates the need for skill and experience—the very assets of the older employee—but inevitably demands a swifter pace which produces greater nervous strain and tends to wear out workmen more rapidly than ever before. As a result, the period during which an industrial worker can be profitably employed, despite the prolonged span of life in general, is constantly growing shorter.[47]

Perceived as unable to adapt themselves to the specific demands of modern chain production, older workers were "discarded and replaced by industry in the same way as out-of-date and worn-out machines."[48] To reinforce the dramatic nature of this exclusion, Epstein then evoked the future fate of these discarded workers: "Many of these wage workers . . . are merely left to tread the narrow path of old age dependency which ultimately winds its way into the high road 'over the hill to the poorhouse.' "[49] This last remark illustrates another key aspect of the reformers' attempt to construct the "need to reform": the constant references to the poorhouse, an institution then commonly viewed as a true symbol of destitution.

From Poorhouses to Pensions?

During the second half of the nineteenth century, many Americans perceived a growing connection between poorhouses and the elderly. Although only 2 percent of the aged actually lived in these institutions,[50] "the nation's public asylums were filled with growing proportions of inmates above age sixty; the elderly came to be viewed as the 'natural' inhabitants of the public institutions."[51] According to Carole Haber and Brian Gratton, the creation of separate social institutions for the mentally disabled and other indigent categories largely explained increasing percentages of elderly residents.[52]

This demographic shift was perceived in the mirror of the poorhouses' increasingly negative image. In the eyes of social reformer

Harry C. Evans, for example, poorhouse had become "a word of hate and loathing, for it includes the composite horrors of poverty, disgrace, loneliness, humiliation, abandonment, and degradation."[53] Concerned with the growing proportions of elderly inmates, reformers constantly referred to poorhouses to promote the idea that old age had become a major source of insecurity and deprivation in American society. In various books and magazines, they argued that the elderly living in these institutions were being "abandoned" and that Americans deserved better than such a harsh treatment after years of hard work.[54] For these reformers, the poorhouses constituted an antimodel for social reforms designed to solve the apparent socioeconomic problems related to industrialization and urbanization. Pensions were framed in opposition to the repressive poorhouse and were depicted as the only way to maintain the elderly at home, that is, to preserve their social and economic dignity.[55] According to social reformers such as Epstein, however, existing voluntary pension plans were generally inadequate for preventing old age poverty while maintaining the elderly's autonomy and dignity.[56]

The first private plans had been created by the railroad industry during the last quarter of the nineteenth century.[57] These pensions primarily served managerial goals such as fighting turnover, increasing workers' obedience, and generating organizational efficiency. During the first three decades of the twentieth century, a growing number of firms established similar pension plans consistent with the idea of welfare capitalism crystallizing at the time. Based on the assumption that employers should retain control over the labor force, welfare capitalism appeared as the paternalistic side of scientific management. During the shift from economic laissez-faire to business management, advocates of welfare capitalism argued that employers should be more proactive in both managerial regulation and economic protection: "In the 1910s and 1920s, organizations such as the National Civic Federation, the Taylor Society, the Special Conference Committee, the Industrial Relations Counselors, and Metropolitan's PSB promoted pecuniary welfare programs as tools of effective bureaucratic administration."[58] These advocates of welfare capitalism contended that employers should fight both labor unions and governmental interventions in order to exert maximum control over the workforce. In the United States, early-twentieth-century welfare capitalism represented a paternalistic model that could grant security to workers in exchange for peaceful labor relations and higher productivity rates. Moreover, welfare capitalism could improve the public image of American capitalism, which had been seriously damaged during the Progressive Era. Offering private benefits to workers illustrated the "human side" of American capitalism.[59]

Beyond the optimistic rhetoric associated with welfare capitalism, social reformers pointed out that private benefits were uncertain and offered protection to only a small portion of the American workforce. In 1920, for example, private pension plans covered less than 5 percent of the private workforce.[60] And because more than 75 percent of the private pension plans created before 1930 were noncontributory, they appeared more as a gift from the employer than as a genuine source of economic security. According to Epstein, most workers were denied benefits because of the high level of labor market mobility prevailing at the time:

> In most of the schemes studied, the minimum length of service demanded of a worker before retirement ranges from 20 to 25 years. If we bear in mind that authoritative statistics show that less than 4 percent of the male workers in industry stay with the same employer for twenty years or over and less than 3 percent of the women remain as long, it is difficult to see how the total number of workers who can qualify for industrial pensions under such rules can grow to such proportions as to materially reduce the great army of indigent aged in this country.[61]

From this perspective, private provisions could not successfully fight poverty and economic insecurity among the elderly. The same remark applied to labor union–sponsored pensions, which were even less developed at the time.[62]

While emphasizing the inadequacy of private pension plans, reformers also argued that private savings and other forms of self-reliance could not genuinely shield workers against the risk of old age destitution. In his book *Social Insurance,* for example, Rubinow stressed the limits of personal savings as a source of old age security. For him, saving was not a reliable protection against old age dependency for six specific reasons: (1) old age was a long-term condition that required continuous saving over a long period of time, (2) wageworkers did not know in advance how much money they had to save to prove adequate; (3) emergencies might force workers to use their savings before retirement; (4) the remoteness of old age prevented necessary savings early in one's life course; (5) average amounts saved at the time in the United States were "ridiculously small as compared to the amounts needed for a sufficient income at old-age;" and (6) "special savings for old age would only be possible through a persistent, systematic, and obstinate disregard of the needs of the working-man's family, which would make the preaching of such special savings a decidedly immoral force."[63] Fighting the idea that self-reliance and personal savings could prevent massive old age deprivation, Rubinow and other social reformers attacked the old liberal idea that private property and self-reliance should constitute the only foundation for economic security. Like European reformers of the time, they rejected the individualistic approach to economic protection and emphasized social responsibility.[64] Noting the inadequacy of "possessive individualism,"[65] reformers also underlined the limits of voluntarism, an approach to social protection associated with welfare capitalism and fraternal societies.[66]

Using the lacunae of private provisions as a starting point, many reformers thus pushed for the enactment of public pension provisions. While discussing European precedents, reformers also framed their discourse around the need to reform in a way that could appeal to the American public. Drawing on an ideological repertoire where personal autonomy represented a core issue, they formulated a normative discourse about social order to justify the adoption of public pension programs. Against the image of deprivation and dependency associated with the poorhouse, many social reformers supported governmental intervention taking the form of public pensions, which could enable elderly individuals and couples to maintain an autonomous lifestyle in the comfort of their homes.[67] Formulated as a response to the discourse about voluntarism and "rugged individualism," the arguments in favor of public pensions were rooted in traditional American images about personal autonomy and responsibility.

The debate concerning old age insecurity gradually entered the public arena. During the 1910s, the United States witnessed the multiplication of state commissions dealing specifically with aging-related issues

(Massachusetts, 1910, 1915; California, 1917; Ohio, 1919; Pennsylvania, 1919). Yet, even though old age insecurity was slowly moving onto state policy agendas, social reformers concerned by the issue found it difficult to convince other advocates of social insurance and economic regulation to push for the enactment of old age pensions in the United States. For this reason, the pension movement was launched a full decade after the campaigns concerning unemployment and health insurance. One influential organization involved in the construction of the reform agenda during the Progressive Era and the 1920s was the American Association for Labor Legislation. Also important in the campaigns of the pension movement were Abraham Epstein and the Fraternal Order of Eagles.

Reformers at Work: From Social Insurance to Old Age Pensions

During the Progressive Era, reformers and reform-minded academics organized to promote the development of labor regulations, social insurance, and other forms of social policy. Despite widespread fear of political corruption as well as institutional obstacles such as federalism and the Supreme Court's conservative stance on social programs and economic regulation, these reformers attempted to convince citizens, policymakers, and interest groups that only modern public policies such as those implemented in some European countries could advance macroeconomic regulation while improving the condition of wage workers and their families.

The AALL's Agenda and the Doomed Social Insurance Campaigns

Although studies concerning European reforms had been published since the early 1890s,[68] it was the creation in 1906 of the AALL that inaugurated the American social insurance movement. Affiliated with the European-based International Association for Labor Legislation founded six years earlier, the AALL promoted a scientific model of social and economic reform aimed at regulating the capitalist system in a more effective and peaceful manner. Led by economists such as

Richard T. Ely and John R. Commons, this organization rapidly increased its membership and organizational capacities by 1910.[69]

By that time, the AALL was already involved in its first major legislative crusade: the push for the enactment of workmen's compensation schemes at the state level. Related to the widely perceived need to reform the existing court-based compensation system, this first legislative campaign proved highly successful. Between 1911 and 1920, forty-two states enacted public workmen's compensation schemes.[70] Stimulated by the legislative success of this first interstate legislative crusade, the AALL then launched campaigns in favor of unemployment compensation and, more important, health insurance.[71] Opposition from business interests and, in the case of health insurance, the American Medical Association (AMA), fraternal organizations, and commercial insurers meant that the AALL failed to convince state policymakers to support its proposals. Forced to campaign at the state level in order to neutralize enduring constitutional obstacles, the AALL could not effectively fight the "concern of state leaders that employers would leave states that implemented costly social reforms—a concern that gave employers significant influence in state legislative debates."[72] In addition, labor unions—in particular those representing craft workers— generally opposed unemployment and health insurance in the name of labor autonomy. For example, the president of the American Federation of Labor (AFL), Samuel Gompers, rejected any political intrusion into collective bargaining, including social insurance. Defending voluntarism, he argued that workers should protect themselves against social ills.[73] As mentioned in Chapter 1, this negative attitude toward the state mostly represented a reaction against the hostility of the Supreme Court toward unionism.[74] "The AFL's strategy of business unionism was forged during its prolonged struggle with the courts over workers' industrial rights, particularly during the unsuccessful anticonspiracy campaign waged during the three decades following the civil war."[75] Unions' political vulnerability shaped their negative perception of government, which was considered a threat to their own survival. It is tempting to consider this negative attitude toward public policy as a key feature of American welfare state exceptionalism, but European historical data contradict this view. Instead of promoting the development of social insurance during the first three decades of the twentieth century, many European unions opposed the advent of compulsory insurance in the name of labor autonomy. The debate surrounding the enactment of the 1910 French legislation on old age insurance illustrates the potential scope of such labor opposition.[76] It was only after World War II that the vast majority of European labor unions came to support social insurance.

In the context of this ideological opposition closely related to existing institutional arrangements, the AALL campaigns concerning both unemployment and health insurance resulted in a legislative fiasco. Despite the efforts of reformers to frame these proposals in a socially and politically acceptable manner, no legislation was implemented at the state level. The question pertinent to the topic of this book, however, is why this organization decided to fight for unemployment insurance and then health insurance instead of old age insurance in the first place. Two main factors explain the AALL's strategic choices.

First, policy ideas played a crucial role, as most AALL members shared a distinctive paradigm that explains some of their most significant policy choices. These reformers generally perceived social insurance as a tool for persuading employers to prevent socioeconomic risks such as sickness, unemployment, and work accidents. As noted by economist and AALL member John Andrews:

> My own belief is that advocates of unemployment insurance have very often emphasized it merely as a method of relief, but is it not true that the more far-seeing advocates of the insurance method in every branch of social insurance have in mind a very important consideration? . . . I know that Prof. Commons and I in all of the work we have done together have thought first of prevention and second of relief in dealing with each form of social insurance in this country.[77]

According to many AALL reformers, employers would act to reduce the scope of socioeconomic risks if they knew that they would have to compensate wageworkers.[78] Because most AALL reformers did not consider old age as a preventable socioeconomic risk, however, this organization did not push for old age programs during the Progressive Era. In fact, reformers such as Epstein and Rubinow, who energetically supported the idea of public pensions, were marginalized within the AALL, and this organization would only promote such pensions energetically during the 1920s, that is, after its influence had started to fade.[79]

Federalism is a second factor that helps explain why AALL reformers—including Epstein and Rubinow—did not push for old age insurance before the New Deal, including during the 1920s, when old age insecurity became a significant policy issue. Because of the high level of interstate labor mobility in the United States, AALL reformers such as John B. Andrews believed that old age insurance could only take the shape of a federal program.[80] Facing the Supreme Court's opposition to the development of comprehensive federal social and economic legislation, the reformers believed that a purely federal social insurance scheme was impossible at the time. For this reason, in the 1920s, reformers pushed for the adoption of a "model bill" on old age assistance at the state level. This state-by-state strategy illustrates again the crucial role of federalism in shaping reformers' strategies and policy ideas.[81]

The Pension Movement: Framing the Reform Agenda during the 1920s

The movement in favor of old age pensions truly emerged after World War I and the failure of the health insurance campaign launched under the aegis of the AALL. Although the AFL rejected social insurance, this organization supported the idea of old age assistance, which did not involve compulsory participation associated with social insurance.[82] Yet, it was not the AFL that took an active part in the pension movement but state federations and, more important, the United Mine Workers (UMW). In 1919, the UMW actually launched a political campaign in favor of old age pensions that was the origin of the pension movement of the following decade. Then at the peak of its strength, the UMW mobilized to reduce old age insecurity through the enactment of pension bills at the state level. First launched in Kentucky, the UMW's mailing and legislative campaign rapidly spread to Illinois and Indiana. Unfortunately for pension advocates, the UMW's strength started to decline after the beginning of this campaign as employers successfully undermined its organizational capacities. Because of that, the UMW's pension crusade rapidly faded.[83]

Paradoxically, it was during the conservative and prosperous 1920s that old age pensions were durably placed on many state policy agendas. During that decade, Russian-born social reformer Abraham Epstein took the lead of the emerging pension movement. In his campaign for the enactment of old age assistance programs at the state level, Epstein received the support of labor unions and, more important, the Fraternal Order of Eagles, an organization seeking to increase its public profile and its membership.[84] As already discussed, social reformers of the 1920s focused almost exclusively on old age assistance for the poor, not old age insurance for wageworkers. Facing business opposition, enduring institutional constraints, and an unfavorable ideological climate, Epstein and his allies nevertheless drafted a model bill on old age assistance during a conference held in New York in December 1922.[85] The Fraternal Order of Eagles then launched a national campaign to bring this model bill to the attention of twenty-four state legislatures.[86] Despite the efforts of this organization, business opposition remained strong, and only six states had enacted laws by 1927. Moreover, these laws were ineffective because the Eagles supported "county option" bills in order to secure legislative success. This specific provision left the decision to implement and finance old age pensions to the counties, which rarely picked this costly option. Aware of this situation, Epstein had already resigned his position with the Eagles in 1924. Three years later, he also quit the declining AALL to launch his own reform organization: the American Association for Old-Age Security (AAOAS), which would later become the American Association for Social Security.[87] Starting that year, Epstein and his newly created organization adopted a more aggressive and consistent strategy and, just before the beginning of the Great Depression, the pension movement seemed stronger than ever.[88] Although only Wisconsin and Montana were offering old age assistance benefits in 1928, this regenerated pension movement continued to spread the idea that old age insecurity represented a key social and political issue in American society.

An interesting example of this growing political interest in old age insecurity is the situation that prevailed in New York State. There, Epstein worked with Governor Franklin Delano Roosevelt, an advocate of social insurance and old age pensions. In 1930, after the creation of an old age commission, the state legislature enacted comprehensive old age assistance legislation.[89] That year, the United States had been facing the Great Depression for months, and such a radical economic and social transformation accelerated the legislative process in many states, so that there was a multiplication of state old age assistance programs during the first half of the 1930s. Given that the issue of old age security had emerged on many state policy agendas in the late 1920s and that specific bills had been debated in state legislatures, such laws were enacted rapidly in reaction to the Great Depression. This situation contrasts with the one of health insurance and unemployment insurance, two policy alternatives that had moved to the periphery of most state policy agendas after the failure of the AALL's legislative campaigns of the 1910s.[90] This process illustrates the role of timing and agenda setting in the early history of modern American social policy.

Pension Reform and the Federal Government
Before the New Deal, the federal government was not a central player in the field of social policy. As in Canada, constitutional obstacles made the idea of comprehensive federal social policy problematic at best. This was especially true concerning social insurance, which implied the imposition of a compulsory payroll tax that would probably fall victim to the Supreme Court's conservative jurisprudence. The situation seemed more promising in the field of social assistance for deprived mothers. In 1921, Congress enacted the Sheppard-Towner Maternity and Infancy Act, the first federal social welfare program in the United States. This legislation implemented federal matching grants to the states for midwife training, prenatal clinics, and other measures that could help pregnant women and young mothers in order to reduce infant mortality. According to Skocpol, this legislation was enacted because a strong coalition of reformers and women's organizations lobbied for its enactment immediately after American women obtained the right to vote, when elected officials could still imagine that they would vote as a block.[91] Another factor that helps explain the relative success of welfare policies for mothers (that is, state pensions and funding for prenatal care) during the Progressive Era and the 1920s was that business interests did not mobilize strongly against what appeared as modest measures that would not affect labor relations in a significant way.[92] This situation contrasted with the one in the field of old age pensions, which directly involved business interests and labor relations.

Although Congress failed to enact legislation on old age pensions during the 1910s and 1920s, some federal elected officials put forward various bills dealing directly with that issue. As early as 1909, Representative William B. Wilson of Pennsylvania drafted a bill providing means-tested old age benefits to the elderly. It is interesting that the bill created an Old Age Home Guard of the United States Army that required pensioners to "report annually to the Secretary of War on military and patriotic sentiments in their communities. These peculiar arrangements were designed to avoid any constitutional objections to federal pensions."[93] This point is crucial, as it reflects the "constitutional obsession" of American reformers during the first three decades of the twentieth century and beyond. Yet tangible constitutional obstacles did not prevent elected officials from formulating more pension legislation proposals in the years following the defeat of Wilson's bill. Between 1910 and 1927, twenty-four of these proposals were discussed in Congress, reflecting the gradual emergence of the old age insecurity issue on the federal policy agenda. Generally ill conceived, none of these bills was enacted. Starting in 1927, Epstein's AAOAS pressured federal officials to enact an old age assistance matching grants bill similar to the Sheppard-Towner Act. Because most members of Congress were hostile to old age assistance legislation, however, Congress failed to enact matching grants during the 1920s.[94]

Another piece of evidence that old age insecurity had become a significant policy issue after World War I is the enactment in 1920 of the Sterling-Lehlbach Act, a measure that established a pension system covering federal civil servants. As opposed to most private pension plans of the time, this federal system was a contributory measure similar to an old age insurance scheme. Created mainly to favor bureaucratic efficiency while protecting retirees against economic insecurity, the Sterling-Lehlbach Act was the relatively modest outcome of a long campaign launched before World War I. Its passage illustrated the growing public salience of old age and retirement-related issues in the United States.[95] The Sterling-Lehlbach Act also contributed to the modernization of the federal civil service and the creation of a professional bureaucracy. Implemented successfully, this retirement system for civil servants demonstrated that the federal government was able to successfully run a large-scale contributory pension scheme.

Conclusion

During the first decades of the twentieth century, American social reformers faced strong ideological and institutional obstacles that hindered
their attempts to push for the enactment of modern social programs. In
the field of pension reform, the immediate legislative outcomes of the
pension movement launched in the 1920s were relatively modest, especially when compared with the situation prevailing in the mothers' pensions domain.[96] But it must be remembered that although Skocpol
associated mothers' pensions with the emergence of a "matriarchal welfare state," these pensions actually constituted a mere symbolic commitment on the part of the states, which spent relatively little money in
that policy area.[97] In contrast, although it was true that only a few states
had enacted old age assistance programs by the end of the 1920s,
reformers such as Epstein and their allies had been successful in transforming old age insecurity into a significant issue on many states' policy agendas. When the Great Depression struck the country and the
main ideological and institutional obstacles to comprehensive social
reforms gradually declined, the enactment of public pensions was being
debated in many states; such was not the case of health and unemployment insurance, issues that had long moved to the periphery of most
state policy agendas. Favorable timing contributed to the development
of a stronger pension movement during the first half of the 1930s.

Theoretically, this discussion points to the long-term impact of
agenda-setting processes and of policy ideas formulated by social and
economic reformers. Furthermore, such a discussion underlines the
powerful institutional obstacles these reformers faced during the Progressive Era and the 1920s. The next chapter shows how the Great
Depression lessened such institutional obstacles while favoring the
emergence of new actors and policy ideas that would both intensify and
reshape the American debate on aging and pension reform in the 1930s.

CHAPTER THREE

Enacting Old Age Insurance

It is possible to understand the dramatic impact of the Great Depression on American society in the mirror of the Progressive Era's modest social policy legacy. Although most West European countries had implemented sizable social programs during the first three decades of the twentieth century, the United States was ill prepared to face the negative economic consequences of the Great Depression. The election of President Franklin D. Roosevelt in 1932, however, favored a constitutional "regime change" that increased the role of the federal government in American society. Adopted in 1935, the Social Security Act durably transformed the field of social policy. It is interesting to note that this omnibus legislation created a measure seldom discussed before 1934: old age insurance. Never enacted at the state level, such a measure had not gathered much public attention. The synergy of five main factors explains the unexpected adoption of old age insurance in the United States: (1) the shock of the Great Depression itself, which made the need to reform increasingly evident while favoring a decline of business power and an increase in social mobilization; (2) the inception of the Townsend Plan, which helped maintain the issue of pension reform on the federal legislative agenda; (3) the president's will to develop a social insurance scheme as an alternative to both social assistance and the fiscally unsound policy alternative associated with the Townsend Plan; (4) on the policy legacy side, the timid development of private pensions and the absence of old age insurance at the state level—two realities that reduced the potential institutional obstacles to the advent of a purely federal insurance scheme in that specific policy area; and (5) the relative lack of political interest for old age insurance, which increased the autonomy of the president and the Committee on Economic Security in setting the legislative agenda in that domain. Most economic and political actors of the time perceived unemployment insurance and old age assistance as the most important elements of the proposed legislation on economic security.[1]

In this chapter I argue that the Townsend Plan kept the issue of old age insecurity on the policy agenda after the gradual triumph of the pension movement inaugurated a decade earlier by Abraham Epstein and his allies. The emergence of the Townsend Plan reinforced the legitimacy of—and the apparent need for—direct federal intervention in the field of old age security. I also explain the specific content of the 1935 Social Security Act regarding old age pensions and set forth an analysis of the policy paradigm behind the enactment of old age insurance. Finally, I explore the potential impact of gender and race on the legislative process. I first show that there is no direct evidence that existing racial hierarchies motivated the substantial reduction in old age insurance coverage enacted in Congress. I then discuss the relationship between old age insurance and traditional gender roles with a special emphasis on the exclusion of spousal and survivor benefits at an early stage of the policymaking process.

The Elderly, the Great Depression, and the "Need to Reform"

The disastrous social and economic consequences of the Great Depression had a paradoxical character: sudden deprivation in the context of great potential abundance and unprecedented economic optimism.[2] The new era of social insecurity and economic disillusion favored a radical transformation of the American policy agenda and a return to the idea of social insurance. Moreover, the dramatic impact of the Great

Depression on the elderly population helped reformers justify the need to reform in order to improve the socioeconomic status of this particularly vulnerable segment of the population. After 1929, the perceived relationship between old age and economic insecurity became stronger than during the previous decades, facilitating the reformers' ideological task. If the arguments put forward to frame the need to reform were similar to those of the 1920s, the changing economic and social context probably made these arguments seem more persuasive.

The Great Depression and the Decline of Welfare Capitalism

During the darkest moments of the Great Depression, it is estimated that the national unemployment rate was greater than 25 percent.[3] With the absence of a comprehensive "safety net," this high level of unemployment created widespread social and economic insecurity across the nation. In this new socioeconomic context, the elderly population was especially vulnerable. First, economic hardship seemed to further undermine intergenerational solidarity, a trend that had long been discussed by social reformers. In the specific context of the Great Depression, it became difficult for families to make ends meet and to also care for elderly relatives.[4] Second, the Great Depression reduced people's ability to save for retirement. Against the optimistic discourse of the American Bankers Association concerning the gradual increase in personal savings since the turn of the twentieth century, longtime advocate of public pensions Abraham Epstein argued in 1933 that, even before the Great Depression, "workers' savings have gone down rather than increased in the past few decades."[5] Already perceived as inadequate before 1929, personal savings constituted an even more problematic source of economic security at the beginning of the 1930s, when the American banking system faced the most important crisis of its history.

A third factor that potentially undermined the economic status of the elderly population was the relative decline of welfare capitalism and business power after 1929. Although many employers had expressed reservations about the effectiveness of private welfare programs in the 1920s,[6] the Great Depression favored an even more blunt assessment of welfare capitalism's apparent inability to protect the majority of American wageworkers against economic insecurity. This was particularly true in the field of old age pensions, where only about 100,000 elderly individuals were receiving private pension benefits in 1930. In this context, reformers argued, the private sector could not offer a decent pension to even a small minority of workers.[7] As during the previous decades, these reformers exploited the weaknesses of private benefits to stress the need to reform. Contrary to the situation in the 1920s, however, they were not preaching in a conservative desert dominated by the welfare capitalist creed.

Undeniably, the Great Depression and the ensuing political transformations considerably reduced the political influence of business interests in American society. Because investment plummeted rapidly, private firms had less political leverage and the risk of "investment strike" loss was not as threatening for state policymakers facing traditional dilemmas related to interstate competition. Furthermore, "the shift in activity from state capitals to Washington decisively freed policy makers from the shackles of interstate competition. The capacity to formulate national policies gave federal officials an opportunity to cope with the problem of capital mobility—and sharply reduced business' structural power."[8] Finally, an electoral realignment occurred that reduced the political influence of business organizations,[9] which were rapidly forced to reorganize their activities at the federal level in an adverse ideological climate. Although business leaders still played a significant role in American politics, the Great Depression certainly undermined their capacity to oppose bold social and economic reforms. Overall, this radically new political and ideological environment facilitated the work of social reformers during the first half of the 1930s.

Still, the decline of business power and the increasingly perceptible inadequacy of private pensions should not hide the fact that significant transformations of occupational welfare in the United States took place in the 1930s: the gradual shift toward contributory pension plans and the related triumph of the actuarial imperative of financial soundness. Inaugurated during the previous decade, this structural and organizational change reflected the growing role of actuaries in corporate governance. Although many employers remained faithful to the paternalistic, noncontributory method, the number of contributory

plans increased steadily during the 1930s. Besides, the "growing awareness of large and expanding pension liabilities [also] pushed many corporate sponsors toward . . . the decision to fund."[10] Although these
contributory (funded) plans could lead to the recognition of "earned
rights" at odds with traditional business paternalism, the decline of confidence in the private sector and the related ideological dismay of welfare capitalism legitimized the existing public pension movement.

The Pension Movement and the Inadequacy of State Assistance

As mentioned in Chapter 2, old age pensions emerged as a significant issue on states' legislative agendas toward the end of the 1920s,
just before the Great Depression struck the country in a dramatic manner. This new economic context facilitated the rapid enactment of pension bills that had already been debated in many state capitals. By the
end of 1934, as many as twenty-eight states—in addition to the territo-
ries of Alaska and Hawaii—were distributing old age assistance pensions.[11] And because the "county option" had mostly been discarded by
the mid-1920s, many of these programs were functioning on a state-
wide basis.[12]

Related to the new sociopolitical context of the Great Depression,
the multiplication of state assistance programs also revealed the limits
of a purely decentralized response to old age insecurity. Undeniably,
the Great Depression weakened the states' ability to protect citizens
against economic deprivation.[13] Coping with mounting interest charges
and in some cases bankruptcy, many states thus failed to distribute
pensions to all the needy elderly, and many people had to spend time
on waiting lists before receiving benefits. In addition, major disparities
existed between states that enacted old age assistance programs. In
1933, for example, average pension benefits varied from only six dollars per month (Indiana) to thirty (Maryland).[14] Reformers were aware
of these inequalities, and they argued that federal legislation was
needed more than ever to support the states in the struggle against old
age insecurity.[15] Considering that states and localities were facing growing fiscal hardship in the early 1930s, the enactment of bold federal
social reforms increasingly appeared as a logical answer to social and

economic problems that could hardly be addressed solely through voluntary and state-level initiatives.

At that time, a national party realignment led to a genuine "regime change" within the American constitutional order that favored a massive expansion of the federal government's economic role in American society.[16]

Bringing the Federal Government In:
The Townsend Plan

In 1933, the accession of Franklin D. Roosevelt to the presidency and the advent of a large Democratic majority in Congress favored a transformation of the role of the federal government in the United States.[17] Following the massive electoral realignment in the fall of 1932, President Roosevelt and the Democratic Congress pushed for greater federal involvement in the economic and social life of the nation. Launched in 1933, the New Deal became the label for this centralization of American polity that simultaneously increased the president's role during peacetime. Although Roosevelt was unable to accomplish some of his policy objectives while facing "countervailing forces within the government,"[18] many significant measures were enacted during his first few months in the White House. In addition to economic planning legislation (Agricultural Adjustment Act, National Recovery Administration), Congress enacted relief measures aimed at fighting massive unemployment (Federal Emergency Relief Act, Civilian Conservation Corps, Public Works Administration, Civil Works Administration). Depicted as temporary devices consistent with "American values," these bold public work initiatives represented the main source of "emergency relief" in the absence of unemployment insurance.[19] Coherent with the idea of work ethics, these programs directly contributed to the rapid increase in federal social spending during the 1930s.[20]

A symbol of the expansion of the federal government, public work initiatives such as the Civil Works Administration progressively transformed the relationship between government and society. Traditionally removed from the everyday life of most American citizens, the federal government suddenly became a key source of support for millions of them. In the space of two years it became the last possible "life buoy" for the victims of the Great Depression.[21] Although work relief programs were designed as temporary measures, they created new social expectations about the role of the federal government, which became associated with a discourse on security that transformed social protection into a core economic and political imperative.[22] These new expectations about social protection and the role of the federal government became increasingly present in the claims of specific social and political movements that came about after the election of Franklin Roosevelt to the presidency.

Such movements emerged to protest against widespread economic insecurity and to demand more government intervention to pump up the economy and redistribute income. From Father Coughlin's National Union for Social Justice to Huey Long's Share Our Wealth, these populist organizations formed a heterogeneous political nexus that increased the pressure on the Roosevelt administration to put forward bolder social and economic reforms before the 1936 presidential elections. For the president, Long's campaign in favor of economic redistribution formed the most significant political threat stemming from the left. Huey Long was a politician from Louisiana who had been elected to the Senate in 1930.[23] He seemed especially dangerous for the president because he belonged to the Democratic Party. It is interesting that Long's political platform included redistributive taxation but also social policy initiatives such as public work programs and old age assistance.[24] In 1933 and 1934, other radical figures such as Californian socialist Upton Sinclair and his End Poverty in California (EPIC) movement included the enactment of more generous public pensions in their platforms.[25] An issue already on the policy agenda when the Great Depression struck the country, public pensions increasingly appeared as a necessary response to widespread economic insecurity affecting the elderly population.

Yet, in the mind of one emerging public figure, old age pensions could play a far more crucial role in American society: restoring economic prosperity itself.[26] Also from California, medical doctor Francis E. Townsend claimed to know how to cure the life-threatening economic disease that had afflicted his country since October 1929. Initially formulated in a Long Beach newspaper in September 1933, the Townsend Plan called for the establishment of a federal old age pension of nothing less than $200 a month to citizens aged sixty or over, without criminal records, who agreed to leave the labor market while spending the money within thirty days.[27] This last condition seemed necessary, since the Townsend Plan aimed at pumping up the economy and restoring prosperity. Although Dr. Townsend recognized that his plan would help the elderly, its generosity stemmed from two macroeconomic objectives: increasing the national level of consumption and encouraging the elderly to retire in order to fight unemployment and create jobs for the young.[28]

Far from pushing for a fundamental transformation of social order, Dr. Townsend supported traditional family values and the logic of capitalism while imagining a rapid and simple way to restore economic prosperity. Yet, the Townsend Plan seemed radical because of the spectacular amount of the monthly pension. Because 87 percent of American families had an average annual income of less than $2,500 in 1935, a monthly pension of $200 ($400 for couples) represented a very generous sum in a context of economic deprivation.[29] Predictably, most economists at the time rejected the Townsend Plan as an overly expensive, inefficient, and frivolous scheme that could further hurt the American economy. In an analysis of the plan published by the Tax Policy League, for example, Mabel L. Walker argued that it "would crush business, bankrupt the country, deprive nearly 90 percent of the population of necessities in order to give luxury to less than 10 percent, and would initiate widespread graft. It is administratively impossible and economically suicidal."[30] Beyond academics and professional economists, most interest groups rejected the Townsend Plan in the name of fiscal and economic realism. From the National Association of Manufacturers to the American Federation of Labor, many influential organizations publicly opposed the plan and made clear that it would be a great mistake for Congress to enact it.[31]

In spite of this harsh criticism emanating from experts and interest groups alike, Townsend's movement expanded quickly to become a visible player in the American public arena. The movement's membership increased rapidly after 1933. With 3,000 clubs and half of million members in February 1935, it constituted a growing "army of the aged" that induced fear among several social commentators.[32] Aimed at solving the general economic problems of the nation, this movement mostly attracted elderly individuals looking for a better and safer life in an era of radical insecurity. Dr. Townsend's populist rhetoric and organizational skills, as well as the simplicity and the generosity of his plan, further contributed to the expansion of the movement.[33]

Many things differentiate Dr. Townsend's crusade in favor of old age benefits from the pension movement that had emerged during the 1920s. First, Dr. Townsend's initiative led to the creation of a mass movement grounded in a populist rhetoric distinct from the expert discourse of "scientific reformers" such as Abraham Epstein. Although these reformers attracted political and media attention using mail campaigns and union resources, they seldom organized large popular meetings as Dr. Townsend did in local stadiums. Second, the goals of the two movements were slightly different. If social reformers insisted on old age security per se, Dr. Townsend focused mostly on the macroeconomic objectives of pension reform. From his perspective, old age pensions were more an instrument of economic recovery than a tool aimed at fighting old age dependency. Like the AALL during the Progressive Era, Dr. Townsend attempted—in a far less rigorous manner—to justify social policy in the name of economic imperatives instead of concentrating on the social needs of the population he intended to cover.[34] This did not prevent the elderly from disproportionately supporting a policy alternative that would have significantly improved their living conditions.[35] Third, the proposals put forward by the two movements had little in common. Social reformers of the 1920s and early 1930s pushed mainly for the enactment of relatively modest social assistance programs, whereas the Townsend Plan called for the enactment of a bold policy alternative. As opposed to the state old age assistance model bill associated with Epstein during the second half of the 1920s, the far bolder Townsend Plan thus never represented a serious policy alternative for most policymakers. More important, Dr. Townsend supported the enactment of a *federal* pension program—as opposed to grants-in-aid to the states. Dr. Townsend's almost exclusive focus on the federal level of government illustrated—and reinforced—the growing federalization of social policy debates in American society. Although states and local governments were still playing a central role in providing social benefits, the federal government had become a growing source of hope for deprived citizens and those speaking in their name. This is related to the fact that, perhaps for the first time in a period of peace, American citizens could perceive the concrete and profound impact of federal policies on their everyday lives.[36] Because of these new popular expectations concerning the federal government's role, policymakers needed to act swiftly in order to receive electoral credit for answering new social protection demands.

Beginning in 1933, Dr. Townsend and his "army of the aged" helped keep the issue of old age insecurity at the center of the national policy agenda. Probably more than Epstein and other scientific reformers, the increasingly public profile of the Townsend Plan encouraged politicians to back federal public pension proposals.[37] Yet, the plan had little chance to be enacted because economists and policy experts rejected it almost unanimously. An unrealistic policy alternative, the Townsend Plan paved the way to more realistic alternatives that could answer widespread concerns about old age insecurity without moving the federal government away from fiscal conservatism.[38] Considering that states faced growing fiscal difficulties and that the electorate seemed to support the idea of public pensions, both parties openly backed the enactment of old age pension legislation in the spring of 1934, barely six months before the next congressional elections.[39] Among the two dozen legislative proposals debated in Congress that year, the Dill-Connery bill had the best chance to be enacted rapidly.[40] Regularly debated in Congress since 1930, that legislation called for federal grants-in-aid to the states that were distributing old age assistance pensions. With a budget of approximately $10 million a year, the Dill-Connery bill constituted an attempt to preserve the decentralized organization of old age assistance while reducing the states' financial burden by one third.[41]

During that spring of 1934, however, President Roosevelt made it clear that he would not support the Dill-Connery bill. Interested in fighting the Townsend Plan, he also had a greater plan in mind: using the popularity of noncontributory pensions to secure the enactment of a much more ambitious legislation on economic security that would include social insurance programs such as unemployment compensation and a contributory old age pension program.[42] This attempt to include federal funding for state old age assistance programs in the administration's bill could also become a way for the president to claim credit for the enactment of such popular alternatives as part of *his* legislation. This proved especially significant because President Roosevelt remained concerned about gaining reelection in 1936.[43] Respecting the president's will and wishing to facilitate the development of the administration's omnibus legislation, the Democratic majority in Congress never enacted the Dill-Connery bill.

Paving the Way for Old Age Insurance

On June 8, 1934, President Roosevelt unveiled his ambitious legislative project on economic security. In an address to Congress reviewing the objectives and accomplishments of his administration, he committed himself to the enactment of social insurance programs that would respect state autonomy while providing coverage against specific socioeconomic risks:

> Next winter we may well undertake the great task of furthering the security of the citizen and his family through social insurance. This is not an untried experiment. Lessons of experience are available from States, from industries and from many Nations of the civilized world. The various types of social insurance are interrelated; and I think it is difficult to attempt to solve them piecemeal. Hence, I am looking for a sound means which I can recommend to provide at once security against several of the great disturbing factors in life—especially those which relate to unemployment and old age. I believe there should be a maximum of cooperation between States and the Federal Government. I believe that the funds necessary to provide this insurance should be raised by contribution rather than by an increase in general taxation. . . . I have commenced to make, with the greatest of care, the necessary actuarial and other studies for the formulation of plans for the consideration of the 74th Congress.[44]

The content of this speech reflects the increasing prominence of the discourse on security that legitimized the enactment of new federal programs during the New Deal. Three weeks later, an executive order created the CES to undertake these studies and prepare the ground for the administration's omnibus legislation.

A Policy Paradigm for Old Age Insurance

President Roosevelt's prescriptions were crucial in shaping the Social Security Act. Without the president's push for social insurance, Arthur Altmeyer argued that "we would probably have today a national noncontributory form of social security in the country."[45] This statement applies especially well to the field of old age security. Of course, the reform campaigns of the Progressive Era had familiarized state policymakers with the concept of social insurance. Yet, if the idea of unemployment insurance was well established by 1934,[46] old age insurance represented anything but a major source of interest among reformers and politicians. No state had enacted an old age insurance program, and reformers such as Andrews had long argued that such a policy could function only as a federal measure.[47] Still facing strong institutional obstacles against federal social policy during the 1920s, reformers thus viewed state pensions as the only politically feasible method to fight old age insecurity.

In 1934, however, President Roosevelt pushed for an old age insurance scheme explicitly designed as an alternative to heavy reliance on social assistance and general revenue financing. The vision at the origin of this policy alternative was slightly different from the two main social insurance paradigms then competing in the field of unemployment compensation: one, the preventive model associated with the AALL and the unemployment program enacted in Wisconsin; the other, the social-needs model associated with Abraham Epstein and the unemployment insurance proposal put forward in Ohio. Although the first paradigm stated that a program based on employer reserves should incite firms to reduce their levels of unemployment, the second paradigm stressed the need to pool risks in order to offer genuine economic security to workers. In Ohio, this second paradigm paved the way to partial general revenue financing.[48] In the decentralized field of unemployment insurance, President Roosevelt and his advisers left the states free to adopt whichever paradigm they preferred. Yet, when dealing with old age insurance, these actors promoted a distinct social insurance paradigm that shaped the elaboration of that federal program.

The social insurance paradigm that the President supported in the field of old age security was largely based on the actuarial principles associated with the insurance industry and some large enterprises operating their own pension plans. Because the federal government had rarely been involved in the field of social policy before 1933, "there were few domestic examples of social provision *besides* private-sector initiatives that New Dealers could draw on, and few policy specialists whose work did not span the public and private sectors."[49] As a student of the Social Security Act has suggested, Roosevelt was probably exposed to insurance principles for the first time in 1921, when he became vice president of the Fidelity and Deposit Company of Maryland, one of the largest surety bonding firms in the United States.[50] Throughout the eight years he spent in the insurance and security business, Roosevelt became familiar with the principles of insurance. During his term as governor of New York (1929–1932), he publicly supported the application of these principles to social risks such as unemployment and old age insecurity.[51]

The policy paradigm that guided the work of the CES in the field of old age security was not an abstract philosophical construction but a set of "programmatic beliefs" dealing with three specific issues: coverage, the contributory method, and general revenue financing. First, the president supported *universal* insurance coverage through the establishment of compulsory contributions. From his perspective, all wageworkers should contribute to social insurance schemes to protect themselves and their families from economic insecurity.[52] This aspect of the paradigm was grounded in the assessment that voluntary—private—provisions could not effectively protect the majority of workers against economic insecurity. Second, Roosevelt embraced the idea of a strict actuarial relationship between contributions and benefits. A strict contributory logic could establish contractual "earned rights" that would protect the social insurance system against a potential ideological attack from the right. According to the president, the contractual logic associated with the contributory method granted "the contributors a legal, moral, and political right to collect their pensions." Because of those "earned rights," he argued, "no damn politician can ever scrap my social security program."[53] Related to the actuarial model that emerged in the private sector during the second half of the 1920s, this logic integrated considerations about actuarial equity and soundness to a long-term political strategy. Third, and consequently, Roosevelt rejected general revenue financing, an option then supported by Epstein and Rubinow, among others. Tied to the idea of self-support, the president's dismissal of general revenue financing in the field of social insurance was grounded in a critique of social assistance, which he depicted as a mere dole. A genuine fiscal conservative, he wanted workers to "purchase" their own economic security instead of depending on taxpayers' money. Considering that the federal income tax still appeared as a relatively modest fiscal tool during the New Deal, the president's concerns about general revenue financing reflected the limited fiscal capacities of the federal government.[54]

It is of interest that insurance companies such as Metropolitan Life had also formulated similar concerns about the contributory method and general revenue financing. As early as 1932, for example, this organization had published an analysis entitled *British Experience with Unemployment Insurance.* In this document, general revenue financing at the center of the British model was harshly criticized in the name of fiscal soundness and self-support.[55] This example illustrates how the president's ideas concerning social insurance were related to actuarial concepts and norms associated with the private sector, especially insurance companies. This traceable influence of ideas emanating from the private sector to Roosevelt and his team reveals two essential paradoxes. First, the genesis of federal social insurance was closely related to the perceived failure of private welfare programs. A compulsory, governmental method to shield workers against economic insecurity, such a social insurance program found some of its legitimacy in the recognition that *private* pensions were unable to provide economic security to the majority of American workers.[56] Second, although the president's insurance paradigm was rooted in private sector methods and metaphors, insurance companies and sponsors of private pension plans were not the driving force behind the policy choices that led to the enactment of federal old age insurance. The President and his team shaped the administration's pension proposals in an autonomous manner. In the field of old age security, the relative political autonomy of the president and the CES toward business interests thus favored the development of a contributory scheme largely modeled on private provisions increasingly perceived as unable to protect American workers against poverty and economic insecurity.

The CES in Action

On June 29, 1934, the president signed the executive order that established the Committee on Economic Security. According to this brief document, "the Committee shall study problems relating to the economic security of individuals and shall report to the President not later than December 1, 1934, its recommendations concerning proposals which in its judgment will promote greater economic security."[57] The CES had four specific—and generally implicit—objectives: (1) formulating detailed recommendations that could immediately inform the drafting of a complete legislative proposal, (2) coordinating the efforts of various federal agencies dealing with economic security issues, (3) gathering the available academic and bureaucratic expertise on social policy into one organization, and (4) through the dissemination of information about social insurance, increasing the political support for the anticipated bill.[58] The committee consisted of Secretary of Labor Frances Perkins (chair of the CES), Attorney General Homer Cummings, Secretary of the Treasury Henry Morgenthau Jr., Secretary of Agriculture Henry A. Wallace, and Federal Emergency Relief Administrator Harry Hopkins. As an executive staff director, Roosevelt appointed Edwin Witte, a professor of economics from Wisconsin,[59] the only state that had implemented an unemployment insurance program by 1934. To assist the five members of the CES, a Technical Board on Economic Security was created. Another economist from Wisconsin, Arthur Altmeyer, chaired the technical board. One of the board's five committees was exclusively dedicated to old age security; it included academics J. Douglas Brown (Princeton University's Industrial Relations Section) and Barbara N. Armstrong (University of California's Law School) and, more important, Murray W. Latimer, then chairman of the Railroad Retirement Board. Well-known reformers Abraham Epstein and Isaac Rubinow, two proponents of general revenue participation in social insurance financing, were not invited to collaborate intensively with the CES. This decision may have reflected the administration's will to promote the contributory method and "fiscal responsibility."[60]

Because the work of the CES has been summarized elsewhere, the following paragraphs briefly analyze its recommendations concerning old age insecurity while discussing the possible interference of business interests in the decision-making process.[61] The CES addressed at least three major "technical issues" while respecting the president's general creed about the contributory method and fiscal responsibility: (1) the relationship between social insurance and social assistance, (2) the specific modalities of old age insurance financing, and (3) the territorial organization of old age benefits in the context of American federalism.

First, the CES clearly favored old age insurance over assistance. Although assistance would still support a significant portion of the elderly population during the years to come, in the long run, old age insurance coverage would increase to protect the vast majority of the elderly population against insecurity:

> Only noncontributory pensions can serve to meet the problem of millions of persons who are already superannuated or shortly will be so and are without sufficient income for a decent subsistence. A contributory annuity system, while of little or no value to people now in these older age groups, will enable younger workers, with the aid of their employers, to build up gradually their rights to annuities in their old age. Without such a contributory system the cost of pensions would, in the future, be overwhelming. Contributory annuities are unquestionably preferable to noncontributory pensions. They come to the workers as a right, whereas the noncontributory pensions must be conditioned upon a "means" test. Annuities, moreover, can be ample for a comfortable existence, bearing some relation to customary wage standards, while gratuitous pensions can provide only a decent subsistence.[62]

This citation reflects the president's idea that "fiscal responsibility" should triumph over "charity." Even though the final CES report recommended federal grants-in-aid to the states, it depicted the contributory method as the only proper way to protect most workers and their families against economic insecurity. Moreover, the above quotation also suggests that old age insurance was meant to become a comprehensive income maintenance program, not a mere tool of poverty alleviation that would only provide workers with the "basic necessities."

Beyond the relationship between insurance and assistance, the CES addressed the issue of old age insurance coverage and financing. Drawing on the idea of fiscal "self-support," the CES recommended the creation of a contributory program in which workers and employers would equally share the payroll tax burden. The program would cover all wageworkers earning less than $250 a month, with the exception of civil servants and railroad workers, who had recently gained protection under the Railroad Retirement Act of 1934.[63] To protect self-employed workers, the CES also recommended the creation of federal voluntary annuities: "There still remains, unprotected by either of the two above plans, professional and self-employed groups, many of whom face dependency in old age. Partially to meet their problem, we suggest the establishment of a voluntary Government annuity system, designed particularly for people of small incomes."[64] This measure would spark much debate during the legislative process.

The CES report also discussed the appropriate tax level necessary to finance old age insurance without hurting the economy. It recommended a gradual payroll tax increase from only 0.5 percent in 1937 to 2.5 percent in 1957. Keeping the initial tax rate at such a low level seemed logical considering the economic context of the time. Yet because the program would not distribute benefits before 1942, it would be a mistake to consider old age insurance as an emergency tool that could stimulate short-term economic recovery.[65] According to the CES report, the program would be "self-supporting" until 1965. After that date, partial general revenue financing would prove necessary if Congress did not alter the tax schedule. The administration itself would successfully push for the elimination of this blatant violation of the president's fiscal conservatism at an early stage of the legislative process.

In the field of old age insurance, CES staff members—including Barbara Armstrong—assumed that the program would essentially cover male breadwinners.[66] In that context, most women would gain indirect protection through their husband's entitlements or receive aid under state old age assistance programs. Although the establishment of survivor benefits would have granted social rights of their own to many American women, the CES rejected this policy alternative for both actuarial and strategic reasons. As Brown recalled:

It was suggested that while a small survivor benefit might be socially desirable where pension payments had begun, it would add materially to the actuarial cost of the plan. The strategic opportunity to develop a closely interlocking system of protection for both the aged and for dependant survivors of all ages was submerged under a cloud of anxiety that even a streamlined plan dealing with the aged alone might fail enactment or court approval.[67]

The decision not to recommend the enactment of survivor benefits was thus related to both fiscal conservatism and political calculus. Brown's words also illustrate how constitutional fears influenced the actions of the CES and the Roosevelt administration in the mid-1930s. At that time, it was uncertain that the Supreme Court would approve the establishment of a federal social insurance program.

This constitutional anxiety was directly related to the proposed territorial organization of old age insurance, which entailed obvious constitutional challenges. According to Quadagno, the five business leaders appointed on the CES's Advisory Council "exerted considerable indirect influence" on that territorial issue.[68] For Quadagno, the fact that the CES supported the establishment of a contributory federal program illustrated the influence of these welfare capitalists on the committee's final recommendations. Knowing about the negative effects of decentralized social policy arrangements, the business members of the Advisory Council pushed for the establishment of a national program. Although there is some evidence that these individuals supported the creation of a purely federal program,[69] this policy choice concerning the territorial organization of old age insurance was directly related to an actuarial logic discussed in Chapter 2: for actuaries and reformers alike, a decentralized old age insurance scheme seemed administratively problematic because of the high level of interstate mobility of the American workforce. According to Altmeyer, a strong consensus rapidly emerged among CES members about the actuarial need for an entirely federal program in the field of old age insurance: "It was soon recognized that, when the actuaries got to advising us, that . . . [a decentralized system] would be impossible. So it never got to the point of debate."[70] Despite the fact that this proposal could turn the Supreme Court against the whole economic security legislation, the CES thus recommended the advent of a federal old age insurance program. Facing the historical evidence available, it is most likely that, without the presence of five welfare capitalists on the CES, the report would still have supported the idea of a federal contributory scheme. After the president formulated the general parameters for the CES's work, interest groups generally proved unable to directly impact its recommendations.[71] This was especially true for old age insurance, a measure that had fostered relatively little public attention before the establishment of the CES.[72] Considering that no old age insurance program had been previously enacted at the state level, no vested interests associated with existing state measures could oppose centralization, which was not the case in the fields of unemployment insurance and old age assistance. In the latter, the CES did recommend the development of grants-in-aid to the states instead of pushing for centralization.[73] Because the president had officially been promoting "a maximum of cooperation between States and the Federal Government," subsidizing state programs was a logical solution considering existing policy legacies.

Although it rapidly became obvious that old age insurance would take the form of a centralized federal program, no one on the committee raised the issue of labor and business participation in old age insurance management. This question, which had been debated in European countries, remained a nonissue for members of the CES and interest groups alike. The CES expressed the will that federal officials alone manage the new program: "The administration of the compulsory old age annuity system we recommend should be vested in the Social Insurance Board. All reserve funds of the system, however, shall be invested and managed by the Secretary of the Treasury, on the same basis as the unemployment compensation funds."[74] Consequently, a federal agency would run the program, and Congress would make the decision concerning coverage and tax levels. Perceived as mere interest groups, business and labor organizations would have to make their impact on federal old age insurance using traditional lobbying strategies. This government-centered model is distinct from European co-management practices that allow business and labor organizations to formally participate in the management of social insurance.[75] The American situation probably reflects the relative disorganization of business and labor interests and the related absence of corporatist tradition in the United States.[76]

Far from pushing for co-management, business interests generally opposed the advent of old age insurance. Considering the declining political influence of business interests during the New Deal, however, this opposition never seriously endangered the enactment of the Roosevelt administration's bill on economic security. Yet economic interests did play a significant role during the legislative process.

Enacting the Social Security Program

The CES report presented to the president on January 15, 1935, formulated detailed proposals concerning old age security (grants-in-aid to the states, federal old age insurance, and voluntary annuities), unemployment insurance, and "security for children." Coherent with Roosevelt's vision, these recommendations rapidly took the form of an omnibus bill. This bill represented a successful attempt to set the legislative agenda while pushing conservative forces onto the defensive side: "Once the CES Report was on the agenda, reasonable counter proposals were costly to submit in both time and dollars. In many cases these costs would have been borne directly by participants rather than diffused through taxpayer support."[77] And because the legislative process moved swiftly to favor the enactment of this complex legislation, business and conservative leaders who had traditionally opposed social insurance found it difficult to organize against it. Considering the many veto points stemming from checks and balances, however, the federal legislative process favored constant bargaining and redrafting, which could have paved the way to significant modifications at odds with the bill's original aims.

A Divided and Poorly Informed Opposition

In early 1935, the House Committee on Ways and Means (CWM) and the Senate Finance Committee (FC) organized public hearings about the new bill. Testimony to these two committees revealed a lack of consensus about old age insurance and other key components of the proposed legislation. Yet, it is important to note that old age insurance drew far less attention than unemployment insurance. Then little known in the United States, old age insurance did not appear as a central issue for most testifiers. Moreover, apart from CES members and reformers such as Abraham Epstein, those testifying seemed ill informed about the legislation and the technical issues at stake. This was especially true concerning business representatives, whose statements generally seemed imprecise and uninformed. Because of their weak presence in Washington until the New Deal, business organizations had yet to develop the resources necessary to quickly analyze federal legislation while consulting with their members.[78] In the case of the economic security bill, the lack of time and preparation was another factor that could explain this situation. Most testifiers had only a few weeks—and sometimes less—to analyze this complex bill and take a specific stance about the proposed measures.[79]

In general, business representatives criticized the bill on economic security and, more specifically, the idea of permanent social insurance schemes that would reduce economic freedom and constitute a significant fiscal burden for employers. The main issue at stake here was the payroll tax, which was perceived as unfair and economically counterproductive in the context of the Great Depression. James A. Emery, representing one of the most influential business organizations in the country, the National Association of Manufacturers, stated:

> I wanted to call the attention of the committee to the fact that as a practical matter the tax in many instances cannot be passed on; it will not be absorbed. And, secondly, it is not levied on the basis of ability to pay, because it makes no distinction between business operating at a loss or a profit, so the pay-roll tax will be the same in many businesses, particularly smaller businesses whose capital has suffered severe losses in the course of this depression, and they have reached the cracking point, where the strain will be too great for them to bear, especially because they may be engaged in a line of enterprise in which the labor cost runs into the higher brackets.[80]

In his seventeen-page-long testimony to the CWM, however, Emery only mentioned the term *old age* twice, and like most business representatives, he focused almost exclusively on unemployment insurance. This illustrates a relative lack of interest toward old age insurance on the part of business representatives.

Less harsh than Emery in his critique of the proposed legislation,

U.S. Chamber of Commerce president Henry Harriman formulated a more cautious yet equally superficial assessment of the bill. Instead of condemning the proposed measures, he simply suggested that Congress wait until economic conditions improved before enacting such an expensive legislation. Furthermore, although he explicitly supported social insurance, he suggested excluding agricultural and domestic workers from both old age and unemployment insurance programs because it would prove "practically impossible to collect the tax on, for instance, the casual worker—the man who comes in and works in your garden for a day or two, or he shovels snow."[81] Concerning old age insurance, Harriman also argued that employers who were already offering private pensions should have the right to opt out from the future federal program: "I would certainly permit existing private annuity plans to be continued as a substitute for the Government plan, under proper regulation and if they are suitable."[82] These two controversial issues would prove to be crucial during the rest of the legislative process.

Despite the fact that Harriman formulated relatively moderate critiques of the proposed bill during his testimony to the Finance Committee, his Chamber of Commerce would soon take a radical stance against the economic security bill and most other New Deal policies.[83] Considering this and other historical evidence, it seems that the vast majority of employers disliked old age insurance and, more generally, the debated legislation on economic security.[84] Furthermore, business support for the future Social Security Act represented a form of "strategic accommodation." Because other debated policy alternatives such as the Townsend Plan represented a stronger threat to their economic interests, some employers supported the proposed bill as a "lesser evil," not a great political achievement. This strategy illustrates the relatively weak political power of business in the mid-1930s.[85] Unable to prevent the enactment of measures they had always opposed, business representatives could either compromise in order to alter policy outcomes or take a radical yet desperate stance against the New Deal and, more precisely, the economic security bill.

During the testimony, dissatisfaction with old age insurance and the economic security bill also came from the left. Proponents of radical policy alternatives attacked the bill as a far too modest response to social insecurity and economic depression. Perhaps the most vocal of them was Herbert P. Benjamin of the National Council for Unemployment and Social Insurance, who was a supporter of the Lundeen Plan, a socialist proposal that called for the establishment of a federal program under which each elderly, unemployed, or deprived citizen would immediately receive a minimum of ten dollars a week, plus three dollars for each dependent. Violent in tone, his testimony dealt almost exclusively with unemployment-related issues.[86] More diplomatic in his approach, Dr. Townsend gently pushed for the enactment of his own plan, but instead of rejecting the bill on economic security as a whole, he thought that only the elements dealing with old age insecurity should be abandoned. As an alternative to the old age components of the bill, he supported the enactment of the Old-Age Revolving Pension Plan that had been introduced by Congressman John S. McGroarty (D-California) on January 16, 1935. This bill called for the enactment of a national transaction tax and $200 monthly benefits for citizens aged sixty and over.[87] During his testimony, Dr. Townsend talked almost exclusively about his proposal, and he showed little interest for the debated legislation on economic security.[88] At the beginning of 1935, however, his plan was still regarded as unrealistic and fiscally unsound by most federal politicians, and it had virtually no chance of being enacted.[89] Paradoxically, Dr. Townsend's testimony, as well as the multitude of letters sent to Congress by his supporters, probably helped to keep pension-related issues on the agenda while further justifying the enactment of federal old age insurance, a more "reasonable" alternative to the apparently popular, yet radical, Townsend Plan. As stated by Altmeyer, "his appearance and the flood of letters the committee received tended to create the idea that the real issue lies between the Townsend Plan and the economic security bill."[90] Because few people on Capitol Hill perceived Townsend's plan as a sound policy alternative, his testimony probably reinforced the support for the administration's proposals.

The testimony also revealed that the economic security bill had many supporters. Among them, labor unions were especially well disposed. The president of the AFL, William Green, enthusiastically supported the advent of unemployment and old age insurance. For example, he agreed that both workers and employers should participate in the financing of federal old age benefits: "I agree that the beneficiaries of old age pensions should make contribution along with industry towards the old-age pension fund."[91] It is interesting that this is the only direct reference made to old age insurance in his fourteen-page-long testimony to the CWM. Like business officials, Green seemed more interested in unemployment insurance than in old age security. Yet, his longer testimony to the Senate's Finance Committee contained a discussion about old age assistance grants-in-aid to the states as well as federal old age insurance. Green supported both measures, but he also pushed for the enactment of several amendments to improve the economic security granted under federal old age insurance. For example, he suggested higher payroll tax levels to finance more generous benefits.[92] Green's bold support for the application of social insurance principles to economic risks such as unemployment stood in stark contrast, however, with traditional AFL opposition toward governmental intervention and compulsory insurance. Because the federal government had become more sympathetic toward unions since President Roosevelt came to power, the AFL came to adopt a more positive vision of governmental intervention in social policy and economic regulation.[93] Yet, labor officials played only a marginal role in the elaboration and the enactment of federal old age insurance. For the AFL, unemployment insurance remained the true legislative priority, just beside collective bargaining.[94]

In sharp contrast to the relatively superficial discussion of old age insurance that characterized most testimony, some witnesses, although sympathetic to the administration's bill, formulated detailed critiques of this component of the economic security bill. Among them, Abraham Epstein was certainly one of the most credible and respected. As the founder of the American Association for Social Security (formerly the American Association for Old-Age Security), he asked Congress to adopt a cautious approach to old age insurance. From his perspective, payroll tax and benefits should remain low during the first years of the program. "I would rather start mildly and softly, but soundly. Give us, first, this pension of $15 a month. Do not rush us to $25, and when that money is wasted, have another Congress come along and rip the whole system out. Start modestly. You will have time enough to make increases a year from now."[95] Moreover, like Harriman and Marion Folsom,[96] Epstein argued that domestic and agricultural workers should be temporarily excluded from old age insurance for both administrative and political reasons:

> So, for God's sake, start mildly, start modestly. Let me tell you that no other country on earth—not only the big countries like ours, but other countries that are not spread out as ours are—no other country dared to try to include the agricultural workers and the domestic servants at first. And if that is so, why should you, with such an immense country like ours, with such a problem of administration to tackle, why should we undertake all these things and then fail in the administration of them so that it will all come back to us to plague us for the next generation. . . . Frankly, I do not want the farmers to come in here and fight us. We will have enough of a fight with the manufacturers' association. Why take on the farmers at the same time? We have had enough of a fight for the last 20 years.[97]

The first of Epstein's arguments would soon justify the exclusion of these two professional groups from old age insurance. Yet, it is worth noting that Epstein had little direct political leverage in 1934–1935. Excluded from the CES, he had become a vocal outsider in a world now dominated by appointed policy experts such as Altmeyer and Witte. Paradoxically, the name of Epstein's organization (American Association for Social Security) may have inspired members of the CWM, who renamed the bill the Social Security Act (instead of the Economic Security Act) in order to distinguish their revised version from the administration's original proposal.[98]

At this point, it is possible to draw some conclusions concerning the opposition to the bill expressed during the congressional testimony. First, there is little doubt that although most business representatives rejected all or at least some key aspects of the Social Security Act, the declining power of business during the New Deal had considerably reduced the chances of business interests to defeat the bill. Second, testimony from both labor and business officials showed that old age insurance was rarely a central policy issue for them. Even Dr. Townsend did not bother discussing the case of old age insurance, a measure that never constituted a major item on the policy agenda (at either the state or the federal level) before the publication of the CES report. Third, unions' support for the administration's bill reveals a transformation of American labor politics; the unions became faithful supporters of federal social policy.[99] Fourth, the debate surrounding the enactment process further shows that independent reformers such as Epstein and Rubinow had been marginalized in a highly centralized policymaking process in which governmental appointees were the most essential source of advice and expertise. Independent reformers who could not join the civil service—as a consultant or a federal employee—lost ground in the New Deal policy landscape. Finally, one could conclude that the opposition to the Social Security Act was divided between politically weaker business interests and proponents of policy alternatives labeled as radical. In spite of this divided opposition, the political strength of the president and the Democratic domination in Congress did not prevent the enactment of provisions that significantly altered the content of the proposed legislation.

The Legislative Fate of Old Age Insurance

The testimony before the CWM ran from January 21 to February 12, 1935. Then the CWM revised the administration's bill, taking into account some concerns expressed during the testimony. One of these concerns dealt with the inclusion of agrarian and domestic workers in the old age insurance program. Henry Harriman (U.S. Chamber of Commerce), Abraham Epstein (American Association for Social Security), and Marion Folsom (Eastman Kodak and CES Advisory Council) had argued in their testimony to the FC that the inclusion of these workers in the old age insurance program should be delayed because of administrative problems related to high labor mobility and uncertain tax collection. In his testimony to the CWM, Secretary of the Treasury Henry Morgenthau also voiced administrative concerns about this inclusion:

> The national contributory old age annuity system, as now proposed, includes every employee in the United States, other than those of governmental agencies or railways, who earns less than $251 a month. This means that every transient or casual laborer is included, that every domestic servant is covered, and that the large and shifting class of agricultural workers is covered. Now, even without the inclusion of these three classes of workers, the task of the

Treasury in administering the contributory tax collections would be extremely formidable. If these three classes of workers are to be included, however, the task may well prove insuperable. . . .[100]

Grounded in the administration's obsession for "fiscal soundness," the exclusion of these workers was coherent with a key aspect of Roosevelt's social insurance paradigm. Paradoxically, universal coverage, another component of the president's vision, had to be sacrificed in the name of fiscal responsibility and sound management.[101] Morgenthau's recommendation to the CWM, perceived as a temporary measure, was grounded not in racial prejudice but in fiscal and actuarial conservatism.[102] Other countries, such as Britain and Canada, also excluded agricultural and domestic workers at the beginning of their social insurance experiments in order to avoid such administrative complications.[103] Even today, collecting payroll taxes from domestic workers represents a major policy challenge in the United States and abroad.[104] Since Morgenthau appeared as an implicit spokesman of the then powerful president, his recommendations to the CWM carried a lot of weight. In the absence of social and political mobilization against this exclusion—as was the case in Sweden in the early twentieth century[105]—the CWM had all the necessary latitude to modify the bill and reduce coverage in a significant manner.

Although the decision to exclude agrarian and domestic workers disproportionately affected African Americans,[106] there is no direct evidence that race represented a significant factor at the origin of the CWM decision to temporarily exclude these workers from the old age insurance program. As opposed to what authors such as Lieberman and Quadagno have argued,[107] southern Democrats did not strongly impact the CWM decision. On the CWM, only four of the eighteen members were from the southern states, and these individuals made no special effort to promote the exclusion of agrarian and domestic workers. Within the CWM and the Congress as a whole, the temporary exclusion of these workers was not challenged in any significant way: "Both parties and all regions of the country, voted in favor of the exclusion—not just Southerners."[108] Furthermore, about 75 percent of agrarian and domestic workers excluded from old age insurance coverage were white. If the CWM decision was aimed at excluding African Americans from coverage, would it have made sense to penalize more than 9 million white workers to achieve this goal? The truth is that members of these occupational groups did not seek to gain coverage and that farm owners certainly wanted to escape from the new payroll tax. As DeWitt argues, "members of Congress (of both parties and all regions) supported these exclusions simply because they saw an opportunity to [avoid] imposing new taxes on their constituents."[109] Witte's account largely confirmed this view.[110]

Mary Poole recognizes that "racist southerners" were not behind such exclusions. Yet, she also discards the administrative concerns surrounding the exclusions, arguing that members of the Roosevelt administration like Morgenthau used these concerns as an excuse to legitimize a decision grounded in unspoken racial hierarchies.[111] Although she is right to state that CES staff members conducted research that seemed to invalidate many of such concerns, Poole fails to recognize that these became a significant *political* issue during the congressional testimonies and that, in the United States, institutional legacies exacerbated doubts about the administrative capacities of the federal government (Chapter 2). Genuine administrative concerns, not hidden racial hierarchies, were the main factor behind the exclusion of these workers.

As this decision on coverage shows, the bill derived from the CES report represented everything but a legislative "sacred cow" for the Roosevelt administration. During Morgenthau's testimony, for example, he suggested a second major modification to the administration's bill that would directly influence another decision of the CWM. Once more in the name of fiscal responsibility, Morgenthau asked the CWM to modify the old age insurance tax schedule to avoid any future general revenue financing.[112] Following Morgenthau's advice, the CWM increased the initial tax rate to 2 percent while altering the tax schedule so that the rate would increase faster than anticipated to reach a maximum of 6 percent in 1949, instead of 5 percent in 1957. These modifications would have the effect of increasing the size of the anticipated trust fund reserves by more than 300 percent. In addition to this new tax schedule, the CWM slightly increased the anticipated replacement rate for low-income beneficiaries of the federal old age insurance program.[113]

Finally, in the field of old age assistance, the CWM modified the provisions concerning grants-in-aid to the states. In order to preserve state sovereignty and to avoid vesting "dictatorial powers in any Federal officials," the CWM eliminated the clause stating that states should pay "a reasonable subsistence compatible with decency and health" to receive federal grants-in-aid. The CWM also relaxed the federal conditions for the approval of state programs, so that "states might impose other conditions for old age assistance than those dealt with in the bill."[114] In addition, the CWM weakened federal administrative requirements and provisions related to the withdrawal of previously approved state old age assistance programs.

Even though the southern Democrats did not significantly impact the decisions of the CWM about old age insurance, there is evidence that in the field of old age assistance the southern Democrats did directly influence the CWM's decisions. Considering the limited fiscal resources and low per capita income of southern states, their representatives wanted to limit the requirements necessary to gain federal aid while maintaining state control over the beneficiaries. Although arguments about fiscal capacities and state sovereignty were genuine ones, there is evidence that racial prejudice motivated southern politicians to fight federal controls in the field of old age assistance.[115] According to Witte, for example, many members of Congress "feared that this measure might serve as an entering wedge for federal interference with the Negro question in the South. The southern members did not want to give authority to anyone in Washington to deny aid to any state because it discriminated against Negroes in the administration of old age assistance."[116] Such issues must be understood in the context of American federalism, which favors competition between the states for economic and fiscal resources. The CES decision to preserve the existing, decentralized old age assistance system paved the way to this push for autonomy motivated by racial prejudice and, perhaps more important, by southern fiscal interests. In this context, the influence of racial prejudice is here related to specific political institutions as well as to the fiscal and economic status of southern states in American federalism. Yet it is possible to argue that, right from the beginning, the administration's bill could not have prevented the massive regional inequalities that would emerge in the field of old age assistance after the passage of the Social Security Act. Far from representing a genuine obstacle to discrimination and inadequate benefits, the defunct clause asking for "a reasonable subsistence compatible with decency and health" would probably have failed to guarantee equal treatment and decent protection across a fragmented and economically stratified federal welfare system. Thus, it would prove misleading to overemphasize the impact of the CWM's decisions regarding old age assistance.[117]

Although the modifications concerning old age assistance did not please the Roosevelt administration, the CWM did not eliminate the three most important measures of the administration's bill: unemployment insurance, federal old age insurance, and old age grants-in-aid to the states. During the deliberations, however, some members of the CWM suggested that the section on old age insurance should be removed from the bill. As a compromise agreed upon by the administration, the CWM only deleted the provisions about voluntary old age annuities. Simultaneously, the president, who kept a low public profile during the legislative process, used his personal influence to convince Democratic members of Congress that his bill represented an indivisible entity. Again, the president imposed his program upon skeptical or indifferent political actors.[118] Although Republican members of the CWM condemned old age insurance in their minority report, Roosevelt's explicit will to preserve *his* program thus represented the best political safeguard against its elimination during the rest of the legislative process.

Beginning on April 11, the House floor debate on the renamed Social Security bill proved relatively uneventful and even monotonous.[119] Although a few conservative and radical voices condemned the bill, its enactment seemed probable considering the overwhelming Democratic House majority. Still, more than fifty amendments were discussed, although few of them gathered much support.[120] Among these amendments, the one associated with Congressman Joseph P. Monaghan (D-Montana) represented a clear attack against federal old age insurance. His proposal called for the replacement of the Social Security bill's old age sections with a version of the Townsend Plan. Like all the other amendments, Monaghan's was defeated. In the House, the opposition to the Social Security bill proved marginal, and the legislation received overwhelming support. On April 19, the House massively voted in favor of the bill. Only 33 members voted against the legislation, whereas 372 supported it.[121]

Less than two weeks later, the Senate FC began to examine and modify the bill. As compared to the CWM, the FC did not alter the legislation in a comprehensive manner. Although the fate of old age insurance remained uncertain during most of the FC's deliberations, the program survived the rewriting, in part because it constituted a more acceptable policy alternative than the Townsend Plan. Still, the FC made a few significant modifications to the bill. First, it restored voluntary federal annuities that had been deleted during the previous stage of the legislative process. Under this system, individuals would have the opportunity to purchase annuity bonds from the federal government while benefiting from a tax exemption. That measure was designed to enable individuals not covered by federal old age insurance to save for retirement. Second, the FC further undermined federal control over state old age assistance programs. Third, instead of supporting the creation of an independent agency, the FC placed the future Social Security Board under the control of the Department of Labor. Finally, and most important, a little-noticed modification directly concerned the future mission of federal old age insurance. For the first time, the bill transformed retirement into a necessary condition for entitlements. In order to receive their benefits, eligible workers would have to exit the job market, otherwise, individuals aged sixty-five and older would still need to pay out the payroll tax until they retired. Supported by the Roosevelt administration, this provision had two main objectives: (1) encouraging the elderly to retire, thus creating more room for younger individuals; (2) preventing "the anomaly that employees over sixty-five may draw old age benefits while earning adequate wages in full employment."[122] In the context of the Great Depression, federal old age insurance explicitly aimed at fighting unemployment and increasing managerial efficiency in the private sector.[123] Because this program would only start to pay benefits in 1942, however, it represented a long-term attempt to restructure the American labor market, not an emergency measure such as the Townsend Plan.

Held from June 14 to 19, the Senate floor debate on the Social Security Act proved more contentious and volatile than that in the House. Many amendments were debated, and some of them constituted a genuine threat against the integrity of the proposed old age insurance program. The Senate enacted three major amendments related to proposed old age benefits. The first one eliminated the voluntary federal annuities that had been previously restored by the FC. Senator Augustine

Lonergan (D-Connecticut) was the origin of this amendment. From his perspective, the federal government should not compete against private insurance companies already offering similar annuities.[124] The enactment of this amendment showed that business power, although weaker than in the previous decade, could still impact New Deal policymaking. The second noteworthy pension-related amendment enacted by the Senate dealt with federal grants-in-aid to the states. Offered by Senator Richard B. Russell Jr. (D-Georgia), this amendment enabled states "which have no Pension-system set-up, and which, therefore, would be unable to take advantage the first year, 1936 . . . to avail themselves of the Federal assistance until such State may have time to adopt a State plan."[125] This issue seemed especially important for states like Georgia, where state constitutional amendments were required before the establishment of any old age assistance program. The third amendment debated in the Senate was certainly the most consequential one because it represented a serious threat to the integrity of federal old age insurance. Associated with Senator Joel Bennett Clark (D-Missouri), this amendment allowed large private firms with more than fifty employees and operating approved pension plans offering more generous benefits than the proposed federal program to withdraw from it. The rationale for this amendment was to preserve generous private pension plans and, indirectly, to subject the federal program to competition. As stated by Senator Alban Barkley (D-Kentucky), "my objection to the Clark amendment is that it sets up two competitive systems of old-age relief."[126] At odds with the idea of compulsory insurance, the Clark amendment represented a serious threat in the eyes of old age insurance supporters.[127] Members of the Roosevelt administration and senators such as Barkley lobbied against this amendment. Noting that it could undermine the foundation of old age insurance, they stressed that it could prove unconstitutional and, therefore, endanger the bill as a whole. In spite of their efforts, however, the Senate finally adopted the Clark amendment on June 19 by a significant majority (51 to 35). On the same day, the Senate passed the amended Social Security bill by a vote of 76 to 6.[128]

Because the House rejected the amendments the Senate had attached to the bill, a Committee on Conference of ten members (five from each assembly) was appointed to even out differences between the two versions of the bill. Although member selection was completed on June 20, deliberations only started ten days later and then dragged on for more than two weeks. Finally, a compromise was found for the contentious issues at stake except for the Clark amendment. Arguing that this amendment could prove unconstitutional and devastate old age insurance, House members refused to recommend its inclusion.[129] Facing this absence of consensus, the conference committee asked staff members to rapidly prepare a more acceptable version of this amendment, which could be enacted later with the bill.[130] This process took more time than expected, but on August 8 the House and on August 9 the Senate finally enacted the Social Security Act without the Clark amendment. Although conferees appointed a legislative special committee to further study this proposal, Congress never reconsidered the amendment.[131]

Conclusion

Pleased with the deletion of the Clark amendment, President Roosevelt signed the legislation on August 14, 1935. In his address upon signing the Social Security Act, he recognized the historical significance of the act, which established a decentralized unemployment insurance system and a purely federal old age insurance program as well as grants-in-aid to the states in old age and family assistance: "If the Senate and the House of Representatives in this hard and arduous session had done nothing more than pass this Bill, the session would be regarded as historic for all time."[132] Establishing the first federal social insurance program in the United States, the legislation directly contributed to the redefinition of the relationship between government and society. And as opposed to public works programs, the Social Security Act created permanent measures that would have enduring social, economic, and political consequences. Although this legislation never called into question the existence of private welfare benefits, its enactment clearly meant that the federal government intended to protect workers against social insecurity while respecting strict fiscal and actuarial imperatives inspired by private insurance practices. For the president and his advisers, the respect of these imperatives would guarantee both the fiscal soundness and the political survival of federal old age insurance.

After its enactment, a significant number of actors still criticized the Social Security Act. If the antigovernmental attacks emanating from the Liberty League and other conservative organizations seemed predictable,[133] a significant number of social reformers also disapproved the 1935 legislation. From their perspective, the Social Security Act represented an unsatisfactory attempt to deal with America's social and economic evils. Among them, Abraham Epstein emerged as the most radical critic of this legislation. For him, the Social Security Act did not entail sufficient income redistribution and, for that reason, could not adequately protect workers against economic insecurity. Bitter over the fact that the CES failed to consult with him, he launched an attack against the legislation, hoping the Supreme Court would invalidate the provisions concerning unemployment and old age insurance.[134] Although more moderate in tone than Epstein, other reformers, such as Eveline Burns, also criticized the bill's apparent insufficiencies.[135] Against the imperative of fiscal responsibility that underlined the legislation, these reformers focused more on the adequacy of benefits and the need for income redistribution. Like Epstein, they also complained that the Social Security Act did not even mention health insurance.[136]

Another stream of criticism toward the Social Security Act emerged from women's representatives. As noted by Mary Anderson from the Women's Bureau, for example, a majority of women would be excluded from old age insurance, a program designed exclusively for independent wageworkers.[137] In the absence of spousal and survivor benefits, social assistance would constitute the only social protection available to a majority of elderly women. The remarks point to a key aspect of the Social Security Act: the relationship between social insurance and traditional gender roles. Although women had the right to participate in contributory insurance programs, these measures were mostly designed to cover the male breadwinner, who could then use his benefits to take care of his spouse and children.[138] As in the decades before, the idea of social insurance was closely related to traditional gender roles, and most elderly women had to rely on their husbands—or on social assistance—for their subsistence.

Because of the exclusion of agricultural and domestic workers, federal old age insurance covered only 45 percent of African American workers—compared to 62 percent for the entire workforce.[139] For that reason, organizations representing African Americans criticized that new program.[140] As demonstrated above, however, racial prejudice traditionally associated with southern Democrats cannot explain this exclusion, which seemed related to fiscal and economic conservatism rather than the pursuit of segregation through new means such as social insurance. Although the exclusion of these professional groups disproportionably affected African Americans, there is no direct evidence that racial prejudice or the mobilization of southern Democrats was the origin of this decision.

Despite its limits, the Social Security Act still represented a bold development in the context of America's constitutional order. Made possible in part by an increase in social mobilization and by a relative decline in business power, the Social Security Act contained only one entirely federal policy: old age insurance, a measure that had never received much political attention before 1934. The Roosevelt administration's will to favor fiscal responsibility largely explains the decision to push for this then little-debated policy alternative. Perceived as an alternative to the unrealistic Townsend Plan, old age insurance was imposed by a handful of experts and politicians, including the president himself. Yet, changes enacted in Congress—frequently following the administration's advice—limited the scope of coverage while creating a large trust fund that would soon spark much controversy.

Theoretically, this chapter underlines the autonomous role of ideational processes in the making of old age insurance. As the Great Depression and the outcome of the 1932 federal elections weakened traditional obstacles to reform like business power, the social insurance paradigm shared by President Roosevelt and his team created a rationale for old age insurance, which unexpectedly moved on the federal policy agenda as a fiscally conservative alternative to the Townsend Plan. There is strong evidence that the nature of this paradigm explains key features of the old age insurance program enacted in 1935.

CHAPTER FOUR

The Politics of Expansion

After 1935, the course of Social Security development in American society was anything but linear.[1] Coming under attack years before the payment of the first benefits, Social Security seemed especially weak during the second half of the 1930s. In a less favorable economic and political context, the Roosevelt administration had to agree on a paradoxical political compromise to save the program: the abandonment of massive advance funding in exchange for benefit increases. Grounded in traditional gender roles, the 1939 amendments shifted the program's logic toward PAYGO financing and income redistribution. Yet, in order to preserve their paradoxical compromise, political actors failed to acknowledge the scope of this paradigmatic shift. And although World War II and its aftermath favored prompt social policy expansion in post-1945 Western Europe, the war-induced return to economic prosperity in the United States actually increased business power while strengthening the conservative coalition in Congress and stimulating the growth of private welfare institutions.

In spite of these potentially menacing transformations, however, Congress finally enacted incremental reforms that helped transform Social Security into a genuine "retirement wage." There is no evidence that anything like a "bureaucratic conspiracy" represented the main driving force behind the postwar expansion of Social Security. Although the officials involved took an active role in shaping the reform agenda through domination over expertise, five other factors are at least as important as bureaucratic mobilization in order to explain postwar policy outcomes: (1) the development of private benefits, which constrained potential business opposition to the program; (2) the nature of American political institutions, which militate against bold reform outside of rare episodes of sudden change such as the New Deal; (3) favorable economic and demographic conditions that made benefit increases possible without massive and immediate tax hikes; (4) the enactment of the 1950 amendments, which favored the emergence of larger constituencies that countered path-breaking reforms such as "flat pension"; and (5) the postwar, liberal consensus that marginalized the opposition to Social Security even within the Republican Party. The expansion of Social Security culminated during the Nixon administration as changes in actuarial assumptions, coupled with exacerbated electoral competition between Congress and the presidency, fueled the program's sudden growth. By then, Social Security constituted an increasingly popular measure that stimulated both interest group mobilization and credit-claiming strategies in Congress. Although from the mid-1960s on federal officials depicted Social Security as a poverty reduction device, they never officially acknowledged the shift toward income redistribution initiated in 1939. Now framed as a poverty alleviation measure *and* a quasi-savings scheme, Social Security thus emerged as a popular yet poorly understood program in postwar American society.

The Hidden Paradigm Shift

Because of the specific financing model enacted in 1935, which declared that federal old age insurance would only start paying benefits in 1942, the program appeared as a frail political entity during the second half of the 1930s. In the absence of beneficiaries, the program was particularly vulnerable to political and ideological attacks. Compensating for this weakness, the newly created Social Security Board (SSB) emerged as a bureaucratic advocate for old age insurance.[2] Established to run this program and other federal measures included in the Social Security Act, this three-person board also promoted the idea of social insurance in American society. The first chairman of the board was John Winant, a former Republican governor of New Hampshire. In 1937, Arthur Altmeyer replaced him as chairman of the SSB, a position he would hold until the abolition of this organization in 1946. After that date, Altmeyer, the former chairman of the CES Technical Board, would still head the new Social Security Administration (SSA) until his retirement in 1953. This situation illustrates the unusual stability of the program's executive leadership, a phenomenon that helped Social Security executives develop political connections as well as unique social insurance expertise. Beginning in the second half of the 1930s, these federal executives pursued an incremental reform strategy to expand Social Security.[3] Yet broad economic and political forces, not only bureaucratic leadership, shaped Social Security development in American society.

The Social Security Board, Electoral Politics, and Agenda Setting

Because old age insurance was the only centralized program of the Social Security Act, federal executives identified themselves with this measure and the related social insurance principles.[4] A year after the enactment of this legislation, "their" program would come under political attack, forcing these executives to step into the public arena in order to promote this measure. This attack came from Republican presidential candidate Alf Landon, who labeled old age insurance a "cruel hoax" in a public address in Milwaukee on September 26, 1936. After recalling the fact that the federal government would not pay old age benefits before 1942, he depicted the program as an "unjust, stupidly drafted, and wastefully financed scheme."[5] For the Republican candidate, the accumulation of a massive reserve fund would pave the way to political abuse and governmental misspending. Implicitly referring to Democrats, he argued, "We have good spenders in Washington. . . . With this social security money alone running into billions of dollars, all restraint on Congress will be off."[6] According to Landon, payroll taxes would never be used to pay pension benefits. This offensive directly exploited the lack of trust toward the government present in the American ideological repertoire. Although the Great Depression had leveled many institutional and ideological obstacles to the expansion of the federal government, fears concerning excessive power concentration remained in American society, especially within business and conservative circles.[7]

Beyond Landon's discourse, other events drew further public attention to old age insurance financing. One thing that happened was that many employers distributed propaganda leaflets against the Social Security Act and the future old age insurance payroll tax.[8] Another was that newspaper articles echoed the Republican candidate's concerns about the intended size of the old age insurance trust fund. As one historian noted, the sheer size of the anticipated reserve fund became a source of fascination: "To have $47 billion held in reserve for such a program staggered the American imagination. The figure represented eight times the amount of money then in circulation in the United States; nearly five times the amount of money in savings banks; enough money to buy all the farms in the United States, with $14 billion to spare."[9] Depicted as a potential threat to democracy and fiscal restraint, the issue of old age insurance funding moved onto the federal policy agenda months before the implementation of the Social Security payroll tax.

The SSB did not wait long to react. First, John Winant, the SSB's only Republican member, immediately resigned to protest Landon's anti–Social Security crusade. Second, the SSB launched an "image management" campaign depicting old age insurance as a sound scheme that would indeed pay pension benefits along the road: "Leaflets and moving picture films intended to educate the people for the post-election registration effort were brought out of hiding and given to the public with a free hand. The Board and its staff, in the last weeks before the elections, vigorously cooperated with the Democratic Party and the labor unions in getting out publicity in defense of the social security plan."[10] Originally scheduled for release after the end of the presidential race, a film entitled *We the People and Social Security* was promptly distributed just days before the election. By November 3, approximately 4 million people had seen it.[11]

In spite of Roosevelt's presidential landslide victory, Social Security financing durably remained on the federal policy agenda after the 1936 election. In January 1937, Senator Arthur Vandenberg (R-Michigan) depicted massive advance funding as an economically unsound measure. Instead, he suggested a shift to PAYGO financing using three different means: beginning to pay benefits earlier, increasing the level of bene-fits, and postponing the payroll tax increase scheduled for 1940.[12] Aimed at reducing the trust fund's size, these measures would thus boost Social Security benefits. The following month, Vandenberg in-vited SSB chairman Arthur Altmeyer to testify to the FC about old age insurance funding mechanisms. After Altmeyer explained the ration-ale behind advance funding, Vandenberg asked him if he would object to the creation of a special commission that could further explore this issue. Facing strong political pressure, Altmeyer agreed with the idea of an advisory group that would report both to the SSB and the FC. At the time, he realized that this second Advisory Council would provide an opportunity to expand Social Security while answering concerns about the anticipated size of the trust fund. In a memorandum to the president, he formulated his opportunistic strategy: "As a matter of fact, I think it is possible not only to offset these attacks on the Social Se-curity Act, but really to utilize them to advance a socially desirable pro-gram, fully in accord with present fundamental principles underlying the Social Security Act and within our financial capacity."[13] Although Altmeyer was right to predict that this Advisory Council could pave the way to expansionist amendments to the Social Security Act, he failed to foresee the significant paradigmatic change it would introduce.

The 1937–1938 Advisory Council and the Hidden Paradigmatic Shift

The Advisory Council met for the first time on November 5, 1937. By that date, the Supreme Court had upheld the Social Security Act, and the crusade against advance funding represented the only imme-diate political threat to the future of Social Security, a program for which the federal government had recently begun collecting the pay-roll tax. Composed of twenty-five members generally sympathetic to the New Deal and the Social Security Act, this second Advisory Coun-cil had to fulfill a far more significant mission than the essentially dec-orative council put together as part of the 1934 CES. Three years later, the implicit task of the new council went far beyond public relations purposes: framing an acceptable political compromise that would preserve and even expand the program while answering concerns about massive advance funding.[14]

Although a consensus rapidly emerged concerning the need to reform Social Security's financial mechanisms, members of the Advisory Council spent much time debating the issue of advance funding. For example, former CES executive-director Edwin Witte defended the basic actuarial choices imposed by Morgenthau and President Roosevelt during the 1935 legislative process. From his perspective, it remained essential to "educate people about the program and against the idea of universal free pensions."[15] Supporting the imperative of fiscal responsibility, Witte found a strong antagonist in the president of Provident Mutual Life Insurance, Albert Linton. Like Landon and Vandenberg, this Republican supporter attacked advance funding in the name of fiscal conservatism and mistrust toward government. In order to reduce the size of the trust fund, Linton put forward a paradoxical solution that would lead to an implicit policy compromise between liberals and conservatives: "To prevent irresponsible raids on the public treasury he would preclude the accumulation of a large reserve fund partly by raiding the treasury (partly also by retarding payroll tax increases); to prevent the giving of unreasonable benefits he would increase unearned benefits to the first annuitants who retired under the system."[16] This paradoxical compromise triumphed because it satisfied both ideological camps, generally for very different reasons. First, some council members were satisfied with the abandonment of massive advance funding. On the right, conservatives approved this idea for the above-mentioned political and fiscal reasons. On the left, Keynesian economists such as Harvard professor Alvin Hansen also welcomed this transformation of old age insurance financing. For these economists, the reserve fund would plague the economy during recession.[17] Second, reformers and the SSB supported expansionist measures necessary to limit advance funding. Finally, the fact that this compromise would also translate into lower payroll taxes helped to secure business support for the compromise.

Even though the Advisory Council finally decided to abandon massive advance funding while increasing benefits, the expansion of the program took the form of a paradigmatic shift grounded in the idea of "family protection." Supporting the development of spousal and survivor benefits, the council did advocate a more redistributive vision of social insurance that implicitly contradicted the individualistic actuarial model that had triumphed in 1935.[18] "The Advisory Council of 1937–1938 shifted the whole concept of what became the OASDI program from a hybrid compromise between private savings and social insurance to a clear-cut concept of social insurance. The new focus became adequacy and the protection of the family unit."[19] In the name of social adequacy and "family protection," the Advisory Council recognized that married couples should receive more generous benefits than singles, thus abandoning the strict relationship between one's contributions and benefits. This restructuring of the program at the expense of actuarial equity was widely accepted within the council's ranks.[20] Yet, the push for the creation of spousal and survivor benefits represented more an attempt to protect male breadwinners than a genuine recognition of women's specific needs. For most members of the Advisory Council, these two types of benefits would increase men's capacity to provide for their families after retirement and even after death.[21] For this reason, members of the council agreed that, in the case of the spousal benefit, "the supplementary allowance was to be paid to the husband on the behalf of a wife."[22] Instead of empowering women, members of the Advisory Council thus supported traditional gender roles and, more directly, the economic and familial power of the male breadwinner.[23]

The council's report put forward a genuine transformation of old age insurance that represented a sharp yet largely hidden departure from principles that had guided its elaboration only three years earlier. First, the Advisory Council recommended that the payment of benefits begin in January 1940 instead of 1942. Second, it supported the payment of a spousal benefit equivalent to 50 percent of the husband's benefit. Covering only women aged sixty-five and older, this measure would increase the husband's benefit instead of granting genuine social rights to wives. Yet, women with a significant working record would still receive their own benefits: "Should a wife after attaining age 65 be otherwise eligible to a benefit in her own right which is larger in amount than the wife's allowance payable to her husband on her behalf, the benefit payable to her in her own right will be substituted for the wife's allowance."[24] In spite of this remark, the spousal benefit represented a distinct disjoining of the relationship between contributions and benefits. In the name of "family protection," the program would become more redistributive. Third, following the same redistributive logic, the Advisory Council recommended the creation of a special benefit for widows. After reaching age fifty-five, the widow of a covered worker could receive a monthly pension bearing a certain relationship to her husband's benefit. Dependent children and younger widows taking care of at least one dependent child would also qualify for benefits. Fourth, the council supported the enactment of a disability insurance scheme protecting workers against a major economic risk: the loss of income related to permanent disability. Fifth, the Advisory Council called for the integration of most professional categories excluded in 1935—agricultural and domestic workers and employees of private, nonprofit religious, charitable, and educational institutions. Finally, the council argued in favor of future general revenue financing for Social Security while recommending the maintenance of a modest "contingency fund" dedicated exclusively to the payment of federal old age benefits.[25]

Less than a month after the publication of the council's report, the SSB published its own report, *Proposed Changes in the Social Security Act.*[26] Dealing with all the provisions included in the bill, its content showed that the SSB openly supported the Advisory Council's main recommendations concerning old age insurance. Although the SSB refused to recommend the immediate integration of agricultural workers into the federal program, its general recommendations were consistent with the political compromise. The SSB and—indirectly—the Roosevelt administration thus agreed to reject massive advance funding while expanding Social Security. Tacitly putting aside the strict contributory model adopted in 1935, the SSB also suggested ways to improve grants-in-aid to the states in the field of old age assistance.

Despite this implicit repudiation of the fiscal imperatives put forward a few years earlier, the president accepted the recommendations of the SSB. On January 16, 1939, he invited Congress to enact amendments to the Social Security Act that would increase the generosity of the old age security components of this legislation:

> I particularly call attention to the desirability of affording greater old age security. The report suggests a two-fold approach, which I believe to be sound. One way is to begin the payment of monthly

old-age insurance benefits sooner, and to liberalize the benefits to be paid in the early years. The other way is to make proportionately larger Federal grants-in-aid to those states with limited fiscal capacities, so that they may provide more adequate assistance to those in need. This result can and should be accomplished in such a way as to involve little, if any, additional cost to the Federal Government.[27]

Although the last sentence represented a reaffirmation of Roosevelt's fiscal conservatism, the president clearly accepted the compromise and put aside his obsession for individual equity and actuarial soundness in order to save "his" program. To explain his willingness to compromise, one must turn to the economic and political transformations that had taken place since the 1936 presidential election. In the months following this landslide Democratic victory,[28] Roosevelt began to lose political capital. Four related factors account for this decline in presidential power and autonomy. First, the abandonment of his court-reform bill in July 1937 seriously damaged his aura of legislative invincibility.[29] Second, growing dissatisfaction within the Democratic coalition undermined the political authority of the president. Although some moderates blamed Roosevelt for supporting sit-down strikes of the Congress of Industrial Organizations (CIO), southern Democrats opposed civil rights measures that could have undermined the segregated social and economic order prevailing in their region. Third, the 1937 recession ruined the economic progress made since 1933.[30] Finally, in this bleak economic context, the 1938 elections boosted the power of the conservative coalition in Congress, thus making new policy experiments unlikely.[31]

In January 1939, a few weeks before his speech about the SSB report, Roosevelt had explicitly ended the "experimental" phase of the New Deal: "We have now passed the period of internal conflict in the launching of our program of social reform. . . . Our full energies may now be released to invigorate the processes of recovery in order to preserve our reforms."[32] It is in this context that we can understand the president's support for what would become the 1939 amendments to the Social Security Act. Instead of launching bold reform initiatives in a favorable political context, the president had to compromise in order to preserve his policy legacy.

The Enactment of a Paradoxical Compromise

The legislative process leading to the enactment of the 1939 amendments proved far less contentious than the debate surrounding the ratification of the Social Security Act, as reformers and conservatives had forged a political compromise over financing and benefit issues months before the beginning of the legislative process. Moreover, Dr. Townsend's constant push for bolder public pensions maintained the pressure on Congress to enhance Social Security provisions. As in 1935, letters sent to Congress by Townsend's supporters further established the need to reform.[33] After public hearings, during which Henry Morgenthau "calmly backed away from the reserve method of financing that had incited so much controversy,"[34] the CWM modified the administration's proposals and rejected the proposed integration of professional categories such as domestic workers into Social Security. Moreover, the CWM extended the concept of agricultural workers to exclude more workers. As Altmeyer recalled, the committee's chairman, Robert Doughton, explained the decision to exclude even more agricultural workers than in 1935 in the following way: "Doctor, when the first farmer with manure on his shoes comes to me and asks to be covered, I will be willing to consider it."[35] Although some farmers had already sent letters to Congress in favor of their integration into the federal program, no mass movement emerged to fight for the integration of most occupational categories excluded in 1935. There is no evidence that racial prejudice was at the origin of this decision to maintain their exclusion from old age insurance.[36]

On June 2, 1939, the CWM finally issued its report concerning the proposed amendments to the Social Security Act. The floor debate did not lead to the enactment of any amendment, and the House easily passed the bill as recommended by the CWM on June 10.[37] The fact that only two representatives voted against that bill showed how broad the consensus was surrounding the paradoxical bipartisan compromise that had gradually emerged since Senator Vandenberg had initiated the second Advisory Council in January 1937. Although the Senate adopted two amendments aimed at increasing old age assistance grants-in-aid paid to poorer states, the enactment of the proposed bill always seemed certain. On July 13, the Senate thus passed the bill by a vote of 57 to 8.[38] After a brief period of discussion, House and Senate members agreed on a conference report. The president signed the 1939 amendments on August 10.

Clearly, the content of this legislation transformed the functioning of old age insurance before that program had actually started to pay benefits, and the measures adopted indubitably altered the very nature of Social Security. Against the financial imperatives imposed by the administration a few years earlier, Social Security emerged as a much more redistributive program than the one established in 1935. No longer centered on actuarial equity and advance funding, the new version of the program included spousal and survivor benefits, two measures rooted in traditional gender roles that favored income redistribution from singles to married couples. Rejecting the Advisory Council's idea that new benefits would only enhance the rights of male breadwinners, Congress also recognized spousal and survivor benefits as entitlements, "as matters of rights for women themselves."[39] Despite the exclusion of divorced women and the recognition of traditional gender roles embodied in the 1939 amendments, they represented a significant step forward for American women. Yet, it is impossible here to follow Mettler's interpretation and talk about the gradual integration of women to "national social citizenship" because the 1939 amendments never transformed Social Security into a universal, citizenship-based program. Although the program proved more redistributive than before, benefits were still formally derived from the payroll tax. In 1939, as had been true four years earlier, the Social Security Act never embodied the principle that social rights were grounded in American citizenship.[40]

Despite the fact that the 1939 amendments reshaped the program's functioning, the actors who agreed on this winning compromise seldom acknowledged the true meaning of this paradigmatic shift. The first way to look at this successful attempt to hide the true scope of the reform is probably related to the following bargaining logic: "When people want to agree on something, they often overlook the true implications of the thing on which they are agreeing. In such a situation, people tend to excuse other people for abandoning previously held belief."[41] From the administration's perspective, hiding the reform's deep meaning also had the advantage of obscuring the fact that the Roosevelt administration had lost control over the federal policy agenda and had been forced to compromise only a few years after the enactment of the Social Security Act. Another advantage of dissimulating the paradigmatic shift embodied in the 1939 reform was to permit the reproduction of the official discourse concerning "earned rights" and Social Security. According to such an ideological frame, this contributory program rooted in self-reliance and other core "American values" granted "earned rights" to covered individuals. In spite of the redistributive shift enacted in 1939, executive officials still defined Social Security in strict opposition with social assistance.[42] Inconsistent with the concrete functioning of the program, such an ideological frame appeared as a useful mechanism to shield Social Security against potential conservative attacks and to establish a genuine "policy monopoly." It is interesting that this frame was as directly rooted in the American ideological repertoire as Landon's critique of old age insurance. This idea reflects the interactive nature of the framing process discussed in Chapter 1: political actors from opposite camps mobilize the same basic symbols and representations to convince the public to support their policy alternatives. Hence, opponents and supporters of various social programs must draw on shared beliefs and representations—or what are perceived as such—in order to justify (or attack) existing social programs. During the post–World War II era, government officials would largely stick to the official discourse about "American values" and "earned rights," thus reinforcing the ideological frame surrounding Social Security. In the absence of the public discourse about fraternity and solidarity ever present in many European societies, American reformers framed an individualistic discourse in order to justify modern, redistributive social policies whose functioning is at odds with the old liberal logic of "possessive individualism."

Private Benefits and Incrementalism

The enactment of the 1939 amendments to the Social Security Act ended the debate over the size of the trust fund, yet it did not guarantee the long-term survival of the program. Still covering little more than 60 percent of the workforce, Social Security would face more challenges during the conservative 1940s, notably because of Congress's unwillingness to increase both benefits and the payroll tax. Although no significant reform was enacted during that decade, new economic trends radically altered the political environment and the meaning of Social Security. To understand the fate of the program during and after the 1940s, I will first turn to the impact of World War II on the American economy before discussing the swift development of private benefits and their impact on the politics of Social Security.

Stuck in Neutral: War, Prosperity, and Congressional Inaction

In many advanced industrial countries, the tragic military conflict with the Nazi regime favored a push to expand social protection, which materialized in an increased sense of interdependence, shared citizenship, and national solidarity.[43] During and immediately after the war, the Beveridge Report and other official publications constructed the need to reform—and expand—social protection in the context of economic planning and reconstruction.[44] In most Western European countries, postwar social policy reforms led to the emergence of more generous public pension systems that gradually became universal or quasi-universal. Despite the variations between national pension systems, they all created new constituencies as a greater number of occupational groups gained public pension coverage. In social insurance countries such as Belgium, France, and Germany, several occupational groups gained coverage under separate pension schemes that commonly reflected prewar pension arrangements.[45] In these countries and elsewhere, labor unions and business interests were granted a central role in the management of public pension programs.[46] In an increasingly favorable economic context, powerful unions and labor parties supported the expansion of these programs.[47] Furthermore, growing pension constituencies meant that pension reform became a central electoral and political issue. This situation encouraged elected officials to pursue credit-claiming strategies in the field of pension reform. Claiming responsibility for the expansion of public pensions, politicians competed to receive the electoral rewards associated with broader coverage and more comprehensive benefits.[48]

In the United States, World War II did not favor such a massive expansion of Social Security.[49] Instead of justifying the need to reform that program in order to boost benefits and universalize coverage, the

war stimulated an immediate return to economic prosperity that reduced unemployment and, consequently, the perceived necessity to
enact new measures similar to those adopted previously as a response
to the Great Depression.[50] In the war's favorable economic context,
American business—with the support of the conservative coalition in
Congress—also regained much ideological and political power after
more than a decade of decline. Related to a dramatic increase in military spending and the direct wartime collaboration between business
and government, the private sector's new economic and political vitality acted against a rapid expansion of federal social policy.[51] Immediately after the war—when, as a reaction against fascism, left-wing
parties became politically successful in many Western European countries—the United States entered a more conservative political era.
Because Republicans and, more generally, the conservative coalition
gained much ground in Congress after the 1942 legislative election,
comprehensive social policy reforms became more and more unlikely
as economic prosperity and conservative opposition reduced the perceived need—and capacity—to expand social benefits.[52]

In spite of such trends, federal officials formulated expansionist reform
proposals through the publication of wartime documents similar to the
Beveridge Report.[53] In 1942, for example, the National Resources Planning
Board (NRPB) issued a special report that recommended nothing less
than the centralization of social assistance and the establishment of
national health insurance as well as the launching of new public work
initiatives. In addition to these bold reform proposals, the report advocated the expansion of federal old age insurance, notably the integration
of new professional categories into the program.[54] Far from enacting such
ambitious proposals, Congress abolished the NRPB and other executive
planning agencies shortly after the 1942 congressional elections, after
which "conservatives in Congress were strong enough to roll back the
New Deal."[55] It is in this context that we should understand the fate of
Social Security reform during and immediately after World War II.

First, the wartime period brought relative inaction on the part of
Congress, which simply froze the old age insurance payroll tax. Between
1942 and 1947, Congress turned back scheduled tax increases no fewer
than seven times.[56] Because of the swift return to prosperity, the reserve
fund had increased faster than expected, thus reducing the short-term

need for tax hikes.[57] Moreover, limited pension costs and a high ratio of contributors to beneficiaries made tax hikes *unnecessary* in the short run. Because elected officials rarely "seek to increase taxes if they can avoid it" and public pressures to expand the reserve fund were negligible, the option to freeze taxes emerged as the obvious policy alternative, at least from a short-term perspective.[58] Although the decision to freeze taxes early in the program's life meant that people would have to contribute more down the road, this logic easily prevailed in spite of concerns about the financial future of Social Security.[59]

Second, current Social Security financing mechanisms came under attack during the 1940s. On the one hand, in 1944, the Senate—under the guidance of Senator Vandenberg and the SSB—formally authorized general revenue financing in case of actuarial unbalance. This meant that the federal government would subsidize the Old Age and Survivors Insurance (OASI) trust fund if the payroll tax alone proved unable to cover all benefit payments. According to Leff, this symbolic gesture was directly related to the above-mentioned tax freeze: "To Senator Vandenberg, it represented a declaration of good intentions, to show that he was not using the tax cut to slash future benefits; for the SSB and sponsor Senator Murray, it was a way to hold Senator Vandenberg to his promises of future solvency while underlining their concern that some provisions be made for the future deficits generated by the freeze."[60] At that time, however, general revenue financing represented a long-term threat to the program's structure, not an immediate menace. On the other hand, a bolder and more threatening policy alternative emerged during the 1940s: flat pensions. By eliminating the relationship between benefits and taxes, this measure would have totally altered the nature of Social Security. For that reason, the SSB and its political allies opposed proposals advocating a shift to a "flat pension." In March 1940, for example, Altmeyer convinced the president to forbid Paul McNutt, then head of the Federal Security Agency, to give a speech that would have formulated an alternative to Social Security dangerously similar to (but more modest in scope than) the Townsend Plan.[61] During the 1940s, the SSB and the presidency would fight other attempts to undermine the program's financing and benefit structure. Emanating from Congress, organized labor, the Townsend Plan, and even the Democratic Party, variations on the flat pension theme failed to gain the support of congressional committees that opposed them in the name of fiscal responsibility.[62]

Considering this crucial role of congressional committees and presidential leadership during and after the war, the efforts of the SSB to undermine these proposals may not have been as instrumental to the survival of Social Security as several authors have argued. In a controversial book, for example, Cates formulated a genuine "conspiracy theory" explaining why Social Security survived and developed as a social insurance scheme during and after World War II. For him, the SSB ensured institutional status quo through bureaucratic and political machinations that eliminated more redistributive alternatives from the policy agenda.[63] Although the SSB certainly helped to restrict the number of reform options debated during the 1940s and early 1950s, private benefits, electoral competition, and policy legacies had a significant impact on Social Security development during the 1940s and 1950s.

The Great Integration: Expanding Private Benefits

During and immediately after World War II, the expansion of private social benefits altered the environment in which reformers had to justify the need to reform federal social policies.[64] Vital federal decisions were at the origin of this expansion. Under the pressure of private businesses and insurance companies, the federal government implemented tax incentives and regulations that stimulated the multiplication of private social benefits in the United States.[65] In 1942, the Revenue Act codified previously enacted changes to the federal tax system that created special tax exclusions for employer-sponsored pension benefits. This key legislation formulated the rules of the game regulating the distribution of private pension benefits. The Revenue Act of 1942 also allowed the integration of private pension plans with Social Security, permitting employers to factor federal benefits into the calculation of private pensions. Even though tax increases enacted during the 1940s gradually increased the value of special tax exclusions, the Revenue Act failed to guarantee an egalitarian distribution of private pension coverage and benefits.[66] Considering that the initial Social Security wage ceiling was only $3,000 per year, many employers established plans offering complementary protection to better-off workers while enjoying increasingly generous tax deductions. This logic led to a rapid expansion of private plans during the 1940s. As corporate pension contributions grew by 500 percent between 1941 and 1945, the "number of plans increased dramatically from 659 in 1939 to 1,947 in 1942 and 9,370 by 1946."[67] Contrary to the reshaping and rapid expansion of social policy systems in some Western European countries during the late 1940s, the United States had a prompt growth in private benefits that would durably impact the postwar reform environment.[68]

As Jennifer Klein argued, American employers formulated a new discourse to justify these growing private pension benefits. Instead of stressing managerial issues as had been done in the 1920s, employers publicly subscribed to the idea of economic security for American workers. Such a discourse emphasized the fact that public and private benefits were complementary and that the private supplementation of public benefits constituted the "American way." Recognized by federal officials, this business-friendly discourse about security and supplementation helped legitimize private benefits and the related containment of Social Security expansion through the postwar era.[69]

By the late 1940s, the labor movement fervently supported the expansion of private benefits. Partly because of Congress's unwillingness to increase Social Security benefits to compensate for the effects of inflation, labor officials launched a crusade to include fringe benefits in collective bargaining. Witnessing the current multiplication of private benefits, unions thought that this integration would increase their legitimacy in American society. Then representing approximately 30 percent of the workforce, these organizations did face a significant challenge: an open political crusade against the labor movement. Supported by employers and conservative politicians, this counterattack gained much ground after the 1946 congressional elections, which resulted in a Republican landslide. For the first time since 1930, Republicans controlled both houses of Congress. Without losing time, Congress passed the Taft-Hartley Act of 1947, undermining labor's position in collective bargaining. In this context, the inclusion of fringe benefits in collective bargaining represented an attempt to fight back against employers and gain more legitimacy. Consequently, far from representing a mere "depoliticization of labor," the struggle over private benefits had a genuine political meaning.[70]

Launched by the CIO, the United Mine Workers (UMW), and the United Automobile Workers (UAW), labor's crusade first proved difficult, as employers refused to bargain over pensions in spite of massive strikes. In 1946, however, the UMW gained coverage under a generous private plan that had a positive psychological effect on other CIO organizations involved in this pension crusade.[71] In spite of a minor UAW victory against Ford in 1947, one could argue that it was the federal government that permitted the victory of the labor movement and the integration of fringe benefits into collective bargaining. At the end of the 1940s, two major federal decisions made this widespread integration possible. In 1948, the Inland Steel decision of the National Labor Relations Board called for pensions to "lie within the statutory scope of collective bargaining."[72] A year later, the Supreme Court upheld this crucial decision, thus forcing employers to bargain over pension benefits that could no longer be mere "discretionary gratuities."[73] In this favorable institutional context, the UAW launched a series of strikes and, after two years of struggle, succeeded in forcing Chrysler, Ford, and General Motors to grant generous, noncontributory pension benefits in the context of collective bargaining.[74] During the 1950s, other unions gained similar concessions from employers and helped transform private pensions into a collective bargaining item. After the merger between the AFL and the CIO in 1955, the new organization supported the inclusion of fringe benefits in collective bargaining.[75] Overall, labor pension activism during the late 1940s and the 1950s contributed to a spectacular increase in private pension coverage, reaching 41 percent of the private sector workforce in 1960, up from 19 percent in 1946.[76] As opposed to the situation prevailing in social insurance countries such as France and Germany, labor unions thus supported the development of—and identified with—private benefits.

Yet, this fact never prevented the labor movement from promoting the expansion of Social Security. Although unions turned to private benefits when this federal program stagnated during the 1940s, they still actively supported its expansion. In the absence of a genuine labor party, however, unions lobbied as a part of the fragmented Democratic coalition and thus embraced a more modest policy platform than most of their Canadian and Western European counterparts, who were frequently tied to socialist and social democratic parties promoting bolder social and economic reforms.[77] This institutional logic, more than the supposed "depoliticization of labor," shaped the involvement of unions in Social Security politics. Excluded from the management of Social Security, they represented a mere interest group among others within the Democratic electoral coalition supporting the expansion of that program.[78]

Beyond labor mobilization, the expansion of private pension benefits during the 1940s and 1950s had a significant impact on the politics of Social Security reform.[79] If federal decisions and tax policy favored the growth of these benefits, private institutions in turn affected the conditions under which Congress and the presidency dealt with Social Security reform. Because the federal government had established a comprehensive old age insurance program *before* the expansion of large-scale private benefits, private pensions were largely seen as supplementary provisions. At first mostly opposed to Social Security, employers came to understand this program as a standard floor of protection necessary to the growth of private pensions. Because firms took Social Security benefits into account when setting their own pension provisions, they increasingly perceived the expansion of federal old age insurance as a tool of cost reduction. This situation contrasted with the one prevailing in the field of health insurance. Because Congress did not enact a health insurance program during the New Deal, the rapid expansion of private health benefits during the 1940s and 1950s emerged as an alternative—not a supplement—to governmental intervention. For the AMA and most business representatives, the growth of private health insurance showed that federal health insurance was superfluous. Even though feedback effects from private welfare institutions contributed to the consensus surrounding federal old age insurance, they undermined the need for direct federal intervention in the field of health insurance. In this context, old age insurance expanded during the Truman administration, whereas the president's push for federal health insurance failed miserably.[80] Political factors favored the enactment of the 1950 amendments to the Social Security Act and, consequently, the emergence of a large "army of beneficiaries" that would support the program's expansion.

The Fair Deal and the 1950 Amendments

Immediately after the war, President Truman (who had succeeded to the presidency after the death of Franklin Roosevelt in 1945) called for a return to the reform spirit of the New Deal. More precisely, he supported the enactment of national health insurance and the expansion of existing federal social programs.[81] Concerning Social Security, the president called for coverage extension and significant benefit increases. Simultaneously, federal reports advocating the expansion of American social policy formulated analogous recommendations.[82] Considering the favorable economic situation and the end of the war, there was a lot of ground for optimism in the liberal camp.

Unfortunately for the new president and his allies, the 1946 congressional elections temporarily postponed the establishment of new social programs as well as the enactment of major Social Security amendments. As a consequence of this election, Republicans gained control over the House and the Senate, permitting them to block major social reforms. In fact, Congress attempted to reduce coverage, and in 1947, the president vetoed legislation that would have excluded magazine and newspaper vendors from Social Security coverage. The following summer, however, Congress successfully modified the definition of "employee" to exclude these workers.[83] Although modest, this measure illustrated the dominance of congressional conservatism and its negative impact on social policy development.

Yet, to the relief of reform-minded actors within and outside government, three political factors would improve the prospect for social reform and social policy expansion starting in the fall of 1948. First, Truman was elected president in 1948, thus increasing his legitimacy and political capital. At the beginning of the following year, the newly elected president launched the Fair Deal, a reform campaign directly aimed at perfecting the political and economic transformation initiated by the New Deal. Articulating the legacy of the New Deal, Truman thus became an "orthodox-innovator" who attempted, like other presidents before him, to "galvanize political action with promises to continue the good work of the past and demonstrate the vitality of the established order in changing times."[84] Facing the difficult task of remaining faithful to Roosevelt's legacy amid growing conservatism, as well as dissension within the Democratic coalition, Truman nevertheless pushed for the enactment of national health insurance and new amendments to the Social Security Act, measures that could reinforce this coalition in the context of "interest group liberalism." Second, Democrats regained control over both houses in Congress after the 1948 federal elections.[85] Although the conservative coalition remained vocal and southern Democrats powerful, this electoral victory created a window of opportunity for reform. Third, the publication of the third Advisory Council's report in the fall of 1948 further set the agenda for reform, and the 1950 amendments to the Social Security Act were largely inspired by this report.

Postwar advisory councils gathered supporters of Social Security under the tight supervision of the SSA.[86] Established in 1947, this third Advisory Council evaluated the measures enacted as part of the Social Security Act while formulating recommendations to improve them. At the very beginning of its report, the council stated the general philosophy guiding its recommendations: "Public-assistance payments from general tax funds to persons who are found to be in need have serious limitations as a way of maintaining family income. Our goal is, so far as possible, to prevent dependency through social insurance and thus greatly reduce the need for assistance."[87] Rooted in fiscal conservatism and faithful to Roosevelt's social insurance paradigm, this statement must be understood in the policy context of the time. At the end of the 1940s, "only about 20 percent of those aged 65 or over [were] either insured or receiving benefits under the program."[88] This meant that, by that time, old age assistance remained far more significant politically and socially than Social Security. "Twice as many people received welfare as received social insurance, even though Congress had expanded social insurance in 1939. The nation spent more than three times as much on welfare as on social insurance."[89] According to the council, three factors explained this situation: inadequate coverage (less than 60 percent of the working population), "restrictive eligibility requirements for older workers," and meager benefits—twenty-five dollars a month on average for a single person.[90] Facing the prospect of losing the marathon against assistance launched more than a decade earlier by President Roosevelt and the CES, Social Security could become irrelevant in the absence of significant Congressional action.

After justifying the need to reform Social Security, the third Advisory Council recommended the rapid enactment of the following measures, which could make the federal program more generous. First, the council argued for the integration of more occupational groups into the program in order to generalize coverage. Probably the most significant of these groups were independent workers, members of the armed forces, domestic and farm workers, and employees of nonprofit organizations. Second, the Advisory Council called for increased benefits in order to compensate for the effects of inflation that had reduced the real value of Social Security monthly payments since 1939. Third, the council also pushed for relaxed eligibility criteria that would allow more workers to receive old age insurance benefits instead of social assistance ones. Finally, the Advisory Council supported the advent of a disability insurance scheme as part of Social Security.[91] Setting the agenda for reform, the council clearly embraced the idea of social adequacy through improved insurance coverage while respecting the general structure of the program. Considering the favorable demographic and economic context, as well as the presence of significant reserves in the trust fund, Congress could in fact enact most of these recommendations without having to vote potentially unpopular massive tax hikes.[92] Since elected officials rarely attempt to increase taxes if they can avoid it, the prospect of distributing higher benefits to many more voters without dramatic tax increases proved almost irresistible. As in other industrial nations operating old age insurance programs, the PAYGO structure of Social Security allowed elected officials to claim credit for seemingly generous measures while hiding the potential long-term costs of their decisions.[93] In the United States, however, the peculiar integration of private benefits into Social Security also paved the way to its expansion, since a growing number of firms perceived such integration—and therefore Social Security—as a means of reducing their own pension spending.[94]

In his January 5, 1949, State of the Union address, Truman encouraged Congress to act swiftly in order to expand federal social policy. Besides the creation of national health insurance, the president stressed the need to reform Social Security. Like the Advisory Council, he identified two major lacunae that prevented this program from adequately fulfilling its original mission: low benefits and limited coverage.[95] On February 22, the Truman administration transmitted two bills to Congress: one dealing with social assistance, the other with Social Security. A month later, the CWM launched public hearings about the second bill, which embodied the recommendations of the Advisory Council. During the testimony, labor officials showed their unanimous support for Social Security and for the administration's bill. In contrast with the organization's earlier call for a flat pension, CIO representative Philip Murray lauded the proposed legislation on Social Security.[96] On his side, William Green from the AFL remained faithful to this organization's strong support for that federal program.[97] Although both organizations were then fighting over the integration of private pensions with collective bargaining, their commitment to Social Security expansion seemed genuine. Within the business camp, the opposition to the bill was subdued. Predictably, a certain number of conservative witnesses attacked Social Security in the name of personal freedom and self-reliance.[98] In 1949, however, most business organizations supported Social Security, a program that increasingly represented a way for employers to reduce their own pension costs. Because Congress had not increased benefits since 1939, the proposed legislation was generally perceived as a reasonable way to compensate for the inflation-induced decline in the real value of benefits.[99] Moreover, farm organizations and the National Association for the Advancement of Colored People (NAACP) testified in favor of the integration of professional categories such as agrarian and domestic workers. Opposition to this integration was almost nonexistent in the testimonies to the CWM.[100] In their statements, Arthur Altmeyer, head of the Social Security Administration, and several members of the Advisory Council also defended the proposed extension of Social Security coverage.[101]

On August 22, after four months of deliberations, the CWM issued majority and minority reports as well as a new draft of the Social Security legislation.[102] In general, this new draft maintained—or slightly altered—the provisions formulated in the administration's bill.[103] For example, most domestic employees and independent workers would gain coverage under this new legislation. Residents of Puerto Rico and the Virgin Islands would also join the program. In total, the number of participants in Social Security would increase from 35 to 46 million people.[104] Moreover, the new draft reduced the proposed average benefit increase to 66 percent, still enough to compensate for the effects of inflation since 1939. The CWM also preserved the clause on disability insurance but limited its application to permanent disability.

Yet, two decisions of the committee proved more significant. The CWM eliminated the proposed integration of agricultural workers without providing any clear justification. Although groups representing farmers had demanded their integration in their testimony, it seemed that the lack of a "resounding and equivocal voice" supporting this option, as well as enduring concerns about its administrative feasibility, convinced the CWM to postpone legislative action.[105] In fact, the bill's new version excluded approximately 300,000 new farm workers from the program through a redefinition of this professional category.[106] The other significant decision was that the CWM rejected the idea of general revenue financing. In the name of fiscal responsibility, the committee eliminated the 1943 clause that recognized the legitimacy of future general revenue financing for Social Security. For the CWM, Social Security must remain a self-supporting program.[107] Fifteen years after the enactment of the Social Security Act, fiscal conservatism seemed to have won a decisive battle over general revenue financing.

Although three Republican minority members harshly attacked Social Security and pushed for the establishment of a "flat pension" that would replace both old age assistance and insurance, the bill did not encounter any major obstacle on the House floor. After a brief debate and the failure of a Republican attempt to recommit the bill, the legislation was easily adopted by a vote of 333 to 14 on October 3, 1949.[108] After a decade of legislative inertia, many members of Congress finally seemed willing to support the cautious expansion of Social Security.

The Senate only began examining the legislation in January 1950, and in May, the FC finally issued a new draft, which differed considerably from the House's version. First, according to this new draft, the program would cover agricultural employees, a measure previously recommended by the Advisory Council. Second, the Senate committee further liberalized the benefits and the eligibility criteria. Third, provisions concerning disability insurance were eliminated in the absence of satisfactory cost evaluations. Beyond this official explanation, there is strong evidence that pressures from the AMA and insurance companies largely motivated this decision.[109] From June 13 to 20, the Senate examined the new version of the bill. After increasing the wage base from $3,000 to $3,600, the Senate easily passed the legislation by a vote of 82 to 2.[110] On August 1, members of the conference committee finally agreed on a common version of the 1950 amendments to the Social Security Act. In spite of some minor modifications, the Senate's draft finally triumphed.

Consequently, although disability insurance was expelled from the bill, Social Security emerged as a broader and more generous program.[111] Introducing the first large-scale coverage extension since 1935, the 1950 amendments included about 10 million additional workers in the federal program.[112] On average, these amendments increased benefits by 77 percent, a measure sufficient to compensate for the effects of inflation since 1939. Moreover, the 1950 amendments liberalized the eligibility criteria for benefits, resulting in immediate benefit payments to a sizable number of elderly individuals who had not yet met former eligibility requirements.[113] Finally, at age sixty-five, dependent husbands of retired or deceased workers became eligible for spousal/survivor benefits. This constituted a modest expansion of the family benefits created in 1939 and a significant move toward gender-neutral family benefits.[114]

In his speech during the signing ceremony, President Truman welcomed the enactment of the 1950 amendments to the Social Security Act as major progress. Even if these amendments failed to implement disability insurance or extend coverage to farm operators, they roughly doubled the program's annual budget, which indubitably reinforced its economic and political stature.[115] After a decade of legislative inertia, Social Security became a much larger measure, creating growing constituencies in American society. And as Social Security covered more occupational groups, a larger number of African Americans participated in the program after years of exclusion.[116]

Considering the centralized administrative structure of Social Security, African Americans who gained coverage under the program were treated fairly. A procedurally egalitarian program, Social Security generated entitlements formally derived from one's payroll contributions. This logic contrasted with the one prevailing in the decentralized field of social assistance, where racial biases impacted the distribution of welfare benefits and where levels and conditions varied greatly from one state to another. In the mirror of state social assistance programs, Social Security emerged as an administratively efficient and color-blind program that favored the smooth incorporation of African American workers into the federal social policy system.[117] A stigma-free program grounded in a progressive benefit structure, Social Security would help an increasing number of African Americans achieve better retirement security in the name of so-called "earned rights." The expansion of Social Security after 1950 confirmed these positive trends that largely stemmed from the institutional and administrative features of that federal social insurance program.[118]

Social Security Success, National Health Insurance Failure

We have seen that the fate of Social Security around 1950 can be understood in the mirror of the defeat of national health insurance. Between 1948 and 1950, President Truman failed to convince southern Democrats and Republicans to back his health insurance proposal, and Congress did not enact national health insurance legislation. The absence of strong enthusiasm for this reform—even within the labor movement—was partially due to the AMA-led campaign against the "socialization of medicine."[119] The idea that the private and the voluntary sectors would create a comprehensive health insurance system without direct federal intervention also played a crucial role in undermining the support for national health insurance.[120] Even though the private sector had adjusted to the presence of Social Security during the growth of private benefits, national health insurance appeared as a costly alternative to well-grounded voluntary, private insurance. Because the attempt to adopt public health insurance occurred *after* the massive expansion of private benefits, the expansion represented an obstacle to reform. In contrast, since Social Security was enacted years *before* the rapid multiplication of private pension plans, public and private pension benefits were seen as more complementary than antagonistic. This result was largely because employers and workers had come to see private pensions as a supplement to existing Social Security benefits. Differences in timing and historical sequence thus shed new light on the contrasting fate of health and old age insurance during and after the Fair Deal.[121]

After the defeat of national health insurance, Social Security gradually reaffirmed its status as the cornerstone of federal social policy. Considering the growing number of beneficiaries, this program increasingly became the object of credit-claiming strategies on the part of federal elected officials. In a highly competitive electoral context, Democrats attempted to gain electoral support and reinforce their political coalition through the push for Social Security–related measures such as disability insurance and the periodical enactment of ad hoc benefit increases compensating for the effects of inflation. In a favorable economic and demographic context, many elected officials could easily support—and claim credit for—the apparently painless enlargement of this increasingly popular program.[122] As in other advanced industrial countries, favorable demographic and actuarial conditions, as well as business and labor support, stimulated the expansion of Social Security in the postwar era.[123] Although bureaucratic activism also contributed to this expansion, the demographic, economic, and electoral realities were the crucial structural forces driving postwar public pension development.

Using Social Security to gain electoral credit and boost his popularity, President Truman promoted the need to reform that program again only months after the enactment of the 1950 amendments.[124] In July 1952, the Democratic Congress easily passed new amendments to the Social Security Act. This modest legislation increased benefits by 12.5 percent, liberalized the retirement test, and made other minor changes. According to Daniel Sanders, three factors facilitated swift legislative action: "the absence of any major tax bill before Congress in 1952," the expected retirement of CWM chairman Robert L. Doughton and the willingness of several majority members of the committee to enact in his honor further improvement to the bill he had sponsored in 1935, and, finally, "the general increase in prices and wages [that] made possible the financing of benefit increases without any increase in the insurance contribution rate."[125] Even though the 1952 amendments did not lead to a massive benefit increase or the enactment of disability insurance, this legislation showed that the era of legislative inertia had come to an end, at least under Democratic congressional and presidential leadership.

The Road to Bipartisan Credit Claiming: Eisenhower and Social Security

In November 1952, however, Dwight Eisenhower was elected president, and Republicans gained majority in the two houses of Congress.

Despite the fact that the new president pledged his support for the New Deal's legacy, his statements concerning the future of Social Security remained vague. Considering that the 1952 Republican platform proposed the payment of benefits to all elderly Americans,[126] the remark made by Eisenhower on February 2, 1953, could have been interpreted either as support for coverage expansion under the existing program or support for the shift to a universal "flat pension": "The provisions of the old-age and survivors insurance law should promptly be extended to cover millions of citizens who have been left out of the social-security system."[127] Although the 1939 amendments had severely undermined Social Security's strict contributory foundation, the enactment of a flat pension would constitute an explicit—and radical—paradigm shift in Social Security. Fears over the possible move to a flat pension increased as the Chamber of Commerce issued a report supporting this type of measure.[128] More precisely, this report suggested abolishing old age assistance while immediately covering ("blanketing in") all elderly individuals, whether or not they had contributed to the program.[129] Moreover, the new Federal Security administrator, Oveta C. Hobby, appointed an advisory group on public pensions dominated by supporters of the Chamber of Commerce proposal. Facing this apparent threat to the integrity of Social Security, organized labor launched a media campaign to denounce this advisory group. As the AFL *News Reporter* commented cynically, the appointment of this conservative advisory group on Social Security was "like appointing professional arsonists to handle arrangements for National Fire Prevention Week."[130]

Despite changes made in the composition of this advisory group, discontent remained high among supporters of the program, especially after the Chamber of Commerce launched a grassroots campaign in favor of "broadened coverage" that would actually reduce social spending while undermining Social Security's income-replacement nature. Led by Arthur Altmeyer, who resigned from his position as commissioner of Social Security on April 10, 1953, labor unions and other Social Security advocates organized the Citizens Conference on Social Security, publicly showing their opposition to reforms that would significantly alter the program's benefit structure and financing logic.[131] Timely mobilization certainly helped to undermine political support for the Chamber of Commerce proposal, and the administration's advisory group on Social Security finally rejected that proposal while supporting the expansion of the existing social insurance program.[132]

There is no evidence that the president would have supported this proposal in the first place. Considering that his New Republicanism involved an apparent reconciliation between the Republican Party and the New Deal's legacy, attacking the largest federal social program would have proven contradictory to his ideologically moderate stance and his electoral strategy, which consisted of seducing elements of the Democratic electoral coalition.[133] Although sympathetic to conservative Republican ideals, "the new president refused to take on New Deal Liberalism or Fair Deal foreign policy directly, and he carefully held the right wing of his party, zealous in his opposition to both, at bay. Eisenhower proved a master at keeping his personal and partisan political priorities hidden."[134] A strategic accommodation in the context of the ideological domination of liberalism in postwar America, this attitude can be found in the field of Social Security reform. Because the program now covered the vast majority of American workers, the president and the Republican majority in Congress would claim credit for Social Security's coverage extensions and—modest—benefit increases while opposing the enactment of more ambitious reforms such as disability insurance. The president and his "new" Republican Party also supported the development of private benefits alongside existing social programs as a way to indirectly limit their expansion.[135] Resisting bold reforms, most Republicans decided to tolerate the institutional status quo instead of attempting to reverse the course of American history through a return to "old liberalism."

It is in this context that we can understand the president's decision to recommend a new, albeit modest, expansion of Social Security in August 1953. Transmitting the advisory group's report to Congress on August 1, he made clear that further benefit increases and the extension of coverage were part of his policy agenda. Furthermore, he copied traditional supporters of the program and, drawing on the American ideological repertoire, framed Social Security as a genuinely American— and conservative—measure:

Retirement systems, by which individuals contribute to their own security according to their own respective abilities, have become an essential part of our economic and social life. These systems are but a reflection of the American heritage of sturdy self-reliance which has made our country strong and kept it free; the self-reliance without which we would have had no Pilgrim Fathers, no hardship-defying pioneers, and no eagerness today to push to ever widening horizons in every aspect of our national life.[136]

Four months later, in his January 7, 1954, State of the Union Address, the president reformulated these recommendations in the broad context of New Republicanism. His specific statement about Social Security appeared as further recognition of the need to reform the program while preserving its structure:

Our basic social security program, the Old-Age and Survivors Insurance system, to which individuals contribute during their productive years and receive benefits based on previous earnings, is designed to shield them from destitution. Last year I recommended extension of the social insurance system to include more than 10,000,000 additional persons. I ask that this extension soon be accomplished. This and other major improvements in the insurance system will bring substantial benefit increases and broaden the membership of the insurance system, thus diminishing the need for Federal grants-in-aid for such purposes.[137]

This speech and others paved the way to a gradual expansion of Social Security during the second half of the 1950s. Reintroduced in January 1954, the administration's proposals were adopted during the following summer. Signed on September 1, 1954, the new amendments to the Social Security Act were largely derived from these proposals. Perhaps the most important aspect of this legislation was the extension of coverage it promoted. Extending compulsory coverage to farmers and to additional farm and domestic employees as well as specific categories of self-employed workers, these amendments also permitted employees of local and state governments to participate in the program on a voluntary basis. The 1954 amendments further liberalized the retirement test while raising the earnings base to $4,200, an indirect way to increase both taxes and benefits.[138] Although the president and his congressional allies temporarily put the issue of disability insurance aside, the earnings records of disabled workers were "frozen" to prevent them from losing their Social Security benefits because of their medical condition. In addition to creating this genuine Trojan horse for disability insurance, the 1954 amendments represented a major step toward social adequacy and universal coverage. Depicted as a measure grounded in fiscal conservatism, self-reliance, and other core "American values," Social Security emerged as a major electoral issue for both parties. If the Democratic Party still identified itself with the New Deal's legacy, New Republicans and their president followed them in using Social Security politics as a source of potential electoral gains while attempting to contain the expansion of federal social policy.[139]

After Democrats regained majority control of both houses in the 1954 election,[140] the Eisenhower administration lost control over the legislative agenda. During a favorable "window of opportunity," through which the AMA struggled with major public image problems, Congress finally enacted disability insurance against the president's will.[141] Because the measure proved popular and enough members of Congress supported it to override his veto, he had no choice but to sign the 1956 amendments to the Social Security Act.[142] In addition to the establishment of an insurance scheme for permanently disabled workers aged between fifty and sixty-five, these amendments extended coverage to new occupational groups, notably uniformed military personnel and most formerly excluded self-employed professionals. More important, the 1956 amendments created an early retirement benefit for women, who could choose to take an actuarially reduced pension at age sixty-two. This measure did not apply to widows and female dependent parents. Aimed at solving a problem identified in 1939, this measure, as well as disability insurance itself, illustrated an incremental reform strategy that allowed supporters of the program to depict new benefits as modest improvements grafted onto existing measures.[143] Furthermore, the fact that early retirement first applied exclusively to women underlined the enduring weight of gender differences in Social Security politics.

The Social Security–related measures enacted between 1958 and 1960 also followed this logic. Before the end of President Eisenhower's second term, two more series of amendments to the Social Security Act were enacted. In 1958, Congress raised the wage base from $4,200 to

$4,600 while increasing benefits by 7 percent in order to compensate for the effects of inflation. Benefits were also made payable to dependents of disabled workers.[144] Two years later, Congress liberalized the earnings test and, more important, permitted disabled workers to qualify for benefits at any age.[145] Like the 1958 amendments, this measure went along the incremental reform path ever present during the postwar era. Because the growth in private benefits undermined the support for national health insurance, reformers and their labor allies first pushed for modest measures tied to existing programs before gradually enlarging them.[146] After the end of the New Deal's "critical juncture," divided government—and the growth of private benefits—had transformed incremental reform into the prevailing pattern of social policy development in the United States.[147] Social Security thus became a genuine Trojan horse for incremental policy expansion at the federal level.

Rooted in partisan credit claiming, Social Security expansion during the Eisenhower presidency mostly benefited the Democrats, who promoted reform in a far more aggressive manner than the moderate New Republicans. Losing control over the legislative agenda after 1954, the president and his party received little credit for the reforms enacted during the second half of the decade.[148] Distancing himself from Social Security reforms, Eisenhower proved unable to contain expansionist forces stimulated by electoral competition and auspicious demographic and economic conditions. The growing center of the federal social policy system, Old Age Survivor and Disability Insurance (OASDI), gradually became known as Social Security during the postwar era. Although the term *Social Security* first referred to all the social programs enacted in 1935, it gradually took on this more limited meaning during the 1950s. Denounced by Altmeyer,[149] this semantic shift showed how the old age insurance component of the Social Security Act expanded disproportionably compared to other federal social policy areas. The "race to the bottom" generally prevailed at the state level, and decentralized policies such as unemployment insurance and old age assistance remained fragmented and subject to administrative arbitrariness and even discrimination. Besides, no national health insurance had been enacted in the early 1950s despite the efforts of reformers, labor unions, and President Truman. During the 1950s, Social Security thus emerged as the exception within the exception, the only comprehensive federal social insurance program in the United States, a country where public policies generally supplemented private welfare institutions in order to compensate for "market failures."

Electoral Competition and the End of Actuarial Conservatism

During the Kennedy administration, the debate over Medicare dominated the federal social policy agenda at the expense of Social Security reform. Although no benefit increase was enacted during the Kennedy presidency, in 1961 the Democratic Congress passed significant amendments to the Social Security Act that allowed entitled workers to retire at age sixty-two with actuarially reduced benefits.[150] Extending a measure previously reserved to women, Congress still pursued the incremental strategy that had emerged at the beginning of the preceding decade. During the following years, the debate over the "rediscovery of poverty" and, more important, Medicare for seniors (another incremental reform tied to the Social Security Act) dominated the federal legislative social policy agenda at the expense of Social Security. After the assassination of President Kennedy and the following landslide victory of the Democratic Party, social reforms intensified during the first major "critical juncture" since the New Deal. Although Social Security remained a lower profile issue in the middle of the 1960s, the launching of the ambitious War on Poverty would alter the program's social and political meaning while preparing the ground for new benefit increases.

Expanding Federal Social Policy and Reframing Social Security as an Antipoverty Device

Related to the civil rights protest and the "rediscovery of poverty,"[151] President Johnson's Great Society constituted the most ambitious legislative campaign launched since the Fair Deal. Reflecting economic optimism and technocratic faith in the federal government, this campaign formed the apotheosis of "interest group liberalism." From the poor to labor unions and minorities, the Great Society served traditionally Democratic constituencies in order to reinforce the party's electoral coalition.[152] In addition to the War on Poverty and the creation of new welfare programs such as food stamps, the mid-1960s also brought the advent of Medicare, a federal hospital and medical insurance scheme that had long received the support of organized labor and the SSA. Yet, far from moving the federal government beyond a "residual approach" to public health insurance, Medicare left to employers and insurance companies the task of protecting most of the non-elderly population against health insecurity. Considering the multiplication of private health insurance plans since the 1940s, policymakers did not strongly challenge the private sector's powerful "vested interests" and opted for a program that would cover only "bad risks" associated with the elderly population.[153] Since 1965, Medicare has become an increasingly large social insurance program. Yet, its development has not favored the emergence of national health insurance in the United States.

As an exception within the exception, Social Security remained the cornerstone of federal social policy during and after the Johnson presidency. Yet, the War on Poverty impacted the way policymakers perceived, or at least depicted, this federal program. In addition to the traditional discourse on self-reliance associated with the program since the New Deal, Social Security now represented a well-tested and reliable device in the national struggle against poverty. Governmental studies linking this federal program with the decline of poverty affecting the elderly provided substance to this new frame.[154] And as welfare programs related to the War on Poverty came under attack during the late 1960s, Social Security remained popular among the middle class, thus reinforcing its status as the centerpiece of the federal social policy system.[155] Without replacing the rhetoric concerning self-reliance and the contributory logic, the new discourse about the role of Social Security in poverty alleviation further justified the need for benefit expansion without explicitly acknowledging the program's redistributive nature.[156]

In spite of the social turmoil stemming from civil rights and, later, antiwar protest, the political consensus surrounding Social Security remained strong. After the defeat of Republican presidential candidate Barry Goldwater in 1964, few politicians dared attack this quasi-universal social insurance program that received wide support from the middle class and that reduced poverty among the elderly.[157] And as surveys indicated strong popular support for Social Security, new age-based interest groups emerged to defend the interests of the elderly population.[158] During the 1960s, federal policymakers attempted to seduce this growing constituency through the first White House Conference on Aging (1961) and the enactment of the Older Americans Act (1965), among other initiatives.[159] As Social Security transformed retirement into a quasi-universal institution in American society,[160] the expansion of the program stimulated political participation among the elderly and the growth of interest group organizations such as the American Association of Retired Persons (AARP).[161]

Perceived as a reliable source of electoral dividends in an increasingly uncertain political environment, Social Security reform would reemerge on the federal policy agenda during the second half of the Johnson presidency. Increasingly large constituencies created new incentives for politicians to increase Social Security benefits. In addition to the creation of Medicare, for example, the 1965 amendments increased the payroll tax while raising benefits by 7 percent on average. The amendments also liberalized disability benefits while granting special protection to individuals aged seventy-two and older. Under a temporary "transitional insured status" provision, individuals who had contributed for at least three quarters but could not formally qualify for benefits received a special monthly pension of $35 ($52.50 for couples).[162] The year after, a provision attached to the Tax Adjustment Act provided Social Security benefits for all uncovered individuals over age seventy-two, even those who had never contributed to the program. Moreover, starting in 1968, general revenues would finance this special benefit.[163] In the name of poverty alleviation, this measure further undermined the contributory nature of Social Security and reinforced the long-term historical shift toward social adequacy and economic redistribution initiated in 1939. Using a war-related bill to reform the program instead of waiting for the enactment of new amendments to the Social Security Act, Congress further repudiated fiscal conservatism in a way that paradoxically recalled the Chamber of Commerce proposal of 1953. As mentioned above, federal policymakers never formally acknowledged this departure from fiscal conservatism and the strict contributory model.

In January 1967, President Johnson recommended the adoption of traditional amendments to the Social Security Act that would increase benefits by nothing less than 20 percent. The president also suggested raising the monthly amount of the "minimal pension" from $35 to $70 ($105 for couples) while increasing the special benefit for people aged seventy-two and older from $35 to $50. In his message to Congress, he clearly reframed Social Security as a poverty-alleviation program in order to justify the need to reform: "Although social security benefits keep five and one-half million persons above the poverty line, more than five million still live in poverty. A great nation cannot tolerate these conditions. I proposed Social Security legislation which will bring the greatest improvement in living standards for the elderly since the Act was passed in 1935."[164] According to the president, "these proposals will take 1.4 million Americans out of poverty this year."[165] Formulated as part of a general speech concerning programs for older Americans, these proposals represented a clear attempt to please a key political constituency: the growing army of Social Security beneficiaries, a constituency that had emerged as a feedback effect from the program. Considering the materialization of the "gray lobby" in the federal arena during the 1960s, these beneficiaries became more politically active and visible, thus exacerbating the credit-claiming competition taking place between Democrats and Republicans. Acting as a policy entrepreneur, the president pushed for massive benefit increases in order to boost his popularity. Asking for even bolder benefit hikes, labor unions and the gray lobby nevertheless supported the president's proposals. Resisting such interest group pressures, the overwhelmingly Democratic Congress enacted a more modest package as part of the 1967 amendments to the Social Security Act. Among other things, these amendments raised the earnings base from $6,600 to $7,800 while increasing benefits by 13 percent on average. The 1967 amendments also liberalized survivor and disability insurance eligibility criteria.[166] Easily enacted less than a year after the 1968 elections, this reform set the stage for future improvements to the program because labor organizations and other interest groups demanded more generous measures. Changes in actuarial assumptions and decline in business power as well as fierce political competition between Congress and the presidency taking place after the election of Richard Nixon would facilitate the enactment of unexpectedly large increases in Social Security benefits.

Automatic Government, Credit Claiming, and
Electoral Competition

Like Eisenhower, under whom he had served as vice president, Richard Nixon had to hide some of his conservative beliefs in order to successfully navigate in a political field still dominated by liberalism. Learning lessons from Barry Goldwater's ill-fated 1964 presidential campaign, Nixon never openly attacked Social Security. After his slight victory in 1968, he even formulated bold reform proposals such as the Family Allowance Plan. Aimed at seducing blue-collar workers traditionally faithful to the Democratic Party, these plans were part of a long-term coalition-building strategy consistent with Kevin Phillips's analysis in *The Emerging Republican Majority*.[167] Facing a Democratic Congress, the Republican president attempted to gain political credit for the enactment of redistributive measures while altering electoral trends in favor of his party. Because the Democratic Congress proved unwilling to enact his suspiciously liberal Family Allowance Plan, Social Security reform became a key political battlefield for the president. As Eisenhower had done more than a decade before, Nixon attempted to demonstrate his generosity toward the elderly while limiting the scope of Social Security expansion.[168] In his case, the idea of automatic indexation constituted a political tool that could both gain more electoral credit and prevent the Democratic Congress from doing the same thing via the enactment of ad hoc benefit increases.

Unfortunately for the president, three things worked against his strategy to limit Social Security expansion through the rapid advance of "automatic government."[169] First, Democratic leaders in Congress, such as Wilbur Mills (D-Arkansas), resisted automatic indexation, which would have deprived them of a traditional credit-claiming mechanism: enacting ad hoc benefit increases to please key electoral constituencies. There is strong evidence that Mills and his allies in Congress attempted to postpone the advent of "automatic government" to maintain their electoral privileges.[170] Second, changes in actuarial assumptions made bolder benefit increases possible in the short run. Supported by prominent economists from the Brookings Institution as well as Social Security commissioner Robert Ball, the new "optimistic" assumptions broke with the actuarial conservatism that had prevailed since the

1930s.[171] Instead of assuming that wages would not grow in the future, policymakers adopted a "dynamic" actuarial model that created massive *projected* windfalls. These projected windfalls contrasted with the traditional after-the-fact windfalls stemming from conservative actuarial assumptions. What made the actuarial situation unique in the early 1970s was that policymakers could use these projected windfalls in addition to the after-the-fact windfalls still available at the time.[172] This exceptional situation provided members of Congress with a great opportunity to exhibit their apparent generosity toward the elderly. Third, business influence and prestige declined steadily during the Vietnam War. As noted by Edsall, "Public confidence in chief executives of major corporations fell like a stone from the mid-1960s to the mid-1970s. . . . The rate of decline in confidence was sharper than for any other major institution in the United States, public or private, including the executive branch, the press, organized labor, and education—excepting only Congress. . . ."[173] Undermining business power, this decline in public confidence also affected the perception of private benefits. As scandals and rumors of mismanagement emerged during the 1960s, advocates, journalists, and policymakers debated the need to reform federal private pension regulation. This debate finally led to the enactment of ERISA (Employee Retirement Income Security Act) in 1974, a complex legislation that further regulated the pension industry without leading to compulsory private coverage, a measure later enacted in such countries as Australia and Switzerland.[174] Meanwhile, disenchantment with business and private welfare institutions facilitated the enactment of massive Social Security benefit hikes amid business opposition.[175]

It is in this broad context that the debate on Social Security reform took place during Nixon's first mandate. On September 25, 1969, the president asked Congress to review his Social Security proposals. In addition to a 10 percent benefit increase, he pushed for the enactment of automatic indexation: "I request that the Congress remedy the real losses to those who now receive Social Security benefits by increasing payments by 10 percent. Beyond that step to set right today's inequity, I propose that the Congress make certain once and for all that the retired, the disabled, and the dependent never again bear the brunt of inflation. *The way to prevent future unfairness is to attach the benefit schedule to the cost of living.*"[176] Already implemented in Canada, France,

Germany, and other industrial nations, automatic indexation was depicted as a "new security in Social Security."[177]

Interest groups were divided over the issue of automatic indexation.[178] On the one hand, the gray lobby (AARP, the National Council of Senior Citizens [NCSC]) and organized labor supported this measure. Yet, the AFL-CIO's strategy for automatic indexation contradicted the president's. Instead of using this device to limit the growth in Social Security expenditures, organized labor pushed for massive benefit increases *before* the establishment of automatic indexation, thus seeing it only as a method to shield higher replacement rates from future political attacks. On the other hand, business leaders opposed both massive benefit increases and automatic indexation because these measures could reduce the perceived need to fight inflation.[179] Moreover, employers feared that automatic indexation in the public sector would force them to adopt the same measure in the operation of private benefits.[180] Because of the recent decline in business power, however, potential business opposition probably carried less political weight than during the two previous decades.

In this context, the most important obstacle to automatic indexation came from Wilbur Mills and other Democratic members of Congress interested in preserving their most popular credit-claiming tool: ad hoc benefit increases.[181] With the intention of postponing the enactment of automatic indexation, the CWM reported its own Social Security bill early in December 1969. Silent about indexation, this legislation contained a 15 percent benefit increase and more minor adjustments. Later that month, it was adopted as part of the Tax Reform Act.[182] Far superior to the inflation rate, this increase pleased traditional Democratic constituencies, especially organized labor. During the signing ceremony on December 30, 1969, Nixon officially welcomed this benefit increase but insisted on the need to establish automatic indexation in order to improve protection under Social Security.[183]

Yet, after this generous ad hoc benefit increase, the CWM felt free to eliminate automatic indexation from the Nixon administration's Social Security bill. Instead of this, the new version of the legislation would contain another ad hoc benefit increase of 5 percent and relatively minor provisions concerning Social Security financing and eligibility criteria. Under growing pressures from organized labor and the gray lobby, the

Senate FC reestablished automatic indexation as part of the bill and "made indexing somewhat more palatable to legislators' desire to preserve discretion by stating that benefits would rise automatically if Congress had not otherwise acted to change benefits within the last year. . . ."[184] The Senate adopted this revised version of the bill after adding some minor modifications to it. Yet the legislation was not enacted before the end of the session because Mills declined to go to conference.[185]

Between February and May 1971, the CWM examined this legislation as reintroduced by Wilbur Mills (HR 1). Understanding that he could no longer oppose a popular measure such as automatic indexation, this savvy politician finally supported this measure, which was included in HR 1. During 1971, two major "focusing events" made the enactment of automatic indexation almost inescapable. First, in March 1971, the Advisory Council, established two years earlier, published a report that made the need to reform the program and create automatic indexation more pressing than ever. This report indeed depicted automatic indexation as a necessary measure to improve the well-being of the elderly population.[186] Second, the White House Conference on Aging offered a great platform for those actors supporting automatic indexation as both a desirable and an unavoidable measure.[187] Meanwhile, an amendment to the 1971 Debt Ceiling Extension Bill, another war-related measure, provided a 10 percent increase in Social Security benefits, retroactive to January 1 of that year. Because the annual rate of inflation was inferior to 5 percent in 1971,[188] this amendment further improved the program's average replacement rate, which increased from 36.3 percent in 1967 to 43 percent in 1971.[189] The legislation also raised the minimum pension while increasing the yearly wage base from $7,200 to $9,000.[190]

Because of the controversial social assistance provisions included in HR 1, the Senate Finance Committee "fought for over a year before reaching a tentative agreement in June 1972."[191] In the meantime, Wilbur Mills pushed for the enactment of a separate bill that would further increase Social Security benefits by 20 percent.[192] Although the actuarial shift embodied in the 1971 Advisory Council's report made this increase feasible without massive tax hikes, President Nixon opposed this measure. Instead, he suggested a 5 percent raise in Social Security benefits coherent with his containment strategy.[193] On June 30, Congress finally adopted both automatic indexation and a 20 percent benefit increase that were attached to the 1972 Debt Ceiling Extension. According to the *Congressional Digest,* two factors explain Congress's decision to attach these Social Security provisions to this war-related bill: "President Nixon, who opposed a 20-percent increase as inflationary, would be unlikely to veto a bill that contained a debt limit increase. And HR 1, the bill under which a proposed benefit increase was then being considered, faced an uncertain future because of controversy over its welfare provisions."[194] Again, a war-related measure helped to accelerate Social Security expansion. And, because the increase in benefits was part of legislation necessary to the pursuit of the Vietnam War, the president had little choice but to sign it.[195] In Nixon's speech upon signing this bill on July 1, 1972, he claimed credit for the enactment of automatic indexation:

> One important feature of this legislation, which I greet with special favor is the automatic increase provision which will allow social security benefits to keep pace with the cost of living. This provision is one which I have long urged, and I am pleased that the Congress has at last fulfilled a request which I have been making since the first months of my Administration. This action constitutes a major break-through for older Americans, for it says at last that inflation-proof social security benefits are theirs as a matter of right, and not as something which must be temporarily won over and over again from each succeeding Congress.[196]

Yet, in his speech, the president barely acknowledged the enactment of the 20 percent benefit increase, a measure that definitely illustrated the failure of his containment strategy.[197] Before the victory of automatic indexation, Congress had boosted Social Security benefits in a way that Nixon disapproved but could hardly oppose because of his coalition-building strategy and, in some cases, war-related fiscal imperatives. As will be shown below, the functioning of automatic indexation (Cost of Living Adjustments, or COLAs) would further increase the program's replacement rates in the mid-1970s.

Finally, Congress enacted new amendments to the Social Security Act in October 1972. Derived from the administration's bill first examined in 1970 and reintroduced as HR 1 in January 1971, these amendments increased benefits for widows and widowers while liberalizing the earnings test. The legislation also liberalized disability and Medicare benefits. For example, disabled workers who had been on federal disability insurance rolls for at least two years gained coverage under Medicare, a measure first designed exclusively for OASI beneficiaries. This provision further illustrated the incremental reform strategy pursued in the postwar era. More important, the 1972 amendments federalized social assistance for the elderly (Old-Age Assistance; OAA), the blind (Aid to the Blind; AB), and the disabled (Aid to the Permanently and Totally Disabled; APTD). Congress nationalized and merged these programs for the following reasons: unifying the income assistance system, eliminating enduring interstate disparities in benefit levels and eligibility criteria, and reducing "the stigma of welfare by administering the program through the Social Security Administration."[198] This last point shows how crucial it seemed to associate social assistance for the "deserving poor" with the SSA, an organization in charge of a most popular social insurance program: Social Security. Beginning in January 1974, eligible individuals would receive uniform federal benefits through the SSA. Less ambitious than Nixon's defeated Family Assistance Plan, yet grounded in similar principles, the Supplemental Security Income (SSI) paid monthly benefits of $130 for singles and $195 for couples, relatively modest figures by mid-1970s standards. Because of the extension of Social Security coverage during the 1950s, however, old age assistance now represented a comparatively modest policy area that attracted relatively little political attention.[199] As compared to Social Security, SSI had thus become a low profile measure offering modest benefits.[200] Although the SSA now administers the SSI, programs for the poor have remained "poor programs," even at the federal level.[201]

If Congress reshaped old age assistance during the Nixon presidency, ad hoc benefit increases enacted between 1967 and 1972 altered the very nature of Social Security in a gradual, yet decisive, manner. During the 1950s and the first half of the 1960s, benefit increases mostly compensated for the effects of inflation. After 1967, Congress voted disproportionately high benefit hikes (13 percent in 1967, 15 percent in 1969, 10 percent in 1971, and 20 percent in 1972), at least when compared with inflation rates. Mainly for that reason, the average replacement rate for Social Security gradually increased during Nixon's first term. Between 1969 and 1971, for example, the real value of benefits (that is, net of inflation) increased by 23 percent.[202] After 1974, high inflation rates coupled with COLAs further amplified the real value of benefits, thus transforming Social Security into a "retirement wage" similar to those established after 1945 in countries such as France, Germany, and Sweden.[203] Although private benefits represented a significant aspect of America's pension system, private pensions never covered more than 50 percent of the workforce, and public confidence toward them declined during the 1960s and early 1970s. More than ever, Social Security represented the true foundation of the American pension system and by far the most crucial source of economic security for the elderly. Paradoxically framed as an efficient tool in the war on poverty *and* a genuinely American program grounded in self-reliance, Social Security truly became the "third rail of American politics." As the popularity of the program soared, the political consensus that had surrounded Social Security since the mid-1950s became widespread and few voices emerged to condemn the program.

Conclusion

Far from being the sole product of a well-orchestrated "bureaucratic conspiracy," the expansion of Social Security during the postwar era was largely the result of powerful economic and electoral logics related to the program's institutional structure. As in Canada and Western Europe, favorable economic and demographic conditions made credit-claiming strategies feasible in a competitive electoral context in which social policy reform emerged as a key source of political dividends.

Yet, a few trends distinguished the American experience from the one then prevailing in most advanced industrial societies. First, federal political institutions, especially checks and balances, certainly encouraged reformers and liberal politicians to pursue the incremental reform strategy that favored the postwar expansion of Social Security. The fragmentation of federal power made comprehensive reforms unlikely outside of periods of turmoil, and as opposed to the situation in countries such as Canada where political power was highly concentrated in a parliamentary system, incrementalism became the chosen form of postwar Social Security expansion in the United States.[204] The expansion of Social Security itself encouraged policymakers, particularly members of the then powerful congressional committees, to enact a series of seemingly modest reforms and, in some cases, to depict original measures such as disability insurance as incremental reforms to preserve the broad coalitions necessary to enact legislation. Second, in order to increase popular support for Social Security and neutralize potential conservative attacks against it, federal officials regularly depicted that program as a measure grounded in self-reliance long after the program had moved to a more redistributive stage of its development following the enactment of the 1939 amendments. Although federal policymakers explicitly reframed the program as a poverty-elimination device after 1965, public understanding of Social Security remained low, and its redistributive nature largely hidden.[205] Even though claiming credit for Social Security's increased generosity, policymakers from both parties seldom acknowledged the gradual transformation of the program. On a theoretical level, the hidden paradigm shift of 1939 and, later, the ideological efforts to conceal the increasingly redistributive nature of Social Security point to the significant role of ideas and frames in the politics of expansion.

Third, the development of private benefits created an unusual situation in which a large, contributory public pension program served as the foundation for the growth of massive private benefits. Although this trend may have slightly reduced the need for comprehensive reforms in the 1940s and 1950s, expanding private benefits did not constitute an obstacle to the development of federal social insurance, as opposed to the situation prevailing in the health sector. The growth in private benefits reinforced business support for Social Security. Finally, labor unions, which were forced to push for the expansion of private benefits in the absence of congressional action during the 1940s, identified themselves as much with private pensions as with Social Security. In the postwar era, they thus fought for the expansion of both public and private pension provisions, which may have prevented unions from favoring the enactment of bolder Social Security reforms. The relatively limited role of organized labor in postwar Social Security politics stemmed from two distinct institutional realities: the absence of corporatist practices and a formal labor role in Social Security management as well as the absence of genuine American labor parties similar to the ones that played such a crucial role in other industrial countries.

CHAPTER FIVE

The Politics of Retrenchment

As opposed to the dynamic of expansion that took place during the postwar era, pension reform moved to a new historical stage in the late 1970s and early 1980s: the politics of retrenchment. From short-term budgetary shortfalls to long-term demographic fears, specific economic and ideological factors justified the need to reform public pension systems through the enactment of painful measures such as benefit costs and tax hikes. Ranging from the increase in retirement age to the modification of indexation schemes, a limited number of frequently technical policy alternatives have been debated in most advanced industrial societies.[1] Yet, because massive public pension programs have generated powerful constituencies, pension retrenchment is a risky business for elected officials. In order to shield themselves from blame, they mobilize strategies that spread the responsibility for unpopular decisions or hide the negative consequences of the proposed reforms. And when politicians do take responsibility for their actions, they may reduce the scope of protest stemming from unpopular retrenchment measures.[2] In many cases, however, the best political strategy is inaction, as policymakers attempt to seek support from beneficiaries and their political allies.

During the 1960s and early 1970s, the status of Social Security in the United States as the centerpiece of the federal social policy system was confirmed. As discussed earlier, a significant increase in Social Security benefits and the enactment of automatic indexation took place during the Nixon presidency. A feedback effect of the program's expansion, the emergence of an "army of beneficiaries," represented a new source of political risks for politicians keen on reducing benefits or even dismantling the program.[3] Social Security development in the United States is a path-dependent process that is hard—yet not necessarily impossible—to reverse.[4]

In the late 1970s and early 1980s, however, the United States became one of the first advanced industrial countries to implement significant cutbacks in its public pension system. At a time when countries such as Canada and France were still debating expansionist pension proposals, the United States suddenly shifted toward retrenchment. As a response to the advent of a short-term fiscal crisis in Social Security, federal officials attempted to reduce benefits and increase revenues while avoiding a massive electoral backlash against them.

This chapter studies the genesis of the 1977 and 1983 amendments to the Social Security Act, changes that were enacted in a context during which the need to reform the program seemed obvious from a fiscal standpoint. Yet this need to reform never translated into significant policy shifts, and Social Security survived the era of fiscal crisis despite payroll tax hikes and significant, yet largely indirect, benefit cuts such as the gradual phasing in of an increase in retirement age between 2000 and 2022. Overall, the United States acted earlier than most other advanced industrial countries in order to improve the financial situation of Social Security, and the 1977 and 1983 reforms have proved so successful that, as opposed to the situation prevailing in other advanced industrial countries, no short-term fiscal crisis has occurred since the mid-1980s.

From Expansion to Retrenchment

During the 1970s, American society experienced a "confidence crisis" related to Watergate, the Vietnam War, and a gradual deterioration of economic conditions following the 1973 oil crisis. In the field of social policy, the mixed results of the War Against Poverty and the emergence of neo-conservatism exacerbated this confidence crisis, which undermined the liberal faith in social progress through technocratic reforms.[5] Although this confidence crisis had a negative effect on the apparent legitimacy of the federal government, Social Security remained a widely popular program covering the vast majority of the working population.[6]

Yet Social Security became a source of political and economic concerns during the Carter presidency, only a few years after the sharpest benefit increases in history came into effect. Considering higher-than-expected inflation and unemployment rates, Social Security suffered from significant actuarial imbalance: "Beginning in 1975, annual outgo from the OASDI trust funds exceeded annual income and the deficits were expected to grow in the future. The disability fund was expected to be depleted by early 1979 and the OASI fund in the early 1980's."[7] In fact, the reforms enacted during the Nixon presidency directly contributed to this situation because a flawed indexation system favored an unexpected augmentation of replacement rates for new beneficiaries. "The adequacy of financing for the 1972 law relied on the assumption that wage growth would continue at a rate roughly twice that of inflation. When wage growth failed even to match inflation in the 1970s, it resulted in a badly under-financed Social Security program."[8] The main problem with the 1972 law was that the benefit formula's percentages that determined benefits for future Social Security recipients also changed in order to reflect consumer prices. During a period of soaring inflation, both the Consumer Price Index and the wage rates would increase, "with the result of producing larger than anticipated initial benefit levels for future beneficiaries."[9] Because this "double indexation" boosted the real value of Social Security payments for new beneficiaries, replacement rates went beyond what most policymakers had expected. Without a change in the indexation system enacted in 1972, replacement rates for some beneficiaries would actually exceed 100 percent, an unacceptable rate by any standard! Additionally, replacement rates were still expected to increase more rapidly than average wages in the future. Paradoxically, the original indexation system that President Nixon supported in order to contain the future expansion of Social Security actually contributed to enhancing the real value of benefits while undermining the financial balance of the program.[10]

This financial situation, and the increasingly loud media discourse surrounding it, rapidly pushed pension reform to the center of the federal policy agenda. Similar to the fiscal crisis that would later affect public pension programs in other advanced industrial countries, this actuarial imbalance made the need to reform Social Security more and more obvious. Largely because Social Security had long been depicted as a quasi-savings scheme, many Americans did not know that "depletion" only meant that the government would have to increase taxes and/or cut benefits to fix a short-term solvency problem in the context of a PAYGO system.[11] The lack of popular understanding about the program's functioning may have exacerbated the political impact of this fiscal crisis.

Social Security's problematic fiscal situation became a significant political issue during 1976, the last year of the Ford presidency, when the 94th Congress debated legislation (HR 14430) that would have stabilized future replacement rates through a revision of the indexation formula.[12] Even if Congress had never adopted that bill, this episode illustrated the shift from the postwar politics of expansion to the politics of austerity. In turn, this shift altered the structure of constraints and incentives surrounding Social Security reform. Although the postwar politics of Social Security expansion had been associated with credit-claiming strategies, fiscal austerity meant that politicians increasingly perceived reform as a source of political risks because policy alternatives such as benefit cuts and tax hikes, which were put forward as ways to solve anticipated fiscal unbalances, are generally unpopular.[13] Although this shift from expansion to austerity has occurred in most advanced industrialized societies, the United States was one of the first countries to enter the era of austerity. And, because of divided government and the two-year election schedule in Congress, adopting a coherent and long-term reform strategy has proven especially difficult in the United States. Power fragmentation and tight electoral schedules associated with the American political system militate against policy planning and long-term reform initiatives. Perhaps for that reason, it is difficult to enact "preventive" actions when no short-term fiscal crisis is in sight. Paradoxically, since 1965, the federal government has used seventy-five-year actuarial projections to assess the long-term financial status of the program.[14] This period is longer than the one used in most other advanced industrial countries. The amalgam of a short-term political time frame and long-term actuarial projections is a distinctive characteristic of Social Security policymaking in the United States.[15]

At the beginning of the Carter administration, reform increasingly seemed unavoidable as the mass media started to spread pessimistic accounts about the future of Social Security.[16] Some of these accounts anticipated a dramatic collapse of Social Security, and their sensational character certainly contributed to the social construction of the need to rescue that endangered program. From this perspective, inaction itself became a source of political risks, as surveys indicated that the population massively supported the idea that Social Security "cannot be allowed to go broke."[17] Considering that explicit, short-term benefit cuts represented an especially unpopular option, increasing tax revenue emerged as the most realistic policy alternative aimed at rapidly improving the financial situation of Social Security. Yet tax hikes also represented an unpopular policy alternative, and the electoral calendar convinced the Carter administration to push aggressively for reform in 1977, which was not an election year. As Secretary of Health, Education, and Welfare Joseph Califano recalled, "It was clear that a major part of the immediate solution was more tax revenue, and I knew we would have to move fast because it was critical to get the Congress to act in 1977. No election year was going to pass a multibillion-dollar tax increase, even for senior citizens, one of the most potent lobbies in Washington."[18] This reference to the gray lobby, which had already become a debated topic in the mid-1970s, pointed to the political fears generated by the advent of an increasingly large and politically organized army of Social Security beneficiaries.[19]

In order to improve the long-term fiscal situation of the program, *indirect* benefit cuts were considered. Already debated under the Ford administration, the alteration of the indexation system represented the most logical way to reduce benefits.[20] On May 9, 1977, President Carter officially supported this type of adjustment while pressing Congress to act rapidly in order to restore the long-term fiscal balance of Social Security. In his speech, he also recommended, among other things, using general revenue financing in a countercyclical fashion and transferring revenues from the Medicare trust fund to the OASI and Disability funds.[21] Beyond these direct responses to the fiscal crisis in Social Security, the president pledged to fight gender discrimination. Not related to the fiscal crisis, his call for gender fairness stemmed from recent Supreme Court decisions and from a growing awareness about gender equality in American society.[22] In 1977, the key gender-related issues concerned the status of divorced and widowed beneficiaries.

The day after the president's speech, the hearings before the CWM Social Security Subcommittee began.[23] In July, Congress began examining the bill containing the administration's Social Security proposals (HR 8218). Because congressional elections would take place in 1978, the need to rapidly enact this potentially unpopular measure became more and more pressing during the fall of 1977. In October, the House finally enacted a new version of the original bill (HR 9346). The Senate easily adopted a revised draft of that bill early in November. After the conference committee achieved an agreement without much trouble,[24] the president signed the legislation on December 20, 1977. In his speech, President Carter mentioned four reasons that legitimized the enactment of such a painful set of amendments to the Social Security Act: a flawed indexation formula that needed to be fixed, long-term demographic changes related to the decline in birth rates, "the worst depression since the Great Depression," and, finally, the fact that "a vast majority of Americans did not believe that their social security benefits would be there when they needed them."[25] In order to shield himself and the Democratic Party from blame, benefit reductions and tax hikes were depicted as unavoidable measures and actions necessary to save Social Security. Describing the federal political elite as courageous, he underlined the "spirit of compromise" that favored the enactment of the 1977 amendments.

This legislation both increased revenues and reduced future benefits. First, in addition to a slight increase in the OASDI payroll tax, the wage base would gradually increase from $22,900 in 1979 to $29,700 in 1981.[26] Despite mounting pressure in Congress to roll back this tax hike as the 1978 legislative election approached, the president made clear that it was there to stay.[27] Second, the legislation revised the indexing system enacted in 1972 to reduce the effects of inflation on Social Security benefits. Called "decoupling," this revised system created two distinct indexation procedures: one to calculate the level of initial benefits, and one to adjust existing benefits for inflation. In 1977, "decoupling" represented the least controversial way to reduce the benefits of future retirees because this apparently technical measure was framed as "a restoration of the always intended benefit levels," a justification that even supporters of the program generally accepted.[28] Furthermore, applying this change to workers who reached age sixty-two in 1979 considerably reduced short-term electoral risks that elected officials faced, because current beneficiaries were not affected by any major benefit cut.[29] It was only years later that "notch babies" affected by the measure would start mobilizing against this decision. The notch babies were the individuals who retired during the five-year phase-in period (the "notch") when the decoupling took place. Even if these individuals received more benefits than those who retired after this transition period, many of them perceived themselves as a singled-out population that policymakers had treated unfairly. Notch babies would receive a less favorable treatment than those who had retired before them, and their advocates focused on that situation to mobilize them politically. In spite of numerous congressional hearings and broad media coverage, however, Congress never withdrew the measure that penalized the notch babies.[30]

In addition to specific retrenchment and refinancing measures, the 1977 amendments to the Social Security Act contained several gender-related provisions. First, remarriage of a surviving spouse after age sixty would no longer lead to a reduction in the amount of Social Security benefits. Framed in gender-neutral terms, this measure would disproportionately affect women, whose average life expectancy is higher than that of men. Second, "the duration-of-marriage requirement for entitlement to benefits as an older divorced wife or surviving divorced wife [was] . . . lowered from 20 to 10 years."[31] Mentioned in the president's speech upon signing the amendments, these measures point to the enduring presence of gender-related issues in Social Security politics.

Far from altering the deep institutional logic of Social Security, however, the 1977 amendments preserved the program created during the New Deal. Radical alternatives to social insurance remained off the agenda. Even the idea of a growing reliance on general revenue financing failed to gain support in Congress. Labeled as the "the most dangerous and shortsighted" policy alternative by former president Gerald Ford, general revenue financing fell under massive attacks. As fiscal conservatism triumphed, the decades-old logic of fiscal autonomy held sway. In the same vein, President Carter rejected the proposal put forward by Energy secretary James Schlesinger, who suggested that the federal government "dedicate $32 billion to the trust funds from the wellhead tax on oil and gas that Carter had recommended as part of his first energy program."[32]

Rightly perceived as a very popular program, Social Security became a source of social and political anxiety during a confidence crisis that would finally contribute to the decline of the "Roosevelt coalition" associated with the New Deal legacy. Yet this decline would not lead to a widespread political weakening of Social Security, a program well entrenched in mainstream American society. As the number of beneficiaries increased, Social Security emerged as a sacred cow for elected officials fearing a political backlash against those who would dare attack this federal program. Not uniquely American, these fears have prevailed among the political elite in most advanced industrial societies coping with fiscal austerity. Public pensions are based on long-term commitments, and large contributive programs such as Social Security are extremely difficult to reform because powerful economic interests, as well as the belief in "earned rights," complicate policy change.[33]

Even if President Carter claimed to have ensured the long-term solvency of Social Security, the actuarial assumptions used in 1977 proved excessively optimistic, just as had the ones put forward less than a decade earlier. In a context of economic recession, the prospect of new financial shortfalls became perceptible before 1980, the year during which Congress enacted a major reform of disability insurance meant to control the increase in that program's costs.[34] By the second half of 1978, it already seemed that the recent reform of Social Security could prove insufficient to guarantee even its short-term fiscal equilibrium. In order to prevent future fiscal unbalances, Secretary Califano proposed to tax up to 75 percent of Social Security benefits. He also recommended an increase in the minimum eligibility age from sixty-two to sixty-five, as well as the enactment of other cost-containment measures such as the elimination of the lump-sum death benefit of $255.[35] Traditional supporters of Social Security such as Wilbur Cohen, union representatives, and senior activists organized a campaign against this retrenchment package. The creation of Cohen's coalition, Save Our

Security, symbolized the institutionalized resistance of beneficiaries against explicit, short-term retrenchment measures.[36]

Although Califano's proposals went nowhere, this episode was crucial, as it illustrated the contentious turn in Social Security politics. By the late 1970s, blame avoidance had replaced credit claiming as the driving logic of Social Security politics. Increasing fiscal problems coupled with the election of Ronald Reagan to the presidency would soon exacerbate the contentious—and risky—nature of the new politics of Social Security reform.

A Pragmatic Deal: Social Security Reform under Reagan

One of the main reasons for Ronald Reagan's election to the presidency in November 1980 was the consolidation of a heterogeneous conservative coalition that included libertarians, business leaders, anticommunists, and religious fundamentalists. For different reasons, these forces were dissatisfied with the liberal political regime created between the New Deal and the Great Society. Furthermore, business interests were organizing to regain much of the political influence they had lost since the late 1960s. Through the creation of pro-business think tanks and publications, corporate America supported the spread of neoconservative ideas about market economy and personal responsibility.[37] In an era of economic disillusion and "confidence crisis," Ronald Reagan campaigned to fight bureaucratic "big government" while rejuvenating traditional values and the American capitalist system. During the 1980 presidential campaign, Reagan condemned AFDC and "welfare dependency" yet refrained from attacking Social Security, a program with a broad constituency that represented a source of widespread political risks for conservatives.[38]

Once in power, President Reagan found it difficult to convince Congress to enact his conservative platform, particularly because Democrats still controlled the House.[39] As opposed to the situation prevailing in Margaret Thatcher's Britain, divided government limited the diffusion of conservative legislation.[40] With the exception of the Omnibus Budget Reconciliation Act (OBRA) and the Recovery Tax Act of 1981,

Reagan's "conservative revolution" did not fully materialize.[41] This is especially true in the field of social policy, where no major federal program was terminated. Facing strong opposition from beneficiaries, labor unions, and their congressional allies, conservatives could not "dismantle the welfare state."[42] Yet, this does not mean that during the Reagan presidency nothing significant happened in the field of social policy. In fact, the combined effect of the 1981 tax legislation, economic recession, and significant increases in military spending created massive federal deficits that, in turn, legitimized cutbacks in federal welfare programs. These cutbacks mostly targeted AFDC and food stamps. In the case of food stamps, for example, eligibility criteria were tightened, depriving more than 400,000 individuals of benefits.[43] Interestingly, Supplemental Security Income was not targeted by major retrenchment efforts. For conservatives, this program never constituted an ideological target, as it was generally believed that most SSI recipients deserved federal aid. Still, SSI benefits remained modest, and no large campaign emerged to significantly increase their real value.[44]

The Origin of the National Commission on Social Security Reform

In a new context of budgetary constraints, Social Security represented an obvious target, at least from a strictly fiscal perspective.[45] Since 1969, Social Security revenues and expenditures had been computed as part of the federal budget. For that reason, improving the financial stature of that program would have a positive impact on the *perception* of the federal budget. The enduring fiscal problems that Social Security faced in the early 1980s increased the temptation to pursue a retrenchment strategy in that policy area. As in the late 1970s, unexpected fiscal shortfalls were largely due to high inflation and unemployment.[46] Widely discussed in the media, this new fiscal crisis endangered the program's survival while keeping Social Security reform on the federal agenda. In the House of Representatives, J. J. Pickle (D-Texas), chairman of the Social Security Subcommittee of the CWM, even formulated a legislative package that would have included a gradual increase in retirement age and other painful measures. As some Republicans openly supported this idea, House Democratic leaders had little incentive to rapidly enact these potentially unpopular measures while sacrificing "opportunities to generate blame against the administration by proposing cuts themselves."[47]

If the alarming fiscal situation of the program made the need to reform increasingly pressing, reforming Social Security undeniably represented a risky business for Republicans. Democrats, who still controlled the House of Representatives, accused Republicans of plotting against the boldest and the most popular federal social program in the United States. Considering the apparent power of elderly voters and their allies, a cautious approach to Social Security reform was taken. As Democrats continued to depict the Reagan administration as a threat against Social Security, every Republican move in that policy domain was met with suspicion.[48]

Like Secretary Califano a few years earlier, the Reagan administration was involved in a political learning process that reinforced its cautious behavior in the field of Social Security reform. In the early days of the Reagan administration, a key event would remind conservatives about the political risks associated with the new politics of Social Security reform. This turning point in political learning occurred immediately after May 12, 1981, the day when the secretary of health and human services unveiled Social Security reform proposals that had been approved by the president.[49] Among the measures put forward by the administration, the most significant one dealt with early retirement provisions: the relative value of those benefits would decrease from 80 to 55 percent of the regular Social Security pension. This measure would have become effective as soon as January 1982 and would have affected all beneficiaries aged sixty-two and older. Therefore, as opposed to what had occurred in 1977, current beneficiaries were directly targeted by the proposal. Although the administration plan's was more modest than a legislative proposal emanating from Democratic ranks, labor unions and the gray lobby reacted with anger to the administration's plan. Under the umbrella of Wilbur Cohen's Save Our Security coalition, these interest groups launched a media campaign against the plan. On May 21, a day after the Senate unanimously condemned the plan, President Reagan withdrew it while expressing his will to consult with Congress and examine all the available options to preserve the financial integrity of Social Security.[50]

On September 24, 1981, the president announced the creation of a National Commission on Social Security Reform. For him and his advisers, this bipartisan commission could shield the administration and the Republican Party against unilateral blame emanating from Democratic ranks.[51] Moreover, if enacted, a bipartisan agreement would spread the blame generated by unpopular measures among political actors from both parties. An original bargaining mechanism for the political actors and the interest groups involved in Social Security reform, the commission had a different mission than the more traditional advisory councils that had existed during the postwar era. Instead of examining broad policy alternatives, the main objective of the new commission was to formulate realistic, bipartisan legislative proposals that could be enacted in a timely manner in order to avoid an electoral backlash.[52] In a way, this objective was similar to the one of the 1937–1938 Advisory Council, which directly paved the way to the 1939 amendments to the Social Security Act.[53]

The Commission in Action: Debating Reform Proposals

On December 16, 1981, an executive order officially created the National Commission on Social Security Reform. The president appointed five of its fifteen members, leaving the House Speaker and the Senate majority leader with five appointments each. Although key Republican officials such as Representative William Archer (Texas) and Senator Robert Dole (Kansas) were appointed, Democrats were also represented on the commission. Furthermore, figures traditionally associated with Social Security joined the commission's ranks: former Social Security commissioner Robert Ball, AFL-CIO president Lane Kirkland, and Representative Claude Pepper (D-Florida). Appointed by the president, economist Alan Greenspan chaired the commission, and the group informally became known as the Greenspan Commission.

Immediately after the appointment of the commission, the president signed a bill correcting a potentially unpopular "mistake" contained in the most recent budget agreement: the termination of the regular minimum benefit for *current* Social Security beneficiaries.[54] Signed on December 29, 1982, that legislation also embodied an action-forcing device that would increase the pressure on the National Commission on Social Security Reform: the OASI trust fund was allowed to borrow from the Medicare and the disability funds, but only until December 31, 1982. In order to avoid serious fiscal shortfalls, a reform had to be implemented before the following summer.[55]

Before the congressional election of November 1982, the commission essentially served the purpose of minimizing political conflict surrounding Social Security. The commission met only seven times between February and October, and no genuine negotiation took place during these mostly informal meetings.[56] Between November 11 and 13, less then two weeks after the elections, members of the commission finally debated the various reform options on the table. Committed to avoiding controversy and to facilitating the rapid enactment of its recommendations, the commission never considered radical alternatives to the current PAYGO system,[57] for example, the shift to forced savings that had been recently enacted in Chile.[58] Instead, its members discussed technical measures aimed at improving Social Security's short- and long-term financial situation. The commission surveyed two types of alternatives: refinancing measures that could increase Social Security revenues and retrenchment measures that could reduce anticipated spending. Within and outside the commission, Republicans and business leaders preferred benefit reductions, whereas Democrats and traditional supporters of Social Security, such as labor officials, preferred revenue increases.[59] As in other advanced industrial countries, political bargaining over public pension reform involved potential quid pro quos between revenue increases and benefit reductions.[60] As opposed to the situation prevailing in social insurance countries such as Belgium, France, and Germany, labor unions and business interests were not among the most central players in the U.S. Social Security bargaining process. This reflects the lack of a managerial role for "social partners" and the absence of corporatist tradition in the United States.

Among the refinancing measures, the best known also proved the least appealing politically: increasing the payroll tax and/or the wage base. Because Republicans and their new president had long campaigned in favor of tax cuts, Democrats found it difficult to sell a massive payroll tax increase, especially if it would materialize before the 1984 presidential election. Members of both parties feared the negative electoral consequences of a significant Social Security tax hike.[61]

Another way to increase revenues posed a different kind of political threat: the extension of Social Security coverage and, more specifically, the inclusion of federal civil servants in the program. The SSA had long supported the measure, and the inclusion of civil servants in Social Security seemed like a logical step. Why should these workers be excluded from the program they administered? Because many civil servants spent part of their career in the private sector and were entitled to Social Security benefits, inclusion was framed as a rationalization of their pension coverage. Yet the National Federation of Federal Employees (NFFE) opposed inclusion, which would have meant the demise of the autonomous pension scheme for federal employees created in 1920.[62] Finally, the massive use of general revenues financing represented another possible way to improve the fiscal situation of the OASI trust fund. Considering that conservatives opposed this measure in the name of fiscal soundness, however, general revenue financing remained a highly controversial policy alternative.[63]

Benefit reduction options were at least as controversial as the refinancing ones. Among the benefit reduction options, the increase in retirement age could be justified in reference to greater life expectancy. Since people were living longer on average, they would also work longer. As a policy option, the increase in retirement age seemed particularly risky because the AFL-CIO and the organizations of elderly citizens would certainly denounce it as unfair and socially regressive. Because of the electoral alliance between Democrats and union officials, as well as the need to build a bipartisan compromise, this policy alternative seemed potentially divisive. As opposed to the increase in retirement age, the taxing of retirement benefits above a specific level represented a more appealing source of political compromise, as both ideological camps could depict the measure in opposite ways: "Liberals could claim it was a tax increase as well as a way to hit the rich with their fair share of the compromise; conservatives could claim it was a benefit cut."[64] Yet, because Social Security benefits had been explicitly excluded from federal income taxation since the early 1940s, such a measure would not be popular among voters, especially elderly ones.[65] Finally, adjustments in the indexation system could prove politically savvy since most voters are generally unaware of such technical changes.

Unfortunately for the president, members of the commission failed to reach consensus in November 1982. On the one hand, they agreed on the definition of the problem and the policy objectives of the future reform. For them, reform seemed necessary in the short run in order to improve the financial situation of the program and restore public confidence in it. On the other hand, both camps proved unable to build a large consensus around the two proposals put forward at the mid-November meetings. In this context, the president had to intervene in order to increase the likelihood of a compromise barely six weeks before the deadline he had set for the publication of the commission's final report. To facilitate the advent of a compromise, the president extended that deadline until January 15, 1983.[66]

In the weeks preceding the new deadline, a secret round of negotiations took place among the president, congressional leaders, and key members of the commission such as Robert Ball.[67] To show its will to compromise, the White House put forward a moderate proposal that included tax hikes and the inclusion of federal civil servants in Social Security. Because the meetings were kept secret, participants could discuss potentially unpopular measures without fearing immediate popular reactions. Facing strong pressure to strike a realistic deal, those involved in this bargaining ultimately agreed on a set of propositions. Using his political connections and his deep knowledge of the program's functioning, former Social Security commissioner Robert Ball played a major role in the elaboration of this bipartisan reform plan.[68] Finally, on January 15, the commission approved this secret reform plan by a large majority of twelve votes against three. A few days later, the long-awaited publication of the commission's report made this plan public.[69]

After stating that Social Security faced both short- and long-term financial difficulties, the report stated: "The members of the National commission believe that Congress, in its deliberation on financing proposals, should not alter the fundamental structure of the Social Security program or undermine its fundamental principles."[70] In order to improve the financial situation of the program while respecting these principles, the commission proposed a complex mixture of relatively modest measures. Perhaps the most controversial recommendation formulated in the report was the inclusion of nonprofit and new federal employees into the program. According to the report, this inclusion would have a positive financial effect on Social Security, both from a short- and a long-term perspective. Concerning coverage, the commission also recommended that local and state governments that had already "elected coverage for their employees under the OASDI-HI program should not be permitted to terminate such coverage in the future."[71] Furthermore, the commission supported the partial taxation of Social Security benefits for higher-income individuals. In order to help solve short-term financial problems, the report also recommended the postponement of the yearly benefit indexation from June to December 1983, which would represent a cost-saving measure because beneficiaries would lose half a year of indexation. Moreover, the commission suggested that a tax-rate increase originally scheduled to take place in 1985 should become effective in 1984 and that another tax increase planned for 1990 should occur in 1989. Additionally, the commission recommended the gradual increase of the delayed retirement credit from 3 to 8 percent a year.[72] This measure implicitly aimed at encouraging older workers to stay longer on the labor market. Finally, the report formulated several recommendations dealing with gender-related issues, including the status of divorced women. Although modest, these recommendations illustrated enduring concerns about the treatment of women in American social policy.

Everything was done to reduce the scope of controversy surrounding this new legislative package. Apart from the inclusion of federal civil servants, the report generally avoided potentially divisive proposals. For example, the increase in retirement age, which received the support of only seven of the Commission's twelve members, was discussed in the report but was not a part of the official recommendations. A survey conducted shortly after the unveiling of the report confirmed that, although some recommendations proved unpopular, the package as a whole received significant popular support.[73] Because the need to reform the program had long been constructed in the media and the political discourse, a significant portion of the population seemed to acknowledge both the fiscal crisis and the idea that sacrifices were necessary to "save Social Security."

On January 15, 1983, the president asked Congress to enact the commission's proposals quickly in order to restore confidence in the program. In his speech, he underlined the bipartisan nature of the proposed legislative compromise embodied in the Commission's report: "This bipartisan solution would solve the social security problem defined by the Commission. It is my understanding that the Speaker and the Majority Leader find this bipartisan solution acceptable."[74]

Speeding up the Legislative Process

Despite the moderate nature of the commission's proposals and the consensus about the need to reform Social Security in order to solve its short-term financial problems, the president and the other advocates of the report's proposals still faced tremendous political risks as key interest groups opposed the legislation. A good way to gauge this opposition is to discuss briefly the content of the hearings before the Subcommittee on Social Security of the House Ways and Means Committee.[75]

As many feared, the representative of the NFFE attacked the bill based on the commission's recommendations. From the perspective of this organization, which was affiliated with the AFL-CIO, the inclusion of new civil servants in Social Security would not solve the program's financial problems and would destroy the autonomous pension program of the federal civil service that had existed since 1920. "Universal coverage would not help social security; it would destroy a perfectly good staff retirement system, and it would end up costing the taxpayers more in the long term."[76] Like the representatives of the NFFE and the American Federation of Government Employees (AFGE), the president of the AFL-CIO, Lane Kirkland, criticized the proposal about inclusion and argued that the federal government should guarantee that the level of pensions allocated to civil servants under Social Security would remain equivalent to the one available under the existing pension scheme. As a former member of the Greenspan Commission, however, Kirkland had already approved the legislative compromise as a whole. This fact reduced the significance of his critical remarks about the inclusion of civil servants in Social Security. In front of the Subcommittee on Social Security, Kirkland reaffirmed his global support for the proposed legislation.[77]

Like the AFL-CIO, most business organizations adopted a conciliatory attitude toward the proposed reform package. For example, the National Association of Manufacturers supported it as a necessary response to the fiscal crisis in Social Security.[78] Criticizing the anticipated tax increases as well as other aspects of the legislation, the representative of the Chamber of Commerce also formulated a nuanced testimony that recognized the need to reform Social Security as soon as possible.[79] Within the business world, the National Federation of Independent Business (NFIB) emerged as the only major organization that aggressively rejected the proposed legislation. For the representative of this organization, the decisions to accelerate the increase in payroll tax and to tax Social Security benefits for higher-income individuals were unacceptable measures that would further hurt its constituency, especially in the context of a recession. As opposed to the Chamber of Commerce, the NFIB promised to campaign against the legislation.[80]

In this campaign, an even larger interest group joined the NFIB: the AARP. During the hearings, the representative of the AARP adopted a radical stance against legislation that would have reduced the level of Social Security benefits while increasing the tax burden: "The AARP believes the package of recommendations put forward by the National Commission on Social Security Reform is an inadequate as well as inappropriate response to the system's short and long term problems."[81] Because the AARP already had more than 14 million members in 1983, the crusade it launched with the NFIB against the commission's proposals could have represented a serious threat for those who supported the legislative compromise. Because the alliance between the AARP and the NFIB proved artificial in nature, however, these two organizations could not agree upon a realistic legislative alternative to the existing bill derived from the commission's recommendations. This situation undermined the credibility of these two organizations in a context during which the need to reform had already been constructed as unavoidable. In sum, the opposition to the bill remained heterogeneous and unable to offer a credible alternative to the existing bipartisan legislative proposals.[82]

During the first half of 1983, time represented a great challenge for those policymakers supporting the commission's proposals. In a climate of legislative emergency, the Subcommittee on Social Security and, later on, the CWM drafted legislation largely based on these proposals. In early March, the full House of Representatives debated this legislation. In order to facilitate the enactment of this legislative compromise, the House's

Rules Committee—whose chair, Claude Pepper, sat on the Greenspan Commission—limited the number of debated floor amendments to three. This did not prevent the study of a major amendment that would significantly reshape the content of the proposed legislation: a gradual increase in retirement age from sixty-five to sixty-seven scheduled between the year 2000 and 2022. Proposed by Representative J. J. Pickle, this amendment dealt exclusively with the long-term projected deficits of the OASI trust fund. Despite efforts by members of the Democratic leadership to promote Claude Pepper's alternative amendment based on higher tax increases, the House passed the Pickle amendment by a slight majority of 228 to 202. On March 9, the House largely voted in favor of the amended bill (282 to 148).[83]

The Senate's Finance Committee markup began on the following day. In the end, the Senate bill was relatively similar to the House one. Most differences between the two versions concerned technical issues that would not spark much controversy. Yet the Finance Committee replaced the two-year increase in retirement age with a one-year increase coupled with a 5 percent benefit reduction starting in 2000. The committee also eliminated the earnings ceiling on Social Security benefits that supposedly penalized high-income recipients.[84] This bill then moved to the Senate floor, where no cap had been placed on the number of amendments discussed. Fortunately for the supporters of the original compromise, the Senate rejected a controversial amendment that would have cancelled the clause on the inclusion of new federal civil servants in Social Security. In order to calm the anxiety generated by this measure, however, the Senate passed an amendment that made provision for the creation of a supplemental pension scheme for federal employees. In spite of additional modifications enacted on the Senate's floor, the bill remained relatively similar to the House's final draft. On March 23, a large majority of the Senate voted for the amended bill (88 to 9).[85]

During the conference held to harmonize the two versions of the bill, Senate members quickly accepted the increase in retirement age voted by the House. After the other differences were settled, the House and the Senate ratified the 1983 amendments to the Social Security Act.[86] Four weeks later, on April 20, President Reagan signed this legislation in a ceremony meant to underline the bipartisan origin of the pain inflicted to present and future workers and retirees. For that reason,

Democratic leaders and the members of the Greenspan Commission were present at the ceremony. In his speech, the president framed the legislation as a necessary bipartisan effort that would guarantee the long-term fiscal soundness of the program:

> [It is] especially fitting that so many backgrounds—young and old, the working and the retired, Democrat and Republican—should come together for the signing of this landmark legislation. The bill demonstrates for all time our nation's commitment to social security. It assures the elderly that America will always keep the promises made in troubled times half a century ago. It assures those who are still working that they, too, have a pact with the future. From this day forward, they have one pledge that they will get their fair share of benefits when they retire. . . . None of us today would pretend that this bill is perfect . . . but the essence of bipartisanship is to give up a little to get a lot. My fellow Americans, I think that we've got a great deal.[87]

As the content of this speech shows, the Greenspan Commission proved to be an excellent presidential strategy to "spread the blame" among political actors while solving the short-term fiscal crisis in Social Security.[88] Yet the 1983 amendments went further than that because the increase in retirement age dealt exclusively with long-term fiscal issues. A major, yet indirect and different benefit cut, this measure would only affect people retiring in 2000 or later. Because this schedule did not affect current and near-future retirees, it was difficult for labor unions and the gray lobby to mobilize effectively against it.[89] Partly for that reason, the increase in retirement age and, more generally, the 1983 amendments failed to generate a political tempest in Washington.[90]

Beyond the issues of bipartisanship and blame avoidance, the process leading to the enactment of the 1983 amendments illustrated a little-noticed, yet significant, shift in Social Security politics: the decline of the SSA as a central actor in the policymaking process. Marred with administrative and technical problems related to the advent of SSI,[91] the SSA had lost credibility as official actuarial assumptions proved overly optimistic through the 1970s. More important, since the 1972 elections when Social Security commissioner Robert Ball was forced to resign, all the commissioners had been political appointees, not career bureau-crats who strongly identified with the SSA and the programs it managed. Overall, this new appointment pattern reduced the institutional auton-omy and the political influence of the SSA.[92] Furthermore, the Green-span Commission marginalized the SSA, which had long developed a close relationship with the more traditional advisory councils. In a way, the SSA fell victim to the confidence crisis that had affected Social Se-curity since the mid-1970s. In 1982–1983, politicians directly stepped in to strike a legislative compromise *before* a bill reached Congress. It is interesting that the only personality closely associated to the SSA who took an active part in the deliberations of the Greenspan Commission was Robert Ball, a former Social Security commissioner who had long retired from the federal civil service.[93] Ball incarnated the institutional legacy of Social Security because he directly contributed to its postwar expansion. Yet his role in 1983 had little to do with a weakened SSA that struggled to administer an increasingly complex welfare and social insurance system. The shift from expansion to austerity greatly under-mined the political role of an organization that had already been affected by the retirement of its heroic postwar leaders.[94]

One of the greatest allies of the SSA during the postwar expansion of Social Security, the labor movement, had also lost much political ground in the years preceding the enactment of the 1983 amendments. Overall, labor unions had faced a significant decline in membership since the 1960s, and the AFL-CIO was not influential enough to stop the bipartisan logic of retrenchment now dominating the politics of Social Security. Concerning both the status of federal employees and the increase in retirement age, labor unions could not exercise a veto point largely because unions represented only one interest group among oth-ers that did not formally participate in Social Security management. This situation contrasts with the one prevailing in social insurance countries such as France and Germany, where labor unions have long played a managerial role in Social Security. In these countries, labor mobilization has forced right-wing administrations to withdraw unpop-ular reform proposals. In the United States, labor unions do not have the mobilization capacity and the institutional status necessary to effec-tively resist retrenchment efforts.[95] For that reason, elderly voters, not labor unions, are the main source of concern for politicians involved in the American politics of retrenchment. In some Western European countries policymakers have to bargain with labor unions in order to avoid blame and protest waves, whereas American politicians have less to fear from labor unions than from elderly voters and the AARP. Yet, as the enactment of the 1983 amendments shows, the AARP is not an invincible political force, and the bipartisan compromise survived the campaign that this organization launched in collaboration with the NFIB.

In addition to the SSA and labor unions, congressional committees were other key actors of the postwar era whose power had declined significantly between the mid-1970s and the enactment of the 1983 amendments. Referring to the political process leading to these amendments, Edward Berkowitz rightly noted, "Decisions once made within congressional committees, with Representative Wilbur Mills the dominant figure, were now made by the congressional leadership."[96] Two main factors explain this decline. First, in the aftermath of the institutional reforms of the 1970s, congressional committees had lost much of their power and prestige. The 1970 Legislative Reorganization Act initiated this process by forcing committees to hold more public meetings and votes. In the following years, other reforms further reduced the autonomy of congressional committees while increasing the role of party leaders and individual members of Congress.[97] Second, as compared to a bipartisan commission, congressional committees were not the best tool to "spread the pain" among political actors and deflect blame stemming from unpopular retrenchment efforts. Overall, the 1983 amendments witnessed the decline of three of the most powerful actors involved in the postwar expansion of Social Security. In a new institutional and political environment, the president, congressional leaders, and former Social Security insider Robert Ball replaced these actors as the most crucial players in the elaboration of the 1983 reform.

Conclusion

In 1977 and 1983, Social Security faced a short-term fiscal crisis, and Congress enacted payroll tax hikes and significant, yet indirect, cutbacks in Social Security benefits. Facing substantial electoral risks, politicians acted cautiously and, in the case of conservatives, learned from their strategic mistakes before adopting a moderate approach to Social Security reform. As the need to reform the program became more and more pressing, federal officials reduced benefits and increased revenues while avoiding massive electoral backlash against themselves. These reforms never transformed the nature of the program.

Following insight from the historical institutionalist literature (Paul Pierson, R. Kent Weaver), this chapter underlines the enduring weight of the policy legacies created during the New Deal and the postwar era. Social Security generated powerful constituencies, which means that the politics of retrenchment is a complicated and risky business for elected officials. At the ideational level, the increasingly bleak political and media discourse about the fiscal future of Social Security helped create the need to enact adjustments depicted as necessary to "save" that popular yet poorly understood program. Although no new paradigm emerged as a serious challenge to the social insurance program enacted in 1935, this ever-present discourse about Social Security's future points to the subtle yet significant role of ideational processes in the politics of retrenchment.

From a comparative perspective, the United States enacted significant retrenchment measures earlier than most other advanced industrial countries. The enactment of these measures sparked far less social protest than the similar retrenchment initiatives put forward since the 1980s in countries such as France, Germany, and Italy. This difference is largely due to the relatively modest involvement of labor unions in Social Security politics in the United States. Furthermore, divided government certainly helped politicians diffuse blame in moments of fiscal crisis. Although retrenchment proved a difficult business for federal policymakers, they found a way to share the blame for unpopular measures when the need to reform seemed inescapable.

Because the 1983 amendments introduced significant retrenchment measures staged over time, no new fiscal crisis emerged during the remainder of the twentieth century. Yet, as evidenced in Chapter 6, a movement in favor of Social Security privatization, which was more about restructuring than retrenchment, emerged in the 1990s.

CHAPTER SIX

What Future
for Social Security?

During the 1990s, the idea of relying on stock market returns to improve the long-term financial situation of public pension systems gained much ground around the world, particularly after the 1994 publication of the World Bank's report *Averting the Old Age Crisis*.[1] Although stock market–related social security reforms have proved more common in Latin America and Eastern Europe than in advanced industrial societies, the role of financial investment in social security reform has been widely debated, and in countries such as Canada, Sweden, and New Zealand, concrete steps were taken in the late 1990s to move toward—or to increase the scope of—partial advanced funding while investing part of social security money in equity.[2] Although no reform was enacted in the United States, financial investment emerged as a key policy issue during President Clinton's second term. These trends led sociologist Jill Quadagno to suggest the possible advent of a "capital investment welfare state."[3]

The expression *capital investment welfare state* should not hide the diversity of policy alternatives associated with financial investment. In the field of social security reform, one can identify at least two essential financial policy alternatives. One, the shift from social insurance to personal savings accounts, which is known in the United States as

Social Security privatization, has long been popular among conservatives. The other, direct government investment, is a clear alternative to privatization. Without changing the nature of earnings-related pension benefits, direct governmental investment is about moving toward partial advanced funding while investing new pension surpluses in equities.[4]

During the mid-1990s, the politics of Social Security in the United States entered a new phase as the issues of privatization and, to a lesser extent, direct governmental investment came to dominate the debate over the future of that program. Social Security privatization, far more than direct government investment, is a form of policy restructuring that extends beyond the traditional retrenchment efforts embodied in the 1977 and 1983 amendments to the Social Security Act. Instead of increasing taxes or cutting benefits, the objective of Social Security privatization is to transform the very logic under which the program provides benefits to retirees. If powerful vested interests and high transition costs make radical reforms such as full Social Security privatization unlikely, path-departing reforms enacted in countries such as Sweden and the United Kingdom show that modern old age insurance schemes are not always "frozen."[5] More modest reforms adopted in other advanced industrial countries provide more ground to the claim that, although most public pension systems follow a path-dependent logic, significant restructuring and institutional change are possible.[6]

Because of the lack of short-term "fiscal crisis," those interested in restructuring Social Security through the development of private savings accounts have found it difficult to construct the need to reform that program in a comprehensive way. The term *privatization* as applied to Social Security is potentially misleading, as the shift from social insurance to personal savings does not necessarily imply an abolition of the payroll tax or the termination of the government's direct involvement in the field retirement security. Yet, during the 1990s, exceptional stock market performances and conservative mobilization gradually pushed the issue of Social Security privatization onto the federal policy agenda. In that context, conservative experts and political actors who promoted partial privatization against institutional inertia had to draw on the American ideological repertoire in order to convince individuals, as well as interest groups, that Social Security privatization would be the only relevant policy alternative to guarantee the long-term fiscal soundness of the program.

This chapter underlines two original features of the current American debate on Social Security restructuring. First, the issue of Social Security privatization has been framed as an attempt to "save Social Security" while transforming its very nature. Demographic pessimism and a discourse centered on personal and collective gain have been used against the institutional legacy of the New Deal and the postwar era. Second, in order to justify Social Security privatization, those promoting an individualistic vision of security have paradoxically referred to gender and race, suggesting that women and African Americans would gain from such a reform. Although race did not play a direct role in Social Security development, it has become a significant issue in the contemporary debate over Social Security privatization.

A New Policy Paradigm

With the help of economic growth and a favorable short-term demographic situation,[7] the 1983 amendments to the Social Security Act proved successful. Since the mid-1980s, the Social Security trust fund has accumulated sufficient fiscal reserves to ensure the actuarial soundness of the program for the years and even the decades to come.[8] During the 1990s, actuarial provisions became more and more favorable as economic growth increased the sheer size of these reserves. According to the current actuarial scenario, the Social Security trust fund would accumulate surpluses until the early 2010s. Yet, in the long run, population aging and the retirement of baby boomers would further increase the percentage of people aged sixty-five and older in American society. Compared with only 4.1 percent in 1900, this percentage should increase from 12.4 in 2000 to 20 in 2030.[9] Consequently, Social Security's dependency ratio will decrease from five workers per beneficiary in 1960 to only two workers per beneficiary in 2040.[10] In this context, outlays should outnumber revenues, thus eroding Social Security reserves. Since 1988, all the reports of the trustees have underlined the long-term fiscal unbalance in OASDI trust funds.[11] And according to the 2004 trustees' report, for example, the fund would face depletion in 2042.[12] Demographic change is real, and it could undermine the fiscal future of Social Security. If the anticipated fiscal shortfalls are likely to materialize in the future, they also provide some sort of "objective foundation" for the conservative discourse justifying Social Security privatization. The discussion that follows focuses on the ideological aspects of the contemporary debate over Social Security reform, demonstrating that demographic fears have become a crucial political device in the ongoing debate about Social Security reform in the United States.

Despite the lack of an immediate fiscal crisis, a significant movement in favor of Social Security restructuring emerged during the 1990s. If the Concord Coalition, a nonpartisan organization founded in 1992 that advocates fiscal responsibility, has long advocated the "means-testing" of Social Security, many conservatives support partial privatization. Although this approach involves a shift from government-guaranteed, defined-benefit pensions to defined-contribution, personal savings accounts, the term *privatization* often refers to the advent of *forced* savings through required contributions analogous to the current payroll tax. Full privatization of mature PAYGO systems constitutes a highly problematic alternative because of the "double payment" problem: current workers would have to finance the pensions of current Social Security beneficiaries and, at the same time, save for their own retirement. For that reason, partial privatization—diverting only a fraction of the pension contributions to personal savings accounts—seems like a more realistic policy alternative than full privatization. Furthermore, this apparently moderate approach would help preserve the existing survivor and disability benefits while transforming a significant portion, if not all, of the retirement component of Social Security into a set of personal savings accounts. From this perspective, partial privatization would leave behind disability and survivor benefits, two costly components of the federal social insurance system. This could implicitly transform it into a residual system subject to adverse selection.[13]

During the 1990s, exceptional stock market performances and the multiplication of government-subsidized private savings schemes transformed partial privatization into a seemingly moderate, yet conservative, alternative to social insurance.[14] Many different reform plans published during the 1990s were aimed at transforming at least part of

Social Security into a compulsory savings scheme. Beyond the multiplicity of these policy alternatives, one can reconstruct the common policy paradigm that underlies them.[15] Subsumed under a broader, old liberal tradition that supports individualism and market forces against economic redistribution,[16] this policy paradigm states that investing payroll contributions in equity is beneficial to the economy *and* to future retirees because it would create higher "return rates" than Social Security.[17] At odds with the redistributive logic at the foundation of Social Security, this new federal savings scheme, it is argued, would stimulate economic growth by boosting national savings rates.[18] Despite the fact that most conservatives embrace the idea of personal choice, however, they often support *forced* savings as a pragmatic way to bring new money to financial markets while implicitly acknowledging the institutional legacy of Social Security, a program financed through a payroll tax. Partial privatization means that a portion of the existing payroll tax would increase personal savings and feed financial markets. When formulating their ideas, pro-privatization experts and politicians take into account prevailing institutional legacies, including the Social Security payroll tax.[19] Furthermore, managing millions of savings accounts could constitute a magnificent boon for the financial industry. In addition to making direct political contributions to those elected officials supporting partial privatization, many banks and financial services firms have financed think tanks, research projects, and public policy forums that promoted Social Security privatization.[20] Yet privatization could stimulate stock market regulation because financial scandals tend to exacerbate popular discontent and the need to reform the financial sector. The British experience during and after the "misselling scandal" of the early 1990s provides ground to this claim.[21]

The above discussion points to the potentially misleading nature of the concept of *privatization* used in the debate on Social Security restructuring. Because privatization often means forced savings, the creation of personal accounts within Social Security would not necessarily represent a withdrawal of the federal government from the field of old age security but a reconfiguration of its action. Simultaneously, privatization would effectively alter the role of the federal government in that field because the shift from defined benefits to defined contributions represents a transformation—and a potential decline—of the protection offered. Furthermore, this shift would eliminate a major redistributive feature of Social Security in the name of "possessive individualism" and financial investment: benefits weighted according to the income level of each beneficiary. From this perspective, privatization would represent an attack against redistribution and the so-called social adequacy component of the program that has existed since the New Deal. If the word *privatization* underlines the pro-market rhetoric surrounding the financial paradigm, its use should not hide the fact that the creation of personal accounts as part of Social Security would still represent a substantial form of governmental intervention in American economy and society.

The controversy surrounding the 1994–1996 Advisory Council on Social Security illustrates the growing influence of the financial paradigm during the 1990s.[22] Unable to reach an agreement on the content of their final report, members of the council finally published three different proposals aimed at solving Social Security's long-term financing problems.[23] Although six of the thirteen members supported a proposal aimed at maintaining the PAYGO system,[24] two other policy alternatives outlined in the report reflected the growing prominence of the financial paradigm within the Social Security policy community. Five council members embraced the idea of partial privatization.[25] From their perspective, Social Security should "move towards a system of relatively large personal accounts, making a substantial portion of the new system fully funded."[26] Funded with 5 percent of the existing payroll tax, these new accounts would be administered by the private—financial—sector. The remaining two members (Edward M. Gramlich, the council's chair, and Marc M. Twinney) supported a "third-way" alternative that failed to create a consensus within the Advisory Council: the creation of personal savings accounts—alongside the existing PAYGO system—in the amount of 1.6 percent of covered payroll funded exclusively by employee contributions. Distinct from partial privatization, this proposal was aimed at integrating the dominant financial logic into Social Security without taking away existing payroll tax money currently allocated to the PAYGO trust fund. This alternative failed to receive the support of most council members for two opposing reasons: it was not radical enough for council members interested in "carving" private savings accounts out of the existing program, and it was perceived as a Trojan horse for privatization by Social Security advocates such as council member Robert Ball.[27] Overall, the debate about these three proposals helped maintain the issue of Social Security reform on the federal policy agenda.[28]

Framing Social Security Privatization

During the 1990s, think tanks played a central role in the debate about Social Security privatization. This phenomenon was related to the fact that the number of think tanks—especially conservative ones—had increased significantly since the 1970s. Moreover, the decline of the postwar liberal consensus and the related expansion of the conservative movement had favored an explicit politicization of expertise and the multiplication of "ideological tanks" such as the Cato Institute and the Heritage Foundation. Although liberal think tanks also participate in federal policy debates, conservative organizations tend to attract more media and political attention.[29] The involvement of conservative think tanks in the debate over Social Security reform further undermined the power and the prestige of the Social Security Administration, which had been the dominant source of public pension expertise in the United States during the postwar era.

In the debate over partial privatization, conservative think tanks act as policy entrepreneurs that seek to articulate demographic fears (problem stream) with the financial paradigm (policy stream) and coalition-building efforts (political stream). While elaborating different policy alternatives rooted in the paradigm discussed above, these organizations helped conservative politicians and journalists frame the issue of privatization in such a way that it could appeal to the American public. Since the 1980s, conservative think tanks and their political allies have indeed pursued what Butler and Germanis labeled a long-term "Leninist strategy" that could gradually undermine the support for Social Security while favoring the enactment of measures instrumental to the expansion of the financial logic.[30] In order to achieve their long-term goals, conservative experts and politicians have used five closely related devices to shape the policy agenda and promote Social Security privatization: (1) framing pessimistic demographic scenarios to undermine the public's confidence in the program, (2) supporting fiscal measures favorable to the development of private savings schemes that might reduce individuals' reliance on—and support for—Social Security,[31] (3) formulating a moral rhetoric about "intergenerational equity" that suggests that Social Security is not only unsustainable but ethically wrong and at odds with core "American values" such as hard work and self-reliance, (4) depicting privatization as a source of personal gain through higher return rates, and (5) showing that even women and African Americans would gain from privatization. These frames never form a consistent discourse, yet they are all used to justify path-breaking Social Security reforms such as full-scale privatization and partial privatization.

Demographic fears, ever present in the mass media and the discourse of conservative experts and politicians, take the form of a conventional ideological frame depicting a developing demographic time bomb as the elderly population grows in relation to the overall population. This frame portrays the demands of pensioners overwhelming the capacity of Social Security to transfer enough income from the active population to support the elderly.[32] Directly related to these demographic fears, the discourse on "generational equity" has proliferated since the end of the 1980s.[33] For the advocates of generational equity, Social Security takes money away from young workers to finance excessively generous pensions that may not be available to them a few decades in the future. Social Security is depicted as a Ponzi scheme that would likely run bankrupt when baby boomers begin to retire.[34] These ideas are later discussed in the mass media, which frequently relies on think tanks to get more information on Social Security reform.[35] In the absence of a fiscal crisis, conservative experts and politicians attempt to construct the need to reform Social Security while undermining popular confidence in this program.

Alongside the pessimistic demographic discourse concerning the future of PAYGO financing and their rejection of the idea—promoted by federal officials during and after the 1936 presidential campaign—that Social Security is grounded in self-reliance and other "American values," conservative think tanks framed a highly optimistic rhetoric regarding the virtues of financial investment in line with the exceptional stock market performances of the second half of the 1990s and the multiplication of 401(k) plans and Individual Retirement Accounts

(IRAs).[36] Since the 1970s, the federal government has encouraged the development of such personal savings accounts. This development has stimulated the expansion of the private financial industry, which constitutes a precondition for Social Security privatization. Incidentally, financial consulting firms such as Mercer and Watson Wyatt play a noticeable role in the debate over Social Security reform. Many of these firms support partial privatization.[37] Furthermore, decline in union membership and managerial shifts in the private sector have favored a reduction in the number of defined-benefit pension plans. In 2003, the Pension Benefit Guaranty Corporation (PBGC) "insured about 29,500 single-employer defined benefit plans, down from an all-time high of 112,000 plans in 1985. This decline primarily reflects a large number of terminations among small plans."[38] Defined-benefit plans covered only 44.3 million workers in 2003, which amounted to little more than 20 percent of the total workforce.[39] From a conservative point of view, the decline in private defined-benefit schemes supports the idea that Social Security privatization is a positive historical fate consistent with economic rationality and financial progress. More important, the savings plans that frequently replace defined-benefit schemes are not directly tied to Social Security, and their institutional logic is at odds with the one of that program.[40] The expansion of private savings plans exacerbates the duality between guaranteed protection, which is associated with Social Security and other defined-benefit schemes, and personal risk, which is associated with personal savings. For those who oppose social insurance and redistribution, the multiplication of private savings plans may reduce the institutional support for Social Security and pave the way to partial privatization.

To appeal to the public and to further construct the apparent need to reform Social Security, conservative experts and politicians have also framed a discourse that emphasizes anticipated personal and collective gains related to privatization. A fine example of this optimistic and individualistic rhetoric can be found in a short book published in 1998 by the Cato Institute: *Common Cents, Common Dreams: A Layman's Guide to Social Security Privatization.*[41] This book suggested in plain language that the current system is "a bad deal" for individuals and that it will prove unable to provide benefits to future retirees without a radical increase in payroll taxes. A natural alternative to this inefficient bureaucratic system, privatization would enrich Americans through higher return rates. Like Landon's discourse concerning the Social Security trust fund during the 1936 campaign, this book's rhetoric also exploits the lack of trust toward the government present in the American ideological repertoire: individuals, in order to guarantee their economic security, must save instead of trusting the politicians and bureaucrats who manage the PAYGO system. This rhetoric must be understood in the context of the declining trust toward the federal government that has characterized American public opinion since the 1970s.[42] For conservative writers, these popular yet politically manipulated fears represent an excellent starting point from which to construct the need for path-breaking reforms.[43]

Following many other conservative publications about Social Security privatization, *Common Cents, Common Dreams* discussed "the worldwide revolution in social security" to illustrate the idea that Social Security privatization is both feasible and desirable. For example, the authors argued that pension privatization enacted under Pinochet's dictatorship in Chile considerably improved the economic fate of that country's retirees. Stressing that American-educated economists designed the Chilean savings system, they sent the following message to their readers: "If we don't change, we will be left behind."[44] Therefore, privatization was seen as the only solution to social and economic problems associated with population aging. Since the late 1980s, other privatization advocates such as José Piñera have referred to the Chilean experience to convince the public and American political actors that Social Security privatization is a historical fate coherent with American individualistic values. According to Piñera, "The road is clear to replace a Bismarckian program with a system that is so inherently consistent with American values."[45] If the reference to Bismarck implicitly depicted Social Security as an un-American institution, such a discourse also described Chile as a laboratory for the implementation of American—conservative—economic ideas.[46]

Furthermore, *Common Cents, Common Dreams* argued that African Americans should support privatization because of their shorter life expectancy: "Social Security is particularly unfair to African-Americans and other minorities. African-Americans can expect to live far fewer years in retirement than can whites because of their lower life expectancy. . . .

Millions of black men will pay Social Security taxes their entire lives and never receive a dime in benefits."[47] Not an isolated example, this type of discourse about the relationship between life expectancy and Social Security return rates is a recurrent theme in the conservative rhetoric about privatization. For example, in a Heritage Foundation report about Social Security's return rates, William Beach and Gareth G. Davis provided the reader with a striking example that contradicted the common wisdom that this program serves minorities well: "For the low-income African-American male age 38 or younger, the news is particularly grim: He is likely to pay more into the Social Security system than he can ever expect to receive in benefits after inflation and taxes. Staying in the current system will likely cost him up to $160,000 in lifetime income in 1997 dollars."[48] The paradox is striking: even though there is little evidence that race significantly impacted Social Security development in the United States, conservatives who seldom pay direct attention to race in their politics refer to it when eager to undermine the support for Social Security, one of America's truly color-blind social programs.

Finally, the authors of *Common Cents, Common Dreams* state that women, like African Americans and other minorities, should support privatization because a "working woman receives nothing in return for her lifetime of Social Security taxes unless she earns benefits greater than 50 percent of those her husband receives."[49] This reference to family benefits is interesting, as it points to the way the program has interacted with traditional gender roles since the enactment of the 1939 amendments to the Social Security Act. Yet, instead of focusing on the reform of these benefits, conservatives such as Ferrara and Tanner use this issue to promote their favored policy alternative: Social Security privatization. According to those who support this, "privatization of Social Security in fact would offer tangible financial benefits to women. If higher rates of return are realized on investments in the private capital markets, privatization is likely to boost the retirement savings of both men and women."[50] In their attempt to build an electoral coalition against the institutional status quo, conservatives seek to convince women that Social Security privatization is something that would be of benefit to them—as to the rest of the population.

As these examples suggest, ideological arguments about gender, race, and Social Security privatization have proliferated since the mid-1990s.[51]

Instead of focusing exclusively on personal gain, this rhetoric underlines the collective gains allegedly associated with privatization. Paradoxically, those who generally embrace an individualistic creed that leaves little space for a critique of social inequalities have exploited "identity politics" and racial divisions to persuade Americans to support path-breaking reforms. This reality illustrates the highly pragmatic nature of the frames mobilized in order to justify Social Security privatization.

It seems difficult to measure the impact of the campaign in favor of Social Security (partial) privatization on public opinion. For one thing, despite existing trust fund surpluses, confidence in the future of the current program remains low.[52] This trend may in part reflect the massive diffusion of "demographic pessimism" in the United States.[53] A second thing is that, although Social Security remains popular, enduring demographic fears have led a majority of the population to support more significant changes that could guarantee the long-term solvency of that program. Surveys conducted between 1996 and 2000 showed that a significant majority of the population supported privatization, at least when survey questions did not mention potential risks related to that policy alternative. When risks were considered, however, support for privatization dropped, and most citizens opposed it.[54] Although the "Leninist strategy" helped promote Social Security privatization, no widespread consensus over this issue emerged during the 1990s.

In spite of their mitigated impact on public opinion, the arguments discussed above have been instrumental in shaping the American debate on Social Security reform since the late 1980s. Taking a defensive stance, traditional supporters of the program—especially Democrats—have rejected Social Security privatization, arguing that such a program restructuring would transfer financial risks onto the shoulders of American workers while generating high transition costs stemming from the need to simultaneously finance current PAYGO pensions and accumulate money into personal accounts for future retirees. According to liberal economists, even partial privatization proposals (allocating only a fraction of current payroll tax to personal accounts) would prove difficult to finance without a significant payroll tax increase. Small, incremental reforms could be sufficient to guarantee the long-term survival of the existing PAYGO, depicted as the best possible source of economic security.[55] Arguing that conservatives create artificial fears and stressing that the majority of the population still supports Social Security, liberal economists fight "disinformation" in order to end the program's "phony crisis."[56] For liberals, the true issue at stake is not the restoration of "American values" through Social Security privatization but the declining confidence in a program that actually works. Against the individualistic rhetoric concerning "American values," they tend to depict Social Security as a great national "success story" while arguing that the need to reshape it is a pure ideological construction.[57] Finally, supporters of the program reject the idea that Social Security privatization would benefit women and African Americans.[58] According to them, Cato-style arguments about life expectancy fail to take into account the fact that, because women have a higher life expectancy than men, Social Security is a better deal for them. Furthermore, liberals point to the fact that women and minorities disproportionately benefit from disability and survivor provisions, which privatization could jeopardize. Overall, because that reform would terminate—or at least seriously undermine—the redistributive, "social adequacy" character of Social Security, liberals contend that it would be detrimental to women, minorities, and lower-wage workers: "Replacing part of Social Security with individual accounts would be a bad deal for most women, children, African-Americans and other people of color, and all low-wage workers."[59] Women, minorities, and low-income white men should support a federal program that redistributes income while providing them with a genuine source of economic security. From this liberal viewpoint, Social Security privatization would mainly benefit higher-income white men, not those who strongly feel the burden of old age insecurity.

Arguments put forward to legitimize Social Security have changed since the postwar era. Instead of framing Social Security as a source of self-reliance analogous to private savings, supporters of the program now tend to depict it as a redistributive device especially crucial for the poor, women, and minorities. Because the discourse about privatization focuses on personal autonomy and self-reliance, those opposing this policy alternative have reframed Social Security as a collective tool that is generous and redistributive in nature. One can trace this frame back to the 1960s, when Social Security advocates began to depict this program as an effective tool in the war against poverty.[60] Yet the idea that Social Security is a genuinely American program that generates "earned rights" for hard-working citizens and their families is still present in the discourse legitimizing that program.[61] Like their opponents, Social Security supporters use all the arguments available in order to justify their political stance.

Political Risks and Legislative Inaction

In part because of the political risks stemming from divided government and the growing army of Social Security beneficiaries, conservatives moved slowly to convince Democrats and President Clinton that partial privatization would prove both feasible and unavoidable. Most politicians interested in privatizing the program stated that their actual goal was to "save Social Security." During the 1990s, Social Security was rarely the object of frontal, explicit attacks in the federal political discourse. Even those elected officials who advocated a—partial—shift from social insurance to personal accounts rarely stated openly that their goal was to "dismantle" Social Security.[62] Facing significant electoral risks, many elected officials embracing the financial paradigm made significant efforts to downplay the potentially radical character of privatization-related alternatives.[63] The rapid multiplication of congressional hearings on Social Security after 1995 shows that partial privatization emerged as a recurrent issue on the congressional agenda during the second half of the 1990s.[64] Yet, enduring political risks and the president's reluctance to strike a deal on Social Security reform made talk about privatization a safer political option for conservatives than concrete legislative action, a risky business considering that divided government gives the president an institutional veto point. Beyond this institutional obstacle to reform, higher than expected levels of economic growth favored the expansion of the reserve fund while improving long-term actuarial forecast.[65]

Facing the prospect of bold federal surpluses,[66] the president first challenged the Republican-led Congress to "Save Social Security First." At the time, this basically meant using the forthcoming federal surpluses to guarantee the long-term financial soundness of Social Security *instead* of enacting massive tax cuts. This idea of using federal surpluses to save Social Security, at the center of President Clinton's 1998 State of the Union address, appeared as a successful strategy to prevent the Republicans from enacting widespread tax breaks. Yet, there were signs that the president could strike a deal with conservatives over Social Security privatization. As a Democratic president navigating in a conservative political environment, William Clinton had already attempted to forge new electoral coalitions by appealing to both liberals and conservatives.[67] This was the meaning of his Third Way proposals on welfare, which did not prevent the enactment of the genuinely conservative welfare reform of 1996.[68] Furthermore, the president's numerous public references to Social Security reform[69] and his eagerness to lay the foundation for a genuine political legacy beyond the "Lewinsky affair" convinced many journalists and members of Congress that President Clinton might support a bipartisan bill favorable to partial privatization.[70] During the two years following the 1998 State of the Union address, therefore, Social Security reform proposals multiplied, and partial privatization appeared as a significant item on both presidential and congressional policy agendas.[71] An example of such proposals is the bill presented in the spring of 1998 by Senators John Breaux (D-Louisiana) and Judd Gregg (R-New Hampshire) "that would have introduced a mandatory private tier using two percentage points of the existing payroll tax."[72] These legislative proposals generally excluded any payroll tax increase, a measure that has been an enduring political taboo since the Reagan era.[73] This taboo further complicated the attempt to draft a political compromise in the absence of a short-term fiscal crisis. And as the trust fund's "exhaustion date" moved farther into the future, conservatives found it increasingly difficult to construct the need to reform Social Security.[74]

After months of being reluctant to take action, the president formally opposed Social Security privatization in his 1999 State of the Union address, recommending that savings accounts be created *alongside* the existing PAYGO system. He also proposed investing Social Security surpluses in equity.[75] Conservatives strongly opposed such a measure, which had been implemented in Canada during the second half of the 1990s.[76] Considering the political tensions created by the impeachment debate, President Clinton failed to act as a successful pol-

icy entrepreneur in the context of divided government. But the fact
that he promoted the idea of federal savings accounts and the investment of Social Security surpluses in equity illustrates the increasing
popularity, if not the intellectual domination, of the financial paradigm
at the end of the 1990s. More generally, President Clinton's proposal
exemplifies the interactive nature of policymaking. Because of the popularity of financial ideas in the late 1990s, the president prominently
featured financial investment in his reform proposal while rejecting
Social Security privatization. Implicitly, the president acknowledged
the need for greater reliance on personal savings and stock market
investment. Furthermore, his emphasis on the necessity to save Social
Security gave further ground to demographic pessimism. As in other
policy areas, the resident's Third Way approach to Social Security
reform consisted of a skillful mix of liberal and conservative ideas.

Overall, the analysis of the debate concerning Social Security privatization during President Clinton second term shows that the financial paradigm and the related idea of partial privatization gained a new
respect, contrasting with the taboo surrounding this policy alternative
during the 1980s.[77] Even if elected officials embracing the financial paradigm were still careful about their political statements and claimed to
work in order to "save Social Security," it became more acceptable to
support partial privatization and other forms of Social Security–related
financial investments. In the spring of 2000, presumed Republican
nominee George W. Bush did endorse the idea of partial privatization,
"saying that he favored permitting individuals to invest a portion of
their Social Security payroll tax."[78]

The Ownership Society?

Immediately following the election of George W. Bush as president,
conservatives hoped to revivify the idea of Social Security privatization,
yet they decided to push for the enactment of a bold tax cut initiative
first. To gain time and pave the way for future reform, President Bush
appointed a commission on Social Security reform (President's Commission to Strengthen Social Security) composed of people who had to
agree in advance to support a few key principles consistent with the

president's vision.[79] These principles included "no increase in Social Security payroll taxes, voluntary personal accounts, and no erosion of benefits for current and near retirees."[80] The commission's report formulated three sets of reform options that reflected the domination of the financial logic:

> Social Security will be strengthened if modernized to include a system of voluntary personal accounts. Personal accounts improve retirement security by facilitating wealth creation and providing participants with assets that they own and that can be inherited, rather than providing only claims to benefits that remain subject to political negotiation. By allowing investment choice, individuals would be free to pursue higher expected rates of return on their Social Security contributions. Furthermore, strengthening Social Security through personal accounts can add valuable protections for widows, divorced persons, low-income households and other Americans at risk of poverty in old age. Partial advance funding of Social Security should be a goal of any effort to strengthen the system. Advance funding within Social Security can best be accomplished through personal accounts rather than direct government investment. Personal accounts offer numerous economic benefits, including a likely increase in national saving, as well as an improvement in incentives for labor force participation.[81]

This citation reformulated many economic arguments at the center of the financial paradigm outlined above while explicitly rejecting the idea—previously formulated by President Clinton—that the federal government should directly invest trust fund surpluses in equity.

Unfortunately for the supporters of this paradigm, the terrorist attacks of September 11, 2001, relegated the issue of Social Security reform to the periphery of the policy agenda as well as the media agenda. Financial downturns related to these events also revealed the vulnerability of tax-sponsored savings plans closely associated with the idea of partial privatization and the financial paradigm itself.[82] Despite the efforts of conservative think tanks and scholars, the new emphasis on national security stemming from these terrorist attacks temporarily undermined the ideological and political push for Social Security privatization. In this context, as elsewhere, the power of ideas is tied to economic, electoral, and institutional forces that pave the way—or not—to their political success.

Despite these apparent obstacles to Social Security restructuring, President Bush still supported the creation of personal accounts within that program during his second term. This support for the "carving out" option is explicit in his 2004 State of the Union address:

> My administration is promoting free and fair trade to open up new markets for America's entrepreneurs and manufacturers and farmers—to create jobs for American workers. Younger workers should have the opportunity to build a nest egg by saving part of their Social Security taxes in a personal retirement account. We should make the Social Security system a source of ownership for the American people. And we should limit the burden of government on this economy by acting as good stewards of taxpayers' dollars.[83]

This push for Social security privatization is part of a broader crusade that would accelerate the massive development of tax-sheltered savings in the United States. This development would favor wealthier Americans, who constitute one of the most faithful Republican constituencies.[84]

Between 1998 and 2001, conservatives missed an opportunity to materialize one of the policy alternatives related to the now-prominent financial paradigm. Because the content of both the policy and the public agendas changed dramatically after September 11, 2001, it seemed more difficult to restructure Social Security and implement a compulsory—or even a voluntary—federal savings scheme. Ideas can matter, yet their potential success at the legislative level depends on changing socioeconomic trends as well as the ideological construction of the need to reform aimed at shaking institutional inertia that traditionally militates against path-breaking reforms. At the very least, conservatives prevented the enactment of new measures and benefit increases that could have improved existing social protection to help citizens facing new risks related to changing socioeconomic conditions.[85] Furthermore, the focus on privatization marginalized other policy issues such as the future of Social Security's family benefits in the context of changing gender and family relations.[86] Agenda setting is a selection process in which a handful of issues become prominent while others remain backstage. In the case of Social Security, the conservative campaign in favor of privatization marginalized other significant pension-related issues.[87]

With the return to massive federal deficits during the George W. Bush presidency, a long-term shift toward the politics of fiscal austerity is almost certain. Because there are no budget surpluses to finance the costs stemming from partial privatization, this new dynamic is not necessarily good news for those who support Social Security privatization. The return to fiscal austerity, however, does not mean that the current Social Security status quo will prevail in the years to come. First, because "Social Security's trust fund income and outlays . . . are routinely shown both separately and as part of the total budget," one cannot entirely separate budget politics and Social Security reform.[88] In a February 2004 speech, for example, Federal Reserve Board chairman—and former chairman of the National Commission on Social Security Reform—Alan Greenspan argued that changes like a further increase in retirement age will prove necessary to curb the anticipated growth in Social Security spending.[89]

Second, the ideological commitment in favor of Social Security privatization is still strong among conservative ranks, including the Bush administration. This became clear during the 2004 presidential race. Accusing Democratic candidate John Kerry of not having a real plan to "save Social Security," President Bush supported partial privatization as a key aspect of the Ownership Society anticipated in his electoral platform. This rhetoric about ownership is grounded in the idea that private property and personal savings constitute the best—and the most legitimate—sources of security for the individual. This confirms the fact that, for conservatives, Social Security privatization is part of a broader policy agenda that aims at increasing the reliance of citizens on individualistic and market-oriented forms of protection.[90]

Faithful to his long-standing creed regarding Social Security, President Bush backed the idea that individuals should be allowed to channel a portion of the existing payroll tax to personal savings accounts. Arguing that Social Security reform would become a crucial issue during his second term, the president defended partial privatization during the third presidential debate: "I believe that younger workers ought to be allowed to take some of their own money and put it in a personal savings account, because I understand that they need to get better rates of return than the rates of return being given in the current Social Security trust."[91] His optimistic rhetoric about return rates echoed the discourse of conservative experts and think tanks. In his response, Kerry argued that the president's plan was "an invitation to disaster" that would create a "a $2 trillion hole in Social Security" leading to "a cut in benefits of 25 percent to 40 percent."[92] Yet, Kerry himself had little to say about how to "save Social Security." During the primaries, he opposed any increase in retirement age in order to gain ground against his opponent Howard Dean, who "had earlier made the mistake of saying that raising the retirement age to 68 or higher would be a good way to bring Social Security closer to solvency."[93] Kerry could certainly not look like a "flip flopper" over this issue, and he adopted the traditional Democratic stance that consists of warning voters against "Republican plots" to destroy Social Security.

The reelection of George W. Bush to the presidency and the Republican gains in Congress made during the 2004 elections have helped push the issue of Social Security privatization back on the federal policy agenda. President Bush's 2005 State of the Union Address confirmed this return of Social Security reform on the agenda. Furthermore, this address prominently featured demographic pessimism while making the implicit claim that partial privatization was the only way to "save" this federal program: "Social Security was a great moral success of the 20th century, and we must honor its great purposes in this new century. The system, however, on its current path, is headed toward bankruptcy. And so we must join together to strengthen and save Social Security."[94] During the first months of his second term, President Bush constantly referred to the need to reform Social Security, and major media outlets devoted numerous reports to this issue.[95]

Yet, in spite of all this talk about reform, Social Security privatization remained a risky political business. Although they had a significant majority in Congress, Republicans fell short of the sixty-vote threshold that would have allowed them to totally dominate the Senate.[96] Furthermore, despite what Michael Tanner argued, there is no sign that voters gave a mandate to the President to restructure Social Security.[97] Political risks stemming from Social Security privatization have not declined, and as the most recent presidential campaign showed, Democrats are still willing to use this issue against Republicans. From this perspective, any attempt to enact legislation about partial privatization could hurt the Republican party and those members of Congress who would support this policy alternative. Yet, the fact that President Bush's privatization campaign failed and that Social Security is still viewed as "the third rail of American politics" does not mean that legislative action is impossible, given the strong ideological commitment in favor of Social Security privatization among conservative ranks and the demographic aging and fiscal constraints that could keep the issue on the federal agenda, in one way or another. Finally, the decline of defined benefit plans and the ongoing development of government-subsidized private savings schemes is gradually undermining the traditional integration between Social Security and private pension plans. As evidenced in Chapter 4, such integration increased business support for Social Security in the postwar era. The decline of integration could have the opposite effect.

Conclusion

In the absence of short-term fiscal crisis since the mid-1980s, those supporting Social Security privatization have found it difficult to construct a need to reform this program in order to restructure it and favor the triumph of the financial paradigm. During the 1990s, exceptional stock market performances helped conservatives frame an optimistic discourse about personal savings. Exploiting demographic fears and the lack of trust toward the government, conservatives have attempted to convince individuals and specific segments of the population—for example, African Americans—that privatization could benefit them. The numerous references to race in the discourse aimed at justifying partial privatization are ironic because Social Security is a color-blind program, whose historical development was not shaped by racial prejudice and segregation. References to gender in the debate over partial privatization are also interesting because each camp attempts to convince women that its policy alternative is the best for them. In the United States, more than in any other advanced industrial country, the contemporary debate over the future of Social Security has become explicitly tied to "identity politics." Both liberals and conservatives are responsible for that situation.

In the early 2000s, financial optimism declined as fast as stock market performances, and Social Security reform moved off the legislative agenda as issues such as tax cuts, terrorism, and Medicare reform took up more symbolic space in the political arena. As various public statements of the Bush administration as well as the 2004 presidential campaign suggest, Social Security finally moved back to the center of the federal policy agenda. Because Congress passed a significant Medicare reform in 2003, elected officials had more time to debate Social Security reform, as demographic fears, as well as the push for partial privatization, remained ever present in American society. In the absence of a short-term fiscal crisis in Social Security, however, most elected officials were not under strong pressure to take the risk of reforming such a popular program. As a result, no action was taken. This issue is further discussed in the afterword. Overall, partial privatization constitutes an attempt to restructure Social Security beyond traditional retrenchment initiatives. As the experiences of other advanced industrial countries show, social insurance programs are not always "frozen" despite the massive constituencies stemming from them. In the United States, only time will tell if the conservative restructuring of Social Security known as privatization has a real chance of passing the legislative test.

Theoretically, this chapter underlines the tension between resilient institutional legacies and the crystallization of a major ideological challenge to Social Security, which takes the form of the financial paradigm that conservative journalists, politicians, and think tanks promote within and outside the policy arena. So far, these institutional legacies have proved stronger than the conservative will to restructure Social Security amid enduring electoral risks. Yet, as the afterword will reiterate, the absence of legislative action does not mean that nothing has happened in the American pension system since the enactment of the 1983 amendments. Furthermore, the defeat of President Bush's 2005 campaign to privatize Social Security cannot hide the fact that, since the mid-1990s, the privatization agenda has become increasingly prominent in the academic, political, and media debate on Social Security reform.

Even though the political future of Social Security remains uncertain, it is possible to discuss key aspects of this program's history while drawing a few general conclusions about theoretical issues. This chapter returns to these issues, underlines the prominent features of the politics of Social Security, discusses the potential impact of race and gender on this program's development, and shows how the lessons derived from the political and historical analysis of Social Security reform can shed new light on the debate over the future of this program.

A Broader Institutionalist Framework

One of the main arguments put forward in this book is that the growing institutionalist scholarship about social policy reform should pay greater attention to the relationship between ideas and institutions in policymaking. It is possible, while taking business power and other societal forces into account, to also study the political impact of ideas in a systematic manner without abandoning the historical institutionalist assumption that policy feedbacks and formal political institutions affect political behavior in a strong way. Historical institutionalism, although insightful, does not sufficiently emphasize the political role of ideas, at least when dealing with social policy development. This new political history of Social Security suggests that the ideational framework about agenda setting, paradigms, and framing sketched in Chapter 1 enhances the explanatory power of historical institutionalism.

Following Kingdon, I stressed the importance of agenda-setting processes in policymaking. The manner in which—and the timing according to which—specific topics and policy alternatives become significant political issues is crucial to understanding why some ideas are considered by policymakers in the first place. The early history of pension reform during the 1930s and 1940s illustrates the crucial role of agenda setting. First, because pension reform entered most state policy agendas late in the 1920s, this issue was debated in many states when the Great Depression struck the country (Chapter 2). Such favorable timing permitted the rapid enactment of state old age assistance schemes in the early 1930s. Second, after the election of President Franklin D. Roosevelt, the mobilization of the Townsend movement helped maintain the issue of pension reform on the federal agenda. The radical nature of the Townsend Plan encouraged the president to promote his own vision of old age security. This favored the inclusion of a federal old age insurance program in the 1935 Social Security Act.

Policy paradigms are essential to policymaking, and it is vital to take them into account in a methodical way in order to understand the origin of key policy decisions. Experts and elected officials used paradigms as "road maps" that provided them with a structured set of assumptions about the functioning of economic, political, and social processes related to specific policy issues. From the enactment of the program to the current debate over Social Security privatization, the systematic study of policy paradigms helps in understanding policymaking and political struggles. In 1934, for example, the president promoted a specific social insurance paradigm that would largely shape the old age insurance scheme enacted as part of the 1935 Social Security Act (Chapter 3). Without taking this paradigm into account, it is impossible to fully understand the specific content of that legislation. Seven decades after the enactment of the Social Security Act, an alternative financial paradigm has become prominent in American society. Associated with Social Security privatization, this paradigm contains a set of assumptions at odds with the program's redistributive logic. Carefully looking at the specific content of this paradigm is crucial to understanding the nature of the current debate over Social Security privatization.

Distinct from policy ideas (that is, alternatives and paradigms), framing is another significant process ever present in policy debates. The framing process can take two closely related forms. First, in order to justify their policy choices, actors involved in that process draw on the very same ideological repertoire to frame existing programs and debated policy alternatives. The general discourse about personal responsibility and self-reliance used since the late 1930s to legitimize Social Security illustrates that claim. Second, frames are used to construct the need to reform existing programs and institutions. From the progressive discourse about poorhouses and old age dependency to the contemporary rhetoric about "demographic time bombs," there are many examples of this second possible objective of ideological frames.

Just as institutions do, ideas and ideological repertoires create constraints and opportunities for policymakers, and they impact political decisions in subtle yet fundamental ways. Yet, ideas are directly related to specific interests, institutional arrangements, and policy legacies, which they can either reinforce or challenge. The broad institutionalist framework formulated in Chapter 1 could be applied to other empirical cases within and beyond the field of social policy studies.

What Is Specific about the American Experience?

The comparative elements discussed throughout this book underline both the peculiarities and the comparatively common features of the politics of Social Security in the United States. Following the historical institutionalist literature, Chapter 2 underlined the institutional features of the American polity that constrained the activities of reformers. For example, pre–New Deal, American-style federalism exacerbated the potential veto power of business interests. Yet, institutional change occurred during the 1930s, a decade during which business power declined steadily. Chapter 3 showed how the Great Depression reduced the institutional obstacles to reform.

Another original characteristic of the American welfare state is the relationship between private and public social benefits. To a certain extent, the United States shares that characteristic with other liberal welfare regimes such as Australia, Canada, and the United Kingdom. Yet, perhaps more than in any other advanced industrial country, the relationship between private and public benefits is essential to our understanding of Social Security politics in the United States. Chapter 4 explored this issue through a comparison between health care politics and Social Security reform during the Truman presidency. This discussion underlined the role of timing and historical sequence in the development of public and private benefits.[1]

As a PAYGO program, Social Security is rooted in the same basic institutional logic as contributive public pension schemes enacted in other advanced industrialized countries. This means that Social Security creates large constituencies that can mobilize to expand the program or, in the era of retrenchment and conservative restructuring, mobilize to defend the institutional status quo and their perceived "earned rights."[2] Still, as opposed to the situation prevailing in social insurance countries such as France, Germany, and Italy, labor unions are not the primary political force explicitly representing the interests of Social Security workers and contributories. Facing declining membership and being deprived of institutional status within the program, the AFL-CIO does not have the leverage of its European counterparts, who have staged influential campaigns to fight pension retrenchment and restructuring. In the United States, beneficiaries themselves have organized to a great extent in order to preserve Social Security.

Another key difference between the United States and other advanced industrial countries is the fact that a significant movement in favor of Social Security privatization has emerged in the absence of short- and middle-range fiscal crisis. Overall, the American demographic and economic situation is more favorable than the one prevailing in most other advanced industrial societies. Furthermore, because of the flawed indexation system implemented in 1974, federal policymakers have had to deal with the fiscal unbalances in Social Security before most other advanced industrial countries have had to do so. At a time when other nations were still debating the expansion of public pension schemes, the two fiscal crises of the mid-1970s and early 1980s forced Congress to enact reforms that have significantly improved Social Security's long-term fiscal situation. Because of the fragmented nature of American political institutions, talk about major restructuring attempts such as Social Security privatization is probably easier than legislative action.[3] In this context, privatization supporters have to use all the arguments available to construct the need to reform Social Security. As in most other advanced industrial societies, demographic pessimism is a crucial aspect of the conservative rhetoric surrounding the debate over Social Security retrenchment and restructuring. Yet a more specifically American trait is the individualistic discourse framed to legitimize both the expansion of Social Security after 1935 and Social Security privatization since the 1990s.

Those who support Social Security and those who seek to restructure this program draw on the very same ideological repertoire in order to frame their favorite policy alternative. Even during and after the New Deal, when new liberalism had become dominant, no language of solidarity and social citizenship similar to the one formulated at the time in most other advanced industrial countries emerged. Instead, vague references to self-reliance still legitimized social insurance programs. Even during the 1960s, the new discourse about the role of Social Security in the War on Poverty did not replace the traditional, individualistic rhetoric about "earned rights." As the debate on Social Security privatization shows, this rhetoric is especially vulnerable to conservative attacks because it is largely at odds with the concrete, redistributive logic of the program that has become dominant since the enactment of the 1939 amendments to the Social Security Act.

Race, Gender, and Social Policy

Perhaps more than in any other country, race and gender are prominently featured in contemporary American research about social policy development. This probably reflects the central role of identity politics in American society and academic circles. Overall, the study of race and gender is a significant contribution to our understanding of social policy. For too long, scholars failed to even take these two crucial issues into account. Yet, despite their general significance, race and gender do not necessarily have the same political impact in one policy area as in another. In the case of the influence of race during the 1930s, racial prejudice and the mobilization of southern Democrats seemed to have a more direct impact in the field of old age assistance than in the field of old age insurance. Moreover, many students of race and gender should become more aware of the potential confusion between the political origins and socioeconomic effects of social programs. For example, showing that the temporary exclusion of agrarian and domestic workers from Social Security enacted in 1935 disproportionately affected African Americans does not necessarily mean that such a decision was grounded in racial prejudice and segregationist ideas. This is especially true when there is strong evidence that an alternative explanation sheds light on this decision. In the case of the exclusion of agrarian and domestic workers, the alternative explanation is related to the fiscal and administrative concerns formulated during and after the House and the Senate testimonies.

Overall, I must conclude that gender has proved more central than race in the politics of Social Security reform. There is no direct evidence that race significantly impacted the long-term historical development of Social Security, whereas gendered forces did strongly impact at least one crucial Social Security reform: the 1939 amendments to the Social Security Act, which created spousal and survivor benefits at first available only to adult women and children. There is strong evidence that these benefits were grounded in traditional assumptions about family roles and gender relations. Reforms enacted since the 1970s have repealed remaining discriminatory provisions from Social Security, yet the current structure of spousal and survivor benefits represents a legacy of the 1939 amendments and the gendered ideas that were dominant at that time. In the history and the politics of Social Security reform, gendered ideas had simply far more traceable causal weight than racial prejudice.

In the future, students of race and gender could further emphasize the difference between the political origin and the socioeconomic effect of social programs while underlining crucial variations existing between policy areas. Stating that race and gender always determine policy outcomes—even in the absence of direct empirical evidence—would transform these factors into quasi-metaphysical explanations that have little heuristic value.

What Could the Future Look Like?

Social scientists are rarely good at anticipating the future. Yet, the historical and political analysis put forward in this book should help scholars and citizens better understand the logic behind the current debate over the future of Social Security. Because the political and economic context of reform is volatile, it is misleading to depict Social Security as a program that cannot change much over time. In 1972, who would have predicted that Social Security would face a massive fiscal crisis barely three years down the road? If the shift from the politics of expansion to the politics of retrenchment was sudden, who can tell what the politics of Social Security will really look like a decade from now? From this perspective, a cautious approach is needed when it feels tempting to look at what the future can bring.

Global demographic and economic trends such as aging and stock market performances matter a great deal in the politics of Social Security reform, in part because of their impact on agenda setting and the construction of the need to reform. Although this need to reform is a social and political construction, concrete changes in the socioeconomic environment help actors promote specific policy alternatives and frame the issues to their advantage. Yet, there is a major difference between demographic aging, which is a long-term and relatively predictable process, and stock market performances, which can change rapidly and unexpectedly. If demographic aging may facilitate the emergence of a diffuse anxiety about the future of Social Security, stock market performances and economic cycles can swiftly engender new constraints and opportunities for policymakers. Furthermore, the institutional features of Social Security also create political constraints and opportunities that actors involved in the debate over this program's future must take into account when promoting specific policy alternatives such as partial privatization. In addition to the politically active army of beneficiaries that the program generates, those who seek to transform the functioning of Social Security have to acknowledge the existence of the payroll tax and the long-term commitments made to current and future beneficiaries. This reality generates a constraining political environment that explains why most conservatives support partial, instead of full, privatization and why the term *privatization* itself can hide the fact that the issue at stake is the shift to personal savings under significant governmental control and the preservation of the payroll tax, not the full withdrawal of the federal government from old age security.

Ideological battles over the need to reform Social Security will probably continue over the next years and decades. Social scientists can certainly shed an interesting light on this debate by analyzing the frames, the policy paradigms, and the institutional mechanisms that underline this debate. Yet, it is possible to make such a contribution only if we understand that ideational and institutional processes are closely related and that they can both affect policy outcomes in a significant way. Because both ideas and institutions matter, studying ideational and institutional processes simultaneously is the best way to understand the politics of social policy, in the United States and abroad.

In order to understand the contemporary debate on Social Security, one can take a closer look at President Bush's 2005 privatization campaign and place it in its international context. Such a discussion underlines the enduring weight of policy legacies in the contemporary politics of Social Security. These legacies create strong obstacles to reform in the absence of short-term fiscal crisis. Yet, as is suggested below, although the 2005 campaign did not lead to any significant legislative action, it underlines the crucial fact that, since the mid-1990s, Social Security privatization has transformed from a marginal to a mainstream policy alternative. In such a context, conservatives have succeeded in undermining the belief in the sustainability of Social Security while forcing most left-leaning actors to adopt a purely defensive stance. In an era of rapid economic, social, and demographic change, this situation has prevented these actors from launching meaningful efforts to modernize—and even improve the protection offered by—the program they support. Ironically, the aggressive conservative push to privatize Social Security and the defensive reaction it triggered on the left may have only reinforced the program's institutional stasis.

Another Look at the 2005 Episode

During the first half of 2005, President Bush spent much time and energy promoting the need to restructure Social Security. At the ideational level, the "ownership society" offered a coherent blueprint for domestic policy reform that bridged a number of policy issues. "I think government ought to promote an ownership society," the president said. "We ought to encourage more people to own their own home, encourage entrepreneurs to be able to take risk and own their own business—and in this case, encourage Americans from all walks of life, if they so choose, to manage their own retirement account."[1] According to Grover Norquist, president of the conservative group Americans for Tax Reform, the "ownership society" represented a bold attempt at

Republican coalition building: "You can't have a hate-and-envy class if 80 percent of the public owns stock. That makes it impossible for Democrats to govern. It spells the end of their world."[2] This logic applied to Social Security, one of the last major legacies of the New Deal, and a large source of potential capital for the financial industry. Not surprisingly, then, Social Security reform rapidly became the proposed centerpiece of Bush's "ownership society."

As is now well known, in spite of intense framing efforts and a national tour that attracted much media attention, President Bush's Social Security privatization campaign went nowhere.[3] Facing growing public skepticism and attacks from Democrats and other traditional supporters of Social Security, the president suspended this campaign during the summer of 2005. After Hurricane Katrina struck New Orleans in late August, the weakened Bush administration and Republican congressional leadership could hardly revive the privatization campaign.[4] By the end of 2005, Social Security privatization had virtually vanished from the congressional agenda.

Drawing on historical institutionalism, this book shows how powerful institutional factors like the double payment problem and the emergence of armies of beneficiaries have created major obstacles to Social Security retrenchment and restructuring. These conditions particularly apply during times of financial surplus in the program and in the absence of a short-term fiscal crisis.[5] As opposed to the situations prevailing in 1977 and 1983, the short-term fiscal status of Social Security at the beginning of President Bush's second mandate remained favorable, as the program received significantly more money from the payroll tax than it was paying out in benefits.[6] Enduring institutional legacies and the absence of short-term crisis largely explain legislative inertia in the field of Social Security reform. Moreover, in 2005 and early 2006, the declining popularity of the Bush administration and the Republican Party seriously undermined the political forces that generally support Social Security privatization.[7] Finally, as stated in Chapter 6, the long-term demographic and fiscal challenge to Social Security is more modest in the United States than in other advanced industrial countries such as Italy, Japan, and Sweden.

A genuinely serious fiscal situation generated by accelerated population aging is likely to pressure policymakers to take tough decisions.

Hence, in the 1990s and early 2000s, countries facing a less favorable demographic situation like Italy, Sweden, and Japan took major steps to restructure their public pension system and control future Social Security spending.[8] In the United States, however, the push to restructure Social Security is more ideologically driven, with demographic change often representing one argument among others to legitimize path-departing reforms inspired by a coherent, market-oriented financial paradigm.[9]

The British Experiment in Social Security Privatization

Outside the United States, one of the best examples of an ideologically driven campaign in favor of Social Security privatization occurred in Britain during the Thatcher era. At the time, demographic aging was not a major short-term challenge in Britain and, although Prime Minister Thatcher referred to that issue in order to legitimize reform,[10] the conservative push to privatize part of the British public pension system represented a significant aspect of the ideological project that directly inspired President Bush's "ownership society": the idea of "popular capitalism."[11] A mix of populism and old liberalism, "popular capitalism" represented an attempt to increase private ownership in a country that had a large number of public enterprises and public housing tenants when the first Thatcher government took power in 1979. Shortly thereafter, this government began to privatize these enterprises and allow tenants living in public housing facilities to buy their flats and houses at a discounted rate.[12] By 1985, the second Thatcher government attempted to extend this logic of privatization to the public pension system.

At the time, two institutional factors facilitated Prime Minister Thatcher's attempt to privatize—in this case encouraging current participants to "op-out" of—the British old age insurance scheme known as SERPS (State Earnings Related Pension Scheme).[13] First, SERPS had only been in place since 1978, and it had yet to pay benefits when Prime Minister Thatcher pushed for a major reform in the mid-1980s. Second, as implemented in 1978, SERPS offered the possibility to those covered by private pension schemes to "op-out" of that program. Such

institutional features weakened the social and political support for
SERPS by covering only part of the workforce and by leaving the door
open for more liberal opting-out conditions. These two factors contrast
with the contemporary situation in the United States, where Social
Security is a quasi-universal program that has long created a large and
politically active army of beneficiaries.[14]

Yet, in Britain, even a vulnerable and immature Social Security program as well the extensive concentration of power that characterizes
the parliamentary system did not allow the Thatcher government to
abolish SERPS altogether. In 1985, even business interests opposed that
reform, which they perceived as overly radical and too costly for the
private sector.[15] That situation forced the Thatcher government to formulate a more moderate proposal, which was finally enacted in 1986.
The new legislation favored a gradual privatization of the program
through cuts in benefits and the liberalization of opting-out conditions
that would help promote a rapid decline in the number of SERPS participants.[16] Ultimately, the Conservatives paid a political price for that
reform, as thousands of workers who had opted out of SERPS realized
that the financial industry lured them to opt out of the program against
their most basic economic interests in the context of a poorly regulated
financial sector. This situation led to the implementation of tighter
financial regulations that illustrate the potential, yet unintended, consequences of Social Security privatization.[17]

Policy Drift, Legislative Inaction, and the
Future of Social Security

In the United States, the lack of short-term fiscal crisis and the presence
of enduring institutional obstacles to reform have transformed Social
Security privatization into a politically risky enterprise. Yet, as underlined in Chapter 6, the absence of concrete legislative outcomes and the
failure of President Bush's 2005 attempt to privatize Social Security do
not mean that nothing has happened in the field of pension policy since
the enactment of the 1983 amendments. An interesting way to look
at the contemporary American situation is the idea of policy drift.
According to Jacob Hacker, the absence of legislative revision in a par-

ticular policy area does not mean that it is not subject to change, as new economic and social conditions transform the environment in which social programs work and, consequently, their effects upon workers and citizens.[18] In the field of pension policy, for example, the decline of private, defined-benefit schemes potentially undermines the economic security of Americans, as employers shift financial risks onto workers through the development of defined-contribution plans. With the absence of reforms meant to counter these tendencies and increase the protection Social Security offers, many American workers will enjoy less economic security than before. From that angle, the conservative campaign is potentially successful in one major way: by forcing liberals to adopt a defensive stance in the debate over Social Security, they marginalize proposals that could improve the protection offered by Social Security and the lesser known but much needed SSI program.[19] Considering that old age poverty is already higher in the United States than in most other advanced industrial countries, the fact that so few federal politicians actually raise this issue is particularly worrisome.[20] Finally, the contemporary privatization debate intensifies ideological polarization, a situation that is not conducive to the type of bipartisan legislation necessary to improve the long-term fiscal health of Social Security.

Theoretically, the failure of President Bush's 2005 Social Security campaign emphasizes the complex interaction between ideational and institutional processes discussed in Chapter 1. Although the analysis of the enactment of the Social Security Act and of the 1939 amendments underlines the direct causal role of policy paradigms, the growing visibility of the financial paradigm in the contemporary Social Security debate does not mean that it will necessarily translate into major policy change. In order to shape policy outcomes, ideas often need the support of powerful actors operating in a favorable institutional context. This is where the comparison between the British and the American experience is so useful. As mentioned above, in the mid-1980s, Margaret Thatcher and her allies had more institutional leverage to implement conservative financial ideas than President Bush and his Republican allies in Congress had two decades later. Yet, underlining the institutional obstacles to privatization does not mean that Social Security restructuring is impossible in the United States, as political mobilization, framing processes, and changing demographic and economic realities could undermine support for that program and facilitate restructuring. Concerning the role of ideas in policymaking, President Bush's 2005 failure to restructure Social Security according to the financial paradigm should not hide the fact that conservative agenda-setting strategies have a significant impact on the politics of social policy. For example, as suggested above, the fact that conservatives have transformed Social Security privatization into a major political issue may have helped divert attention away from growing economic inequality and insecurity affecting citizens and workers.[21] Forcing liberals and moderates to focus their attention on—and defend—Social Security is perhaps an astute way for conservatives to prevent these actors from aggressively promoting the enactment of new measures aimed at fighting poverty and economic insecurity, both within and outside the existing Social Security framework. In the short run, the ongoing privatization talk may only reinforce the defensive attitude of most left-leaning actors who oppose the conservative project. This situation, in turn, could exacerbate institutional stasis in the absence of major bipartisan proposals capable of adapting Social Security to changing economic, social, and demographic conditions. Yet, in the long run, conservative efforts to restructure Social Security are not necessarily doomed to fail. This is true because these efforts have already transformed a previously marginal policy alternative like Social Security privatization into a mainstream issue that even the president can openly promote. Furthermore, only time will tell if the higher support for Social Security privatization among younger workers will impact future policy debates or decline as these workers grow older.[22] Consequently, the short-term failure of President Bush's campaign should not rule out the possibility that, over time, the enduring conservative push for privatization—in a context of growing demographic and fiscal challenges—could favor a major transformation of Social Security. And that is the uncertain situation in which we find ourselves today, as history and politics continue to drive the discussion over America's largest social program.

NOTES

Introduction

1. In the debate concerning American exceptionalism, some authors have noted the lack of "social citizenship" in the United States. According to Frazer and Gordon, American social policy is grounded in a strict dichotomy between "charity" (assistance logic) and "contract" (contributory logic) that leaves no room for genuine social entitlements derived from citizenship: Nancy Frazer and Linda Gordon, "Contract versus Charity: Why Is There No Social Citizenship in the United States?" *Socialist Review* 22 (July 1992): 45–68.

2. According to Jill Quadagno, the "integration of the middle class" with Social Security is at the foundation of its political success: "Interest-Group Politics and the Future of the U.S. Social Security," in *States, Labor Markets, and the Future of Old-Age Policy,* ed. John Myles and Jill Quadagno (Philadelphia: Temple University Press, 1991), 36–58.

3. For an overview of pension reform in advanced industrial countries, see John Myles and Paul Pierson, "The Comparative Political Economy of Pension Reform," in *The New Politics of the Welfare State,* ed. Paul Pierson (Oxford: Oxford University Press, 2001), 305–333.

4. R. Kent Weaver, *Whose Money Is It Anyhow? Governance and Social Investment in Collective Investment Funds,* Working Paper no. 2003-07 (Boston: Center for Retirement Research at Boston College, 2003).

5. Dean Baker and Mark Weisbrot, *Social Security: The Phony Crisis* (Chicago: University of Chicago Press, 1999); Robert M. Ball and Thomas N. Bethel, *Straight Talk about Social Security: An Analysis of the Issues in the Current Debate* (New York: Century Foundation/Twentieth Century Fund, 1998); Henry J. Aaron and Robert D. Reischauer, *Countdown to Reform: The Great Social Security Debate* (New York: Century Foundation Press, 1998).

6. Paul Pierson, "Increasing Returns, Path Dependence, and the Study of Politics," *American Political Science Review* 94 (2000): 251–267.

7. The following are the major books that deal extensively with the history of Social Security: W. Andrew Achenbaum, *Social Security: Visions and Revisions* (Cambridge: Cambridge University Press, 1986); Jerry R. Cates, *Insuring Inequality: Administrative Leadership in Social Security, 1935–1954* (Ann Arbor: University of Michigan Press, 1983); Martha Derthick, *Policymaking for Social Security* (Washington, DC: Brookings Institution, 1979); Jill Quadagno, *The Transformation of Old Age Security: Class and Politics in the American Welfare State* (Chicago: University of Chicago Press, 1988); Sheryl R. Tynes, *Turning Points in Social Security: From "Cruel Hoax" to "Sacred Entitlement"* (Stanford, CA: Stanford University Press, 1996); Carolyn L. Weaver, *The Crisis in Social Security: Economic and Political Origins* (Durham, NC: Duke Press Policy Studies, 1982). To this list, one can add two biographies written by historian Edward D. Berkowitz about key administrative figures of Social Security: *Robert Ball and the Politics of Social*

Security (Madison: University of Wisconsin Press, 2003), and *Mr. Social Security: The Life of Wilbur J. Cohen* (Lawrence: University Press of Kansas, 1995).

8. Giuliano Bonoli, *The Politics of Pension Reform: Institutions and Policy Change in Western Europe* (Cambridge: Cambridge University Press, 2000); Ann Shola Orloff, *The Politics of Pensions: A Comparative Analysis of Britain, Canada, and United States, 1880–1940* (Madison: University of Wisconsin Press, 1994); John Myles, *Old Age and the Welfare State,* 2d ed. (Lawrence: University Press of Kansas, 1989).

9. This theoretical development, which has affected all aspects of historical and social science research in the United States, is grounded in a critique of traditional perspectives on social and political order that emerged during the 1960s and 1970s in the context of feminist and civil rights mobilizations. Starting in the 1980s, attention to gender and race has increased significantly in the field of social policy research. An interesting way to measure the growing emphasis on gender and race in American social policy research is to compare the various editions of the following textbook: Bruce S. Jansson, *The Reluctant Welfare State,* 4th ed. (Belmont, CA: Wadsworth Publishing, 2000). The original, 1987 edition contains only a handful of references to gender, sexuality, and race, whereas the subsequent editions increasingly deal with these issues.

Chapter 1. Ideas, Institutions, and Social Security

1. For example: T. H. Marshall, *Citizenship and Social Class* (London: Pluto, 1992); Karl Polanyi, *The Great Transformation* (1944; repr., Boston: Beacon Press, 1957); Richard M. Titmuss, *Essays on 'the Welfare State,'* 2d ed. (1959; repr., Boston: Beacon Press, 1963).

2. John Myles and Jill Quadagno, "Political Theories of the Welfare State," *Social Service Review* 76, no. 1 (March 2002): 34–57.

3. In a way, such an eclectic perspective is advocated in John Williamson and Fred C. Pampel, *Old-Age Security in Comparative Perspective* (New York: Oxford University Press, 1993). For the authors, existing theories all contribute to our understanding of pension reform, and no attempt is made to design a better, more synthetic approach to welfare state development.

4. Daniel Béland and Jacob S. Hacker, "Ideas, Private Institutions, and American Welfare State 'Exceptionalism': The Case of Health and Old-Age Insurance in the United States, 1915–1965," *International Journal of Social Welfare* 13, no. 1 (2004): 42–54.

5. For example, Edwin Amenta, *Bold Relief: Institutional Politics and the Origins of Modern American Social Policy* (Princeton, NJ: Princeton University Press, 1998); Gøsta Esping-Andersen, *The Three Worlds of Welfare Capitalism* (Princeton, NJ: Princeton University Press, 1990); Theda Skocpol, *Protecting Soldiers and Mothers: The Political Origins of Social Policy in the United States* (Cambridge, MA: Belknap Press, 1992).

6. Williamson and Pampel, *Old-Age Security in Comparative Perspective,* 6.

7. Clark Kerr, John T. Dunlop, Frederick Harbison, and Charles A. Myers, *Industrialism and Industrial Man: The Problems of Labor and Management in Economic Growth,* 2d ed. (Oxford: Oxford University Press, 1964); Harold L. Wilen-

sky, *The Welfare State and Equality: Structural and Ideological Roots of Public Expenditures* (Berkeley: University of California Press, 1975).

8. Myles and Quadagno, "Political Theories of the Welfare State," 36.

9. Daniel Levine, *Poverty and Society: The Growth of the American Welfare State in International Comparison* (New Brunswick, NJ: Rutgers University Press, 1988); Roy Lubove, *The Struggles for Social Security, 1900–1935* (Cambridge, MA: Harvard University Press, 1968); Seymour Martin Lipset, *Continental Divide: The Values and Institutions of the United States and Canada* (New York: Routledge, 1990). For a critique of Levine, see Theda Skocpol, "Thinking Big: Can National Values Explain the Development of Social Provision in the United States? A Review Essay," *Journal of Policy History* 2 (1990): 425–438.

10. Levine, *Poverty and Society*, 11.

11. John L. Campbell, "Ideas, Politics, and Public Policy," *Annual Review of Sociology* 28 (2002): 21–38.

12. Lipset, *Continental Divide*, 136–151.

13. Skocpol, *Protecting Soldiers and Mothers*, 17.

14. For example: Hace Sorel Tishler, *Self-Reliance and Social Security, 1870–1917* (Port Washington, NY: National University Publications [Kennikat Press], 1971).

15. Béland and Hacker, "Ideas, Private Institutions, and American Welfare State 'Exceptionalism,'" 7.

16. Gøsta Esping-Andersen, *Politics against Markets: The Social Democratic Road to Power* (Princeton, NJ: Princeton University Press, 1985); Walter Korpi, *The Democratic Class Struggle* (Boston: Routledge and Kegan Paul, 1983).

17. Colin Gordon, "New Deal, Old Deck: Business and the Origins of Social Security, 1920–1935," *Politics and Society* 19 (1991): 165–207; Jill Quadagno, "Welfare Capitalism and the Social Security Act of 1935," *American Sociological Review* 45 (1984): 632–647; J. Craig Jenkins and Barbara G. Brents, "Social Protest, Hegemonic Competition, and Social Reform: A Political Struggle Interpretation of the Origins of the American Welfare State," *American Sociological Review* 54 (1989): 891–909.

18. William Domhoff, *State Autonomy or Class Dominance? Case Studies on Policy Making in America* (New York: Aldine de Gruyter, 1996). See also William Domhoff, "Corporate-Liberal Theory and the Social Security Act: A Chapter in the Sociology of Knowledge," *Politics and Society* 15 (1986–1987): 297–330.

19. Béland and Hacker, "Ideas, Private Institutions, and American Welfare State 'Exceptionalism,'" 7.

20. Moreover, in contradiction to the power resource argument, there is no evidence that labor unions have systematically played an instrumental role in the creation of modern social policies outside of Scandinavia: Williamson and Pampel, *Old-Age Security in Comparative Perspective.*

21. For example: Ellen M. Immergut, "The Theoretical Core of Institutionalism," *Politics and Society* 26 (1998): 5–34; Sven Steinmo, Kathleen Thelen, and Franck Longstreth, eds., *Structuring Politics: Historical Institutionalism in Comparative Analysis* (New York: Cambridge University Press, 1992); Skocpol, *Protecting Soldiers and Mothers*; Ann Shola Orloff, *The Politics of Pensions: A*

Comparative Analysis of Britain, Canada, and United States, 1880–1940 (Madison: University of Wisconsin Press, 1994); Ellen M. Immergut, *Health Politics: Interests and Institutions in Western Europe,* Cambridge Studies in Comparative Politics (Cambridge: Cambridge University Press, 1992); Antonia Maioni, *Parting at the Crossroads: The Emergence of Health Insurance in the United States and Canada* (Princeton, NJ: Princeton University Press, 1998); Paul Pierson, *Dismantling the Welfare State? Reagan, Thatcher, and the Politics of Retrenchment* (New York: Cambridge University Press, 1994); Sven Steinmo, *Taxation and Democracy: Swedish, British, and American Approaches to Financing the Modern State* (New Haven, CT: Yale University Press, 1993).

22. Theda Skocpol, "Bringing the State Back In: Strategies of Analysis in Current Research," in *Bringing the State Back In,* ed. Peter B. Evans, Dietrich Rueschemeyer, and Theda Skocpol (New York: Cambridge University Press, 1985), 9.

23. See Notes 17 and 18 for a list of references.

24. Amenta, *Bold Relief: Institutional Politics and the Origins of Modern American Social Policy;* Theda Skocpol and John Ikenberry, "Expanding Social Benefits: The Role of Social Security," *Political Science Quarterly* 102 (1987): 389–416; Theda Skocpol and Edwin Amenta, "Did Capitalists Shape Social Security?" *American Sociological Review* 50 (1985): 572–575.

25. Skocpol, "Thinking Big," 425–438.

26. Skocpol, *Protecting Soldiers and Mothers,* 41.

27. Ibid.

28. Maioni, *Parting at the Crossroads.*

29. Victoria C. Hattam, *Labor Visions and State Power: The Origins of Business Unionism in the United States* (Princeton, NJ: Princeton University Press, 1993), and William E. Forbath, *Law and the Shaping of the American Labor Movement* (Cambridge, MA: Harvard University Press, 1991).

30. Immergut, *Health Politics.*

31. Stephen J. Kay, "Unexpected Privatizations: Politics and Social Security Reform in the Southern Cone," *Comparative Politics* 31 (1999): 406. See also Daniel Béland, "Does Labor Matter? Institutions, Labor Unions, and Pension Reform in France and the United States," *Journal of Public Policy* 21 (2001): 153–172.

32. For example: Skocpol, *Protecting Soldiers and Mothers.*

33. Douglas C. North, *Institutions, Institutional Change, and Economic Performance* (New York: Cambridge University Press, 1990); Paul Pierson, "When Effect Becomes Cause: Policy Feedback and Political Change," *World Politics* 45 (1993): 595–628; Paul Pierson, "The New Politics of the Welfare State," *World Politics* 48 (1996): 143–179; Pierson, *Dismantling the Welfare State?;* Paul Pierson, "Increasing Returns, Path Dependence, and the Study of Politics," *American Political Science Review* 94 (2000): 251–267. On the concept of path dependence, see also Jacob S. Hacker, "The Historical Logic of National Health Insurance: Structure and Sequence in the Development of British, Canadian, and U.S. Medical Policy," *Studies in American Political Development* 12 (1998): 57–130. For a critical discussion about path dependence and institutional change, see Kathleen Thelen, *How Institutions Evolve: The Political Economy of Skills in Germany, Britain, the United States, and Japan* (Cambridge: Cambridge University Press, 2004).

34. For example: Paul Pierson, *Politics in Time: History, Institutions, and Social Analysis* (Princeton, NJ: Princeton University Press, 2004).

35. Béland and Hacker, "Ideas, Private Institutions, and American Welfare State 'Exceptionalism,'" 46 (italics in original).

36. Jacob S. Hacker, *The Divided Welfare State: The Battle over Public and Private Social Benefits in the United States* (Cambridge: Cambridge University Press, 2002).

37. Béland and Hacker, "Ideas, Private Institutions, and American Welfare State 'Exceptionalism.'"

38. Colin Gordon, "Why No Health Insurance in the US? The Limits of Social Provision in War and Peace, 1941-1948," *Journal of Policy History,* 9 (1997), 277–310; Christopher Howard, *The Hidden Welfare State: Tax Expenditures and Social Policy in the United States* (Princeton, NJ: Princeton University Press, 1997); Lucy apRoberts, *Les retraites aux Etats-Unis* (Paris: La Dispute, 2000).

39. Jacob S. Hacker and Paul Pierson, "Business Power and Social Policy: Employers and the Formation of the American Welfare State," *Politics and Society* 30, no. 2 (2002): 277–325. For a classic discussion about the variation in business power over time, see Fred Block, "The Ruling Class Does Not Rule," in *The Political Economy,* ed. Thomas Ferguson and Joel Rogers (1977; repr., Armonk, NY: M. E. Sharpe, 1984), 32–46.

40. Béland, "Does Labor Matter?"

41. The following section is adapted in part from Daniel Béland, "Ideas and Social Policy: An Institutionalist Perspective," *Social Policy and Administration* 39, no. 1 (January 2005): 1–18.

42. Elizabeth S. Clemens and James M. Cook, "Politics and Institutionalism: Explaining Durability and Change," *Annual Review of Sociology* 25 (1999): 442.

43. Béland and Hacker, "Ideas, Private Institutions, and American Welfare State 'Exceptionalism.'" On this issue, see also François-Xavier Merrien, *L'Etat-providence* (Paris: Presses Universitaires de France, 1997).

44. From a different perspective, Robert C. Lieberman discussed the relationship among ideas, institutions, and policy change in the United States: "Ideas, Institutions, and Political Order: Explaining Political Change," *American Political Science Review* 96, no. 4 (2002): 697–712. For an interesting analysis of the growing literature on ideas and public policy, see Campbell, "Ideas, Politics, and Public Policy," 21–38. On this issue, see also Mark Blyth, *Great Transformations* (New York: Cambridge University Press, 2002) and Vivien A. Schmidt, *The Futures of European Capitalism* (Oxford: Oxford University Press, 2002). Throughout the present book, the term *policy idea* refers to specific policy alternatives as well as the principles and causal beliefs in which these proposals are grounded.

45. Hugh Heclo, *Modern Social Politics in Britain and Sweden: From Relief to Income Maintenance* (New Haven, CT: Yale University Press, 1974), 305.

46. Desmond King and Randall A. Hansen, "Experts at Work: State Autonomy, Social Learning and Eugenic Sterilization in 1930s Britain," *British Journal of Political Science* 20 (1999): 78.

47. Béland and Hacker, "Ideas, Private Institutions, and American Welfare State 'Exceptionalism.'"

48. Skocpol, *Protecting Soldiers and Mothers.*

49. Pierson, "The New Politics of the Welfare State," 143–179.

50. Scholars exploring the impact of political institutions on identity formation take into account the link between ideas and institutions. Institutionalist research dealing with labor identity and nationalism provides ground to this claim: Hattam, *Labor Visions and State Power;* André Lecours, "Regionalism, Cultural Diversity, and the State in Spain," *Journal of Multilingual and Multicultural Development* 22, no. 3 (2001): 210–226.

51. Margaret Weir, *Politics and Jobs* (Princeton, NJ: Princeton University Press, 1992), 19.

52. Ibid., 19–20.

53. Peter A. Hall, "Policy Paradigms, Social Learning, and the State: The Case of Economic Policymaking in Britain," *Comparative Politics* 25, no. 3 (1993): 275–296.

54. Ibid.

55. Ibid.

56. King and Hansen, "Experts at Work."

57. John L. Campbell, "Institutional Analysis and the Role of Ideas in Political Economy," *Theory and Society* 27 (1998): 377–409.

58. John W. Kingdon, *Agendas, Alternatives, and Public Policies,* 2d ed. (New York: HarperCollins, 1995). Since the 1970s, agenda-setting studies have investigated the interaction among media, public opinion, and policymakers to explain why public issues rise and fall in importance over time: Stuart N. Soroka, *Agenda-Setting Dynamics in Canada* (Vancouver: University of British Columbia Press, 2002), 166. Historical institutionalist R. Kent Weaver referred to Kingdon's framework in his analysis of the 1996 welfare reform: *Ending Welfare as We Know It* (Washington, DC: Brookings Institution Press, 2000).

59. Kingdon, *Agendas,* 3.

60. Ibid.

61. Soroka, *Agenda-Setting Dynamics,* 7–8. Considering the fragmentation of political institutions in the United States, it seems necessary to distinguish between congressional and presidential policy agendas.

62. For example: Jacob S. Hacker, *The Road to Nowhere: The Genesis of President Clinton's Plan for Health Security* (Princeton, NJ: Princeton University Press, 1997), and Weaver, *Ending Welfare as We Know It.*

63. Kingdon, *Agendas,* 4.

64. One can note that, from an institutionalist perspective, the autonomy of the three streams is probably more limited than Kingdon would argue. As noted by Weir (*Politics and Jobs,* 18): "A historical perspective shows that these streams are linked in important ways over time. Policies from an earlier period can affect each of these streams at a later time. The conception of what the problems are and how they should be defined very often depends on previous policies, which establish some groups as authoritative voices in a particular field and make other perspectives less credible."

65. Ibid., 106.

66. Ibid., 90–164.

67. Kingdon, *Agendas,* 117.

68. Ideas as "road maps" are discussed in Judith Goldstein and Robert O. Keohane, "Ideas and Foreign Policy: An Analytical Framework" in *Ideas and Foreign Policy,* ed. J. Goldstein and R. O. Keohane (Ithaca, NY: Cornell University Press, 1993), 3–30. It is difficult to draw a strict line between cognitive and normative ideas, that is, between paradigms and programs. As opposed to what Campbell has proposed, it seems more accurate to understand paradigms as a form of knowledge and a plan for action.

69. Kingdon, *Agendas,* 122. According to Hendrick Spruyt, specific ideas cannot triumph in the political arena without the support of powerful interests: *The Sovereign State and Its Competitors: An Analysis of Systems Change* (Princeton, NJ: Princeton University Press, 1994).

70. The idea of ideological repertoire refers to a relatively articulated set of cultural symbols and political representations mobilized during policy debates to frame the issues and shape public opinion.

71. Campbell, "Institutional Analysis," 394. As opposed to the technical and epistemological assumptions at the foundation of policy paradigms, these ideas are located at the foreground of the policy debate: Ibid., 385.

72. Ibid. In their book about aging, Lawrence A. Powell, Kenneth J. Bronco, and John B. Williamson offer an interesting discussion about the role of frames in American policy debates: *Senior Rights Movement: Framing the Policy Debate in America* (New York: Twayne Publishers, 1996). For a critical discussion of the concept of frame that warns the reader against a static vision of the role of ideas in public policy, see Margaret Somers and Fred Block, "From Poverty to Perversity: Ideas, Markets and Institutions over 200 Years of Welfare Debate," *American Sociological Review* 70, no. 2 (2005): 260–287.

73. Campbell, "Institutional Analysis," 397. In a sense, the need for policymakers to frame issues using culturally accepted repertoires shows that "public opinion matters." On the role of public opinion, see Paul Burstein, "Bringing the Public Back In: Should Sociologists Consider the Impact of Public Opinion on Public Policy?" *Social Forces* 77 (1998): 27–62.

74. The Social Security Administration (SSA) discourse depicting Social Security as a saving scheme mediated by the federal government is an example of "strategic misconception" related to the framing process (see Chapter 4). Frames may also serve as ideational weapons oriented against enacted or proposed policies. In his book *The Rhetoric of Reaction,* for example, Albert O. Hirschman analyzed three types of conservative frames that have been used since the eighteenth century to undermine the support for egalitarian reforms and, more generally, left-wing political projects: *The Rhetoric of Reaction: Perversity, Futility, Jeopardy* (Cambridge, MA: Belknap Press of Harvard University Press, 2001).

75. Robert Henry Cox, "The Social Construction of an Imperative: Why Welfare Reform Happened in Denmark and the Netherlands but Not in Germany," *World Politics* 53 (2001): 475.

76. On the concept of "policy monopoly," see Frank R. Baumgartner and Bryan D. Jones, *Agendas and Instability in American Politics* (Chicago: University of Chicago Press, 1993).

77. Pierre Bourdieu, "Political Representation: Elements for a Theory of the Political Field," in *Language and Symbolic Power,* ed. J. B. Thompson (Oxford: Polity Press, 1991), 171–202.

78. As noted by Sewell, structures cannot exist without some sort of personal autonomy and historical contingency, and social actors sometimes do more than reproduce the field's rules of the game: William H. Sewell Jr., "A Theory of Structure: Duality, Agency, and Transformation," *American Journal of Sociology* 98 (1992): 1–29.

79. Hacker, *The Divided Welfare State.*

80. On the "politics of assumptions," see Paul Light, *Still Artful Work: The Continuing Politics of Social Security Reform* (New York: McGraw-Hill, 1995). Demographic fears and intergenerational equity will be discussed in Chapter 6.

81. For example: Anne-Marie Guillemard, "Re-Writing Social Policy and Changes within the Life Course Organisation: A European perspective," *Canadian Journal on Aging* 16, no. 3 (1997): 441–464.

82. Hacker, *The Divided Welfare State.*

83. Between 2000 and 2050, public pension expenditure in the United States is expected to increase from 4.2 to 7.0 percent of the GDP, a relatively modest figure by European standards. In Germany and Sweden, for example, public pension expenditure is expected to respectively increase from 11.5 and 11.1 percent of the GDP in 2000 to 17.5 and 14.5 percent in 2050: Giuliano Bonoli, *The Politics of Pension Reform: Institutions and Policy Change in Western Europe* (Cambridge: Cambridge University Press, 2000), 18.

84. Sylvester J. Schieber and John B. Shoven, *The Real Deal: The History and Future of Social Security* (New Haven, CT: Yale University Press, 1999).

85. John Myles and Paul Pierson, "The Comparative Political Economy of Pension Reform" in *The New Politics of the Welfare State,* ed. Paul Pierson (Oxford: Oxford University Press, 2001): 305–333.

86. Andrea Louise Campbell, *How Policies Make Citizens: Senior Citizen Activism and the American Welfare State* (Princeton, NJ: Princeton University Press, 2003).

87. Martha Derthick, *Policymaking for Social Security* (Washington, DC: Brookings Institution, 1979); Brian Balogh, "Securing Support: The Emergence of Social Security Board as a Political Actor," in *Federal Social Policy: The Historical Dimension,* ed. Donald T. Critchlow and Ellis W. Hawley (University Park: Pennsylvania State University Press, 1988), 55–78; Jerry R. Cates, *Insuring Inequality: Administrative Leadership in Social Security, 1935-1954* (Ann Arbor: University of Michigan Press, 1983); Sheryl R. Tynes, *Turning Points in Social Security: From "Cruel Hoax" to "Sacred Entitlement"* (Stanford, CA: Stanford University Press, 1996); Carolyn L. Weaver, *The Crisis in Social Security: Economic and Political Origins* (Durham, NC: Duke University Press Policy Studies, 1982). For a critical discussion of this issue, see Gary P. Freeman, "Voters, Bureaucrats, and the State: On the Autonomy of Social Security Policymaking" in *Social Security: The First Half-Century,* ed. Gerald D. Nash, Noel H. Pugach, and Richard F. Tomasson (Albuquerque: University of New Mexico Press, 1988), 145–180.

88. Edward D. Berkowitz, *Robert Ball and the Politics of Social Security* (Madison: University of Wisconsin Press, 2003).

89. On the crucial role of congressional committees during the postwar era, see Julian E. Zelizer, *Taxing America: Wilbur D. Mills, Congress, and the State, 1945–1975* (New York: Cambridge University Press, 1998). On the concept of credit claiming, see R. Kent Weaver, "The Politics of Blame Avoidance," *Journal of Public Policy* 6, no. 4 (1986): 371–398.

90. According to these authors, the strict dichotomy between "charity" and "contract" leaves no room for genuine social entitlements derived from citizenship: Nancy Frazer and Linda Gordon, "Contract versus Charity: Why Is There No Social Citizenship in the United States?" *Socialist Review* 22 (July 1992): 45–68.

91. The federal income tax expanded only during World War II, years after the enactment of the Social Security Act.

92. In her seminal book on Social Security expansion, for example, Derthick argued that the role of presidents in the politics of Social Security reform appeared to be relatively modest: *Policymaking for Social Security.*

93. Paul Pierson, *Dismantling the Welfare State.*

94. On this opposition, see Weaver, "The Politics of Blame Avoidance," 146–161. On the concept of credit claiming, see David R. Mayhew, *Congress: The Electoral Connection* (New Haven, CT: Yale University Press, 1974).

95. Myles and Quadagno, "Political Theories of the Welfare State."

96. Several well-known accounts dealing with gender or race are Michael K. Brown, *Race, Money, and the American Welfare State* (Ithaca, NY: Cornell University Press, 1999); Linda Gordon, *Pitied but Not Entitled: Single Mothers and the History of Welfare, 1890–1935* (New York: Free Press, 1994); Robert C. Lieberman, *Shifting the Color Line: Race and the American Welfare State* (Cambridge, MA: Harvard University Press, 1998); Suzanne Mettler, *Dividing Citizens: Gender and Federalism in New Deal Public Policy* (Ithaca, NY: Cornell University Press, 1998); Mary Poole, *The Segregated Origins of Social Security: African Americans and the Welfare State* (Chapel Hill: University of North Carolina Press, 2006); Jill Quadagno, *The Color of Welfare: How Racism Undermined the War on Poverty* (Oxford: Oxford University Press, 1994); Julia O'Connor, Ann Shola Orloff, and Sheila Shaver, *States, Markets, Families: Gender Liberalism and Social Policy in Australia, Canada, Great Britain, and the United States* (Cambridge: Cambridge University Press, 1999).

97. On the 1960s, see Terry H. Anderson, *The Movement and the Sixties* (Oxford: Oxford University Press, 1996).

98. Lieberman, *Shifting the Color Line;* Mettler, *Dividing Citizens;* Skocpol, *Protecting Soldiers and Mothers;* Theda Skocpol, "African Americans in U.S. Social Policy," in *Classifying by Race,* ed. Paul E. Peterson (Princeton, NJ: Princeton University Press, 1995), 129–155.

99. Social scientists studying race and gender generally view these categories as social and historical constructions, not purely biological phenomena. What they are interested in is how people understand these categories and how social and political institutions reflect them and the hierarchies they entail. This is the way I refer to race and gender through this book.

100. Quadagno, *The Color of Welfare.*

101. For example, *Social Politics,* the leading journal about gender and social

policy, has published many articles about welfare regimes that discuss the work of Esping-Andersen. The nature of this debate is illustrated in an article by Jane Lewis, a leading feminist scholar: "Gender and Welfare Regimes: Further Thoughts," *Social Politics: International Studies in Gender, State, and Society* 4 (1997): 160–177.

102. Esping-Andersen, *The Three Worlds of Welfare Capitalism.*

103. Brown, *Race, Money, and the American Welfare State,* 11. In the field of gender studies, Mettler explored the dual nature of American social policy during the New Deal: Mettler, *Divided Citizens.*

104. Linda Faye Williams, *The Constraint of Race: Legacies of White Skin Privilege in America* (University Park: Pennsylvania State University Press, 2003), 86.

105. Larry DeWitt, "It Was Not about Race: The Decision to Exclude Agricultural and Domestic Workers from the U. S. Social Security Program" (unpublished paper, July 2004); Gareth Davies and Martha Derthick, "Race and Social Welfare Policy: The Social Security Act of 1935," *Political Science Quarterly* 112, no. 2 (1997): 217–236.

106. In a way, Lieberman has already initiated this process of differentiation in his book, *Shifting the Color Line.* Yet, his book is probably better at measuring social and economic outcomes stemming from institutional and administrative legacies than at explaining policy choices, especially when dealing with Social Security reform.

107. Davies and Derthick, "Race and Social Welfare Policy."

108. For a general discussion of the American and international literature about the relationship between gender and social policy, see Ann Shola Orloff, "Gender and the Social Rights of Citizenship: The Comparative Analysis of Gender Relations and Welfare States," *American Sociological Review* 58 (1993): 303–328, and O'Connor, Orloff, and Shaver, *States, Markets, Families,* 1–42.

109. Mettler, *Dividing Citizens,* 15–16.

110. Skocpol, *Protecting Soldiers and Mothers.*

111. For example: Frazer and Gordon, "Contract versus Charity."

Chapter 2. Setting the Reform Agenda

1. John B. Williamson and Fred C. Pampel, *Old-Age Security in Comparative Perspective* (New York: Oxford University Press, 1993).

2. German chancellor Otto von Bismarck was interested in social policy partly because he admired the way in which French emperor Napoléon III had used modest social programs as social control devices against class discontent: Gaston V. Rimlinger, *Welfare Policy and Industrialization in Europe, America, and Russia* (New York: John Wiley and Sons, 1971), 106.

3. Williamson and Pampel, *Old-Age Security in Comparative Perspective,* 44. In 1925, Britain enacted a contributory pension scheme.

4. Ibid., 80.

5. Ann Shola Orloff, *The Politics of Pensions: A Comparative Analysis of Britain, Canada, and the United States, 1880–1940* (Madison: University of Wisconsin Press, 1993), 14.

6. In Germany, for example, covered workers would not be entitled to old age

benefits before age seventy. In the 1880s, the average male life expectancy was no more than forty-five, and only 20 percent of German wageworkers survived to age seventy: Williamson and Pampel, *Old Age Security in Comparative Perspective,* 27–28.

7. For example, Bruce Ackerman defined three essential transformative moments in U.S. constitutional politics: the 1780s, the Reconstruction, and the New Deal: *We the People: The Foundations* (Cambridge, MA: Belknap Press, 1990).

8. Sven Steinmo and Jon Watts, "It's the Institutions, Stupid! Why Comprehensive National Health Care Fails in America," *Journal of Health Politics, Policy, and Law* 20 (1995): 329–372. For a critique of this reductionist perspective, see Jacob S. Hacker, "Learning from Defeat? Political Analysis and the Failure of Health Care Reform in the United States," *British Journal of Political Science* 31, no. 1 (2001): 61–94.

9. Jacob S. Hacker, "The Historical Logic of National Health Insurance: Structure and Sequence in the Development of British, Canadian, and U.S. Medical Policy," *Studies in American Political Development* 12 (1998): 57–130.

10. Bruno Théret, "Regionalism and Federalism: A Comparative Analysis of the Regulation of Economic Tensions between Regions by Canadian and American Federal Intergovernmental Transfer Programmes," *International Journal of Urban and Regional Research* 23, no. 3 (1999): 479–512.

11. On the idea of a "race to the bottom," see Martha Derthick, "Up-To-Date in Kansas City: Reflections on American Federalism," *PS: Political Science and Politics* 25, no. 4 (December 1992): 671–675.

12. Jacob S. Hacker and Paul Pierson, "Business Power and Social Policy: Employers and the Formation of the American Welfare State," *Politics and Society* 30, no. 2 (2002): 277–325.

13. Jill Quadagno, *The Transformation of Old Age Security: Class and Politics in the American Welfare State* (Chicago: University of Chicago Press, 1988). On the impact of race in the South during the Progressive Era, see Jack T. Kirby, *Darkness at the Dawning: Race and Reform in the Progressive South* (Philadelphia: Lippincott, 1972).

14. Richard E. Ellis, *The Union at Risk: Jacksonian Democracy, States' Rights, and the Nullification Crisis* (New York: Oxford University Press, 1987).

15. Daniel Béland and François Vergniolle de Chantal, "Fighting 'Big Government': Frames, Federalism, and Social Policy Reform in the United States," *Canadian Journal of Sociology* 29, no. 2 (2004): 241–264.

16. Theda Skocpol, *Protecting Soldiers and Mothers: The Political Origins of Social Policy in the United States* (Cambridge, MA: Belknap Press, 1992).

17. Stephen Skowronek, *Building a New American State: The Expansion of National Administrative Capacities, 1877–1920* (New York: Cambridge University Press, 1982).

18. Skocpol, *Protecting Soldiers and Mothers,* 75.

19. Robert M. Maranto and David S. Schutz, *A Short History of the United States Civil Service* (New York: University Press of America, 1991), 46.

20. For example: Quadagno, *The Transformation of Old Age Security.*

21. William Henry Glasson, *History of Military Pensions Legislation in the United States* (New York: Columbia University Press, 1900), 76.

22. Orloff, *The Politics of Pensions*, 136.

23. Ibid.

24. For example: Quadagno, *The Transformation of Old Age Security*, 30–33.

25. Richard F. Bensel, *Sectionalism and American Political Development, 1880–1980* (Madison: University of Wisconsin Press, 1984), 64.

26. Ann Shola Orloff and Theda Skocpol, "Why Not Equal Protection? Explaining the Politics of Public Social Spending in Britain, 1900–1911, and the United States, 1880s–1920," *American Sociological Review* 49 (December 1984): 726–750.

27. Charles Richmond Henderson, *Industrial Insurance in the United States* (Chicago: University of Chicago Press, 1909), 277.

28. Henry Rodger Seager, *Social Insurance* (New York: Macmillan, 1910), 145.

29. Skocpol, *Protecting Soldiers and Mothers*, 156–157.

30. Hacker and Pierson, "Business Power and Social Policy."

31. Orloff, *The Politics of Pensions*, 136.

32. Isaac M. Rubinow, *Social Insurance: With Special Reference to American Conditions* (New York: Henry Holt and Company, 1913), 408 (italics in original).

33. Michel R. Dahlin, "From Poorhouse to Pensions: The Changing View of Old Age in America, 1890–1929" (Ph.D. diss., Stanford University, 1983).

34. Ibid.

35. William Glasson, *Federal Military Pensions in the United States* (New York: Oxford University Press, 1918), 273–280.

36. For example: Michel R. Dahlin, "Symbols of the Old Age Pension Movement: The Poorhouse, the Family, and the 'Childlike' Elderly," in *Societal Impact on Aging: Historical Perspectives*, ed. K. Warner Shaie and W. Andrew Achenbaum (New York: Springer Publishing Company, 1993), 123–129.

37. This was, for example, the case in France at the turn of the twentieth century: Anne-Marie Guillemard, *Aging and the Welfare State Crisis* (Newark: University of Delaware Press, 2000).

38. For a general discussion about this issue, see John Myles, *Old Age and the Welfare State*, 2d ed. (Lawrence: University Press of Kansas, 1989).

39. Hace Sorel Tishler, *Self-Reliance and Social Security, 1870–1917* (Port Washington, NY: Kennikat Press, 1971), xi.

40. Carole Haber and Brian Gratton, *Old Age and the Search for Security: An American Social History* (Bloomington: Indiana University Press, 1994).

41. Abraham Epstein, *Facing Old Age: A Study of Old Age Dependency in the United States and Old Age Pensions* (New York: Alfred A. Knopf, 1922), and *The Challenge of the Aged* (New York: Vanguard Press, 1928); Rubinow, *Social Insurance*, 301–328; Henry L. Seager, *Social Insurance* (New York: Macmillan, 1910), 115–145; Lee W. Squier, *Old Age Dependency in the United States: A Complete Survey of the Pension Movement* (New York: Macmillan, 1912).

42. Seager, *Social Insurance*, 117.

43. Charles F. Thwing and Carrie F. Butler Thwing, *The Family: An Historical and Social Study* (Boston: Lathrop, Lee and Shephard, 1913), 141.

44. Rubinow, *Social Insurance*, 302.

45. Concerning the history of age discrimination, see William Graebner, *A History of Retirement: The Meaning and the Function of an American Institution*

(New Haven, CT: Yale University Press, 1980). According to this author, reformers were right to say that there was a link between new managerial practices and age discrimination. He specified that these tendencies truly materialized only during the 1930s, however, under the auspices of the federal government. For a stimulating discussion concerning the issue, see Haber and Gratton, *Old Age and the Search for Security.*

46. For example: Squier, *Old Age Dependency in the United States,* 272.

47. Epstein, *The Challenge of the Aged,* 4.

48. Ibid., 31.

49. Ibid.

50. Dahlin, *From Poorhouse to Pension,* 40.

51. Haber and Gratton, *Old Age and the Search for Security,* 122.

52. Ibid.

53. Harry C. Evans, *The American Poorfarm and Its Inmates* (Moosehearth, IL: Loyal Order of the Moose, 1926), 5.

54. Lawrence A. Powell, Kenneth J. Bronco, and John B. Williamson, *Senior Rights Movement: Framing the Policy Debate in America* (New York: Twayne Publishers, 1996), 63–67.

55. Ibid.

56. For example, Epstein, *The Challenge of the Aged,* 149–205.

57. Steven A. Sass, *The Promise of Private Pension: The First Hundred Years* (Cambridge, MA: Harvard University Press, 1997), 18

58. Jennifer Klein, *For All These Rights: Business, Labor, and the Shaping of America's Public-Private Welfare State* (Princeton, NJ: Princeton University Press, 2003), 61.

59. For a general discussion concerning welfare capitalism, see Stuart D. Brandes, *American Welfare Capitalism, 1880–1940* (Chicago: University of Chicago Press, 1978).

60. Jacob S. Hacker, *The Divided Welfare State: The Battle over Public and Private Social Benefits in the United States* (Cambridge: Cambridge University Press, 2002), 89. At the beginning of the 1930s, 140,000 out of 6.5 million Americans aged sixty-five and older were actually entitled to private pension benefits.

61. Epstein, *The Challenge of the Aged,* 163.

62. Although labor unions criticized the paternalistic nature of welfare capitalism, the high costs undermined the development of trade union pension plans. According to Latimer, only 18,000 retirees were receiving pensions under these plans as late as 1931: Murray Latimer, *Trade Union Pension Systems and Other Superannuation and Permanent and Total Disability Benefits in the United States and Canada* (New York: Industrial Relations Counselors, 1932).

63. Rubinow, *Social Insurance,* 313.

64. On this issue, see François Ewald, *L'État-providence* (Paris: Grasset, 1986), and Henri Hatzfeld, *Du paupérisme à la sécurité sociale, 1850–1940* (Paris: Armand Colin, 1971).

65. On this concept, which refers to the relationship between individualism and private property in old liberalism, see C. B. Macpherson, *The Political Theory of Possessive Individualism* (Oxford: Oxford University Press, 1962).

66. As opposed to their British counterparts, however, American fraternal societies seldom offered pension provisions to their members. "In Massachusetts in 1907 only three out of 117 fraternal associations had such provisions": Epstein, *The Challenge of the Aged,* 195. In this context, they never formed a significant obstacle to reform, at least in terms of entrenched interests. On the development of fraternal societies in the United States, see David T. Beito, *From Mutual Aid to the Welfare State: Fraternal Societies and Social Services, 1890–1967* (Chapel Hill: University of North Carolina Press, 2000).

67. Powell, Bronco and Williamson, *Senior Rights Movement,* 61.

68. John Graham Brooks, *Compulsory Insurance in Germany* (Washington, DC: U.S. Government Printing Office, 1893); William Franklin, *Workingmen's Insurance* (New York: Thomas Y. Crowell, 1898). On the reformers' relationship to the European experience during the Progressive Era, see Daniel T. Rodgers, *Atlantic Crossings: Social Politics in a Progressive Age* (Cambridge, MA: Harvard University Press, 2000).

69. Between 1908 and 1910, for example, the membership of the AALL increased from 300 to 2,000: David A. Moss, *Socializing Security: Progressive-Era Economists and the Origins of American Social Policy* (Cambridge, MA: Harvard University Press, 1995), 6. In 1911, the publication of the *American Labor Legislation Review* further increased the organization's public profile.

70. Roy Lubove, *The Struggle for Social Security, 1900–1935* (Cambridge, MA: Harvard University Press, 1968), 45–65, and Tishler, *Self-Reliance and Social Security.*

71. On unemployment insurance, see Daniel Nelson, *Unemployment Insurance: The American Experience, 1915–1935* (Madison: University of Wisconsin Press, 1969); Udo Sautter, *Three Cheers for the Unemployed: Government and Unemployment before the New Deal* (Cambridge: Cambridge University Press, 1991). Regarding health insurance, the best history is Ronald L. Numbers, *Almost Persuaded: American Physicians and Compulsory Health Insurance, 1912–1920* (Baltimore, MD: Johns Hopkins University Press, 1978).

72. Daniel Béland and Jacob S. Hacker, "Ideas, Private Institutions, and American Welfare State 'Exceptionalism': The Case of Health and Old-Age Insurance in the United States, 1915–1965," *International Journal of Social Welfare* 13, no. 1 (2004): 42–54. On this issue, see also Hacker and Pierson, "Business Power and Social Policy, 277–325.

73. Samuel Gompers, *Labor and the Common Welfare* (New York: E. P. Dutton, 1919).

74. Victoria C. Hattam, *Labor Visions and State Power: The Origins of Business Unionism in the United States* (Princeton, NJ: Princeton University Press, 1993), and William E. Forbath, *Law and the Shaping of the American Labor Movement* (Cambridge, MA: Harvard University Press, 1991).

75. Hattam, *Labor Visions and State Power,* iv.

76. Bruno Dumons and Gilles Pollet, *L'Etat et les retraites: Genèse d'une politique* (Paris: Belin, 1994). Like its American counterpart, the early-twentieth-century French labor movement was both relatively weak (low membership) and fragmented (ideological divisions). Historically, most unions adopted a

radical and pugnacious attitude toward the centralized French government stemming from their fear of the ever-centralized French government. Such an attitude could not hide their institutional and political weakness. Powerless labor unions tend to oppose collaboration with strong governments: Seymour Martin Lipset, "Radicalism or Reformism: The Sources of Working-Class Politics," *American Political Science Review* 77, no. 1 (March 1983): 1–18, and Gary Marks, *Unions in Politics: Britain, Germany, and the U.S. in the Nineteenth and Early Twentieth Centuries* (Princeton, NJ: Princeton University Press, 1989).

77. John Andrews to Olga Halsey, January 27, 1915, AALL Papers, reel 13, cited in Moss, *Socializing Security,* 59.

78. For example, see "Practical Program for the Prevention of Unemployment in America," *American Labor Legislation Review* 5 (June 1915): 189–191.

79. Moss, *Socializing Security.*

80. John B. Andrews, "Old-age Pensions; Their Basis in Social Need," *American Labor Legislation Review* 19, no. 4 (December 1929): 357.

81. For example: William Graebner, "Federalism in the Progressive Era: A Structural Interpretation of Reform," *Journal of American History* 64 (1977): 331–357.

82. In 1909, for example, the AFL supported a federal bill on old age pensions: Skocpol, *Protecting Soldiers and Mothers,* 233.

83. Quadagno, *The Transformation of Old Age Security,* 64–66.

84. Ibid., 67–68.

85. See John B. Andrews, "Progress in Old Age Pension Legislation," *The American Labor Legislation Review* 13 (March 1923): 48.

86. Louis Leotta, "Abraham Epstein and the Movement for Old Age Security," *Labor History* 10 (Summer 1975): 359–377.

87. Ibid.

88. Ibid.

89. *Old-Age Security Herald,* April 4, 1930, 1.

90. Béland and Hacker, "Ideas, Private Institutions, and American Welfare State Exceptionalism."

91. By 1927, however, politicians knew that such block voting was not the case, and under the pressure of the AMA, Congress did not renew the act: Skocpol, *Protecting Soldiers and Mothers.* One should note that the Sheppard-Towner Act was possible in the first place because the Supreme Court of the time had a more positive attitude toward programs designed to protect women than toward social insurance and labor legislations.

92. Hacker and Pierson, "Business Power and Social Security." Yet, even the modest Sheppard-Towner Act did not survive long: the legislation expired in 1929, barely seven years after its implementation.

93. Lubove, *The Struggle for Social Security,* 135.

94. Leotta, "Abraham Epstein and the Movement for Old Age Security," 372–373.

95. Graebner, *A History of Retirement,* 57–87. For a general discussion concerning the development of public sector pensions in the United States, see Robert L. Clark, Lee A. Craig, and Jack W. Wilson, *A History of Public Sector Pensions in the United States* (Philadelphia: University of Pennsylvania Press, 2003).

96. Skocpol, *Protecting Soldiers and Mothers.*

97. On the modest nature of mothers' pensions, see Linda Gordon, *Pitied but Not Entitled* (New York: Free Press, 1994); Mark H. Leff, "Consensus for Reform: The Mothers' Pension Movement in the Progressive Era," *Social Service Review* 47, no. 3 (1973): 397–417.

Chapter 3. Enacting Old Age Insurance

1. Business and labor interests seemed more concerned with what would become of the Wagner Act on collective bargaining than with an old age insurance scheme that would only have a long-term impact on U.S. labor relations.

2. Gaston V. Rimlinger, *Welfare Policy and Industrialization in Europe, America, and Russia* (New York: John Wiley, 1971). See also James T. Patterson, *America's Struggle against Poverty, 1900–1994*, 2d ed. (Cambridge, MA: Harvard University Press, 1994), 41–42

3. Irving Bernstein, *A Caring Society: The New Deal, the Worker, and the Great Depression* (Boston: Houghton Mifflin, 1985), 21. Three more figures illustrate the radical nature of this economic crisis. Between 1929 and 1933, the GDP fell by 29 percent, consumption by 18 percent, and investment by 98 percent: Robert S. McElvaine, *The Great Depression: America, 1929–1941* (New York: Times Books, 1984), 75.

4. Carole Haber and Brian Gratton, *Old Age and the Search for Security: An American Social History* (Bloomington: Indiana University Press, 1994), 42–43.

5. Abraham Epstein, *Insecurity: A Challenge to America: A Study of Social Insurance in the United States and Abroad* (New York: Harrison Smith and Robert Haas, 1933), 112.

6. Stuart D. Brandes, *American Welfare Capitalism, 1880–1940* (Chicago: University of Chicago Press, 1978), 146.

7. For example: Epstein, *Insecurity*, 143–148.

8. Jacob S. Hacker and Paul Pierson, "Business Power and Social Policy: Employers and the Formation of the American Welfare State," *Politics and Society* 30, no. 2 (2002): 297.

9. Ibid., 298.

10. Steven A. Sass, *The Promise of Private Pension: The First Hundred Years* (Cambridge, MA: Harvard University Press, 1997), 80.

11. Paul H. Douglas, *Social Security in the United States* (New York: Whittlesey House, 1936), 7.

12. "State Action on Pensions for Aged Citizens," *Congressional Digest* 14, no. 3 (March 1935): 71–72.

13. James T. Patterson, *The New Deal and the States: Federalism in Transition* (Princeton, NJ: Princeton University Press, 1969), 32–33.

14. Carolyn L. Weaver, *The Crisis in Social Security: Economic and Political Origins* (Durham, NC: Duke Press Policy Studies, 1982), 59–60.

15. For example: Isaac M. Rubinow, *The Quest for Security* (New York: H. Holt, 1934), 287.

16. Bruce Ackerman, *We the People: The Foundations* (Cambridge, MA: Belknap Press, 1990), 47–50.

17. The Republican Party dominated Congress during the 1920s and early 1930s, but the 1932 elections resulted in a Democratic landslide victory. In the 67th Congress, there were 313 House Democrats facing only 117 Republicans and five independents. In the Senate, 59 Democrats faced 36 Republicans. Yet, these impressive numbers should not hide that fact that the Democratic Party remained divided between liberal and more conservative politicians who frequently held contrasting views on civil rights and economic issues.

18. Stephen Skowronek, *The Politics Presidents Make: Leadership from John Adams to Bill Clinton* (Cambridge, MA: Harvard University Press, 1997), 294.

19. William W. Bremer, "Along the Way: The New Deal's Work Relief Programs for the Unemployment," *Journal of American History* 62 (December 1975): 636–652.

20. In 1938, for example, social spending represented 6.3 percent of the GDP in the United States. Compared to France (3.47 percent) and Great Britain (5.01 percent), this figure shows that the United States was anything but "lagging behind" in terms of welfare state development: Edwin Amenta, *Bold Relief: Institutional Politics and the Origins of Modern Social Policy* (Princeton, NJ: Princeton University Press, 1998), 5.

21. It is worth noting that, in addition to federal aid, states provided some welfare benefits to the unemployed.

22. On this "ideology of security," see Jennifer Klein, *For All These Rights: Business, Labor, and the Shaping of America's Public-Private Welfare State* (Princeton, NJ: Princeton University Press, 2003).

23. Still governor of Louisiana when elected to the Senate, Long waited until January 1932 before traveling to Washington to take his oath of office. For that reason, he only served in the Senate from 1932 until his death in 1935.

24. Alan Brinkley, *Voices of Protest: Huey Long, Father Coughlin, and the Great Depression* (New York: Random House, 1982), 72–73.

25. Upton Sinclair, *I, Governor of California, and How I Ended Poverty: A True Story of the Future* (New York: Farrar and Rinehart, 1933). In his book, Sinclair called for the instauration of a sixty dollar monthly pension to all residents of California aged sixty and older. Although Sinclair never became governor of California, his EPIC movement rapidly gained a large audience beyond the state's borders: Clarence McIntosh, "Upton Sinclair and the EPIC Movement" (Ph.D. diss., Stanford University, 1955).

26. For example, see Jackson K. Putman, *Old-Age in California: From Richardson to Reagan* (Stanford, CA: Stanford University Press, 1970), 51, and Twentieth Century Fund, Committee on Old Age Security, *The Townsend Crusade* (New York: Twentieth Century Fund, 1936), 18.

27. Abraham Holtzman, *The Townsend Movement* (New York: Bookman Associates, 1963), 36. At first, Townsend argued that a new federal sales tax could finance his plan before he finally opted for a tax on economic transactions. On the Townsend Plan see also Edwin Amenta, *When Movements Matter* (Princeton, NJ: Princeton University Press, 2006).

28. It is worth noting that the slogan of the Townsend movement was "Youth for Work, Age for Leisure."

29. Holtzman, *The Townsend Movement,* 45.

30. Mabel L. Walker, *The Townsend Plan Analyzed* (New York: Tax Policy League, 1936), 31.

31. Holtzman, *The Townsend Movement,* 109. The title of Witte's 1935 unpublished report to the CES illustrates the dominant perception of the time: "Why the Townsend Old Age Revolving Pension Plan Is Impossible" (Washington, DC, Committee on Economic Security).

32. For example: Richard I. Neuberger and Kelly Loe, *An Army of the Aged* (Caldwell, ID: Caxton Printers, 1936). It is worth noting that a survey conducted in December 1935 showed that only 3.8 percent of the population as a whole supported the Townsend Plan. Claims concerning its popularity may have been inflated: Twentieth Century Fund, *The Townsend Crusade,* 14.

33. Holtzman, *The Townsend Movement.*

34. The AALL proposals emphasized microeconomic goals such as improving efficiency at the firm level, whereas the Townsend Plan focused on macroeconomic goals such as increasing aggregate demand. I would like to thank Edward Berkowitz for his insight about this issue.

35. Holtzman, *The Townsend Movement.*

36. William Leuchtenburg, *FDR and the New Deal, 1932–1940* (New York: Harper and Row, 1963), 331.

37. For example: "Republican Declaration on Policy," *New York Times,* June 7, 1934, 1.

38. For a discussion about this issue, see Sheryl R. Tynes, *Turning Points in Social Security: From "Cruel Hoax" to "Sacred Entitlement"* (Stanford, CA: Stanford University Press, 1996), 49–50.

39. In 1934, both major federal parties supported the idea of federal grants-in-aid in the field of old age pensions: American Association for Old Age Security, "Both Major Parties Promise Social Legislation," *AAOAS Bulletin* 8 (June-July 1934): 5–6.

40. On the numerous old age pension legislations debated in 1934, see "Efforts Seeking Federal Action on Old-Age Pensions 1909–1935," *Congressional Digest* 14, no. 3 (March 1935): 76.

41. Louis Leotta, "Abraham Epstein and the Movement for Old Age Security," *Labor History* 10 (Summer 1975): 359–377.

42. Douglas, *Social Security in the United States,* 10–11. For the same reason, the president also stated that he would not support proposed unemployment insurance legislation in order to push for his own omnibus bill on economic security.

43. Ibid.

44. "Message to Congress Reviewing the Broad Objectives and Accomplishments of the Administration, June 8, 1934," reprinted in *The Report of the Committee on Economic Security of 1935 and Other Basic Documents Relating to the Development of the Social Security Act: Fiftieth Anniversary Edition* (Washington, DC: National Conference on Social Welfare, 1985), 138.

45. Arthur J. Altmeyer, *The Formative Years of Social Security* (Madison: University of Wisconsin Press, 1965), 258.

46. The year before, the Wisconsin legislature had enacted the first unemployment insurance program in the United States.

47. John B. Andrews, "Old-age Pensions; Their Basis in Social Need," *American Labor Legislation Review* 19, no. 4 (December 1929): 357.

48. On the opposition between these two models, see G. John Ikenberry and Theda Skocpol, "Expanding Social Benefits: The Role of Social Security," *Political Science Quarterly* 102, no. 3 (Fall 1987): 389–416.

49. Daniel Béland and Jacob S. Hacker, "Ideas, Private Institutions, and American Welfare State 'Exceptionalism': The Case of Health and Old-Age Insurance in the United States, 1915–1965," *International Journal of Social Welfare* 13, no. 1 (2004): 42–54. On this issue, see Edward D. Berkowitz and Kim McQuaid, *Creating the Welfare State: The Political Economy of Twentieth-Century Reform,* rev. ed. (Lawrence: University Press of Kansas, 1992), and Daniel T. Rodgers, *Atlantic Crossings: Social Politics in a Progressive Age* (Cambridge, MA: Harvard University Press, 2000), 444.

50. Raymond Richards, *Closing the Door to Destitution: The Shaping of the Social Security Acts of the United States and New Zealand* (University Park: Pennsylvania State University Press, 1994), 138. One of Roosevelt's initial law partners, Langdon P. Marvin, was also a director of the Metropolitan Life.

51. For example: "Roosevelt Pleads for Job Insurance," *New York Times,* March 7, 1934, 34. For a discussion concerning Roosevelt's policy stances during his tenure as governor of New York, see also Bernard Bellush, *Franklin D. Roosevelt as Governor of New York* (New York: AMS Press, 1968), and Daniel R. Fusfeld, *The Economic Thought of FDR and the Origins of the New Deal* (New York: Columbia University Press, 1955).

52. Frances Perkins, *The Roosevelt I Knew* (New York: Viking, 1946), 282.

53. Arthur Schlesinger, *The Coming of the New Deal* (Boston: Houghton Mifflin, 1959), 308–309. See also Perkins, *The Roosevelt I Knew,* 281–283.

54. Mark H. Leff, "Taxing the 'Forgotten Man': The Politics of Social Security Finance in the New Deal," *Journal of American History* 70, no. 2 (September 1983): 359–379. See also Mark H. Leff, *New Deal and Taxation, 1933–1939: The Limits of Symbolic Reform* (Cambridge: Cambridge University Press, 1984).

55. Metropolitan Life, *British Experience with Unemployment Insurance,* Series on Social Insurance, Monograph no. 6 (New York: Metropolitan Life, 1932), 18.

56. The report of the CES formulates many remarks concerning the inadequacy of private provisions: Committee on Economic Security, *The Report of the Committee on Economic Security of 1935.*

57. Franklin D. Roosevelt, "Executive Order Establishing the Committee on Economic Security and the Advisory Council on Economic Security," reprinted in Edwin E. Witte, *The Development of the Social Security Act* (Madison: University of Wisconsin Press, 1963), 201–202.

58. Bernstein, *A Caring Society,* 51.

59. On Witte, see Theron F. Schlabach, *Edwin E. Witte: Cautious Reformer* (Madison, WI: State Historical Society, 1969).

60. On this issue, see J. Lee Kreader, "American Prophet for Social Security: A Biography of Isaac Max Rubinow" (Ph.D. diss., University of Chicago, 1988), 627–636.

61. Witte's personal recollections still represent the best available survey of the CES's activities: *The Development of the Social Security Act* (Madison: University of Wisconsin Press, 1963).

62. Committee on Economic Security, *The Report of the Committee on Economic Security of 1935.*

63. On the Railroad Retirement Act, see William Graebner, *A History of Retirement: The Meaning and the Function of an American Institution* (New Haven, CT: Yale University Press, 1980), 153–180.

64. Committee on Economic Security, *The Report of the Committee on Economic Security of 1935.*

65. J. Douglas Brown, *An American Philosophy of Social Security* (Princeton, NJ: Princeton University Press, 1972), 17–22.

66. On that issue, see Suzanne Mettler, *Dividing Citizens: Gender and Federalism in New Deal Public Policy* (Ithaca, NY: Cornell University Press, 1998), 64–65.

67. Brown, *An American Philosophy of Social Security,* 132.

68. Jill Quadagno, *The Transformation of Old Age Security: Class and Politics in the American Welfare State* (Chicago: University of Chicago Press, 1988), 112. See also Jill Quadagno, "Welfare Capitalism and the Social Security Act of 1935," *American Sociological Review* 49 (October 1984): 632–647. The five business representatives on the Advisory Council were Gerard Swope (General Electric), Morris Leeds (Leeds and Northrup), Sam Lewisohn (Miami Copper), Marion Folsom (Eastman Kodak), and Walter Teagle (Standard Oil). Among these figures, Folsom was certainly the most knowledgeable and influential. On Folsom, see Sanford Jacoby, "Employers and the Welfare State: The Role of Marion B. Folsom," *Journal of American History* 80, no. 2 (1993): 525–556.

69. Brown, *An American Philosophy of Social Security,* 21–22.

70. Arthur Altmeyer, interview by Peter A. Corning, Department of Health, Education, and Welfare, Washington, DC, September 3, 1965, Columbia Oral History Project.

71. On the relative autonomy of the CES, see Ikenberry and Skocpol, "Expanding Social Benefits."

72. Edward D. Berkowitz, "History and Social Security Reform" in *Social Security and Medicare: Individual vs. Collective Risk and Responsibility,* ed. Eric Kingson, Sheila Burke, and Uwe Reinhardt (Washington, DC: Brookings Institution, 2000), 31–55. See also Schlabach, *Edwin E. Witte,* 110–112.

73. Committee on Economic Security, *The Report of the Committee on Economic Security.*

74. Ibid., 29.

75. Daniel Béland, "Does Labor Matter? Institutions, Labor Unions, and Pension Reform in France and the United States," *Journal of Public Policy* 21 (2001): 153–172.

76. On this issue, see Colin Gordon, "Why No Corporatism in the United States? Business Disorganization and Its Consequences," *Business and Economic History* 27, no. 1 (Fall 1998): 29–46.

77. Weaver, *The Crisis in Social Security,* 74–75.

78. I would like to thank Jacob Hacker for his insight about this issue. For

a general discussion about the "chronic disorganization" of business interests in the United States, see Gordon, "Why No Corporatism in the United States?"

79. For a detailed analysis of the opposition and the support for old age insurance in 1935, see Tynes, *Turning Points in Social Security,* 50–59.

80. Quoted in *Hearings before the Committee on Ways and Means, House of Representatives on H.R. 4120* (Washington, DC: U.S. Government Printing Office, 1935), 1027.

81. Quoted in *Hearings before the Committee on Finance, United States Senate on S. 1130* (Washington, DC: U.S. Government Printing Office, 1935), 915.

82. Ibid., 1917.

83. Robert M. Collins, *The Business Response to Keynes* (New York: Columbia University Press, 1981).

84. Hacker and Pierson, "Business Power and Social Security."

85. Ibid.

86. Testimony in *Hearings before the Committee on Ways and Means, House of Representatives on H.R. 4120,* 587–597.

87. Holtzman, *The Townsend Movement,* 91.

88. Testimony in *Hearings before the Committee on Finance, United States Senate on S. 1130,* 1016–1051. See also *Hearings before the Committee on Ways and Means, House of Representatives on H.R. 4120,* 667–700.

89. Holtzman, *The Townsend Movement.*

90. Altmeyer, *The Formative Years of Social Security,* 32.

91. Testimony in *Hearings before the Committee on Ways and Means, House of Representatives on H.R. 4120,* 391.

92. Testimony in *Hearings before the Committee on Finance, United States Senate on S. 1130,* 181.

93. For a discussion concerning this issue, see Edwin Witte, "Organized Labor and Social Security" in *Labor and the New Deal,* ed. Milton Derber and Edwin Young (Madison: University of Wisconsin Press, 1957): 239–274.

94. Furthermore, during his testimonies to the legislative committees, Green did not contest the proposed federal government's full managerial control over old age insurance. On the relative lack of interest in old age insurance in 1934–1935, see Berkowitz, "History and Social Security Reform."

95. Testimony in *Hearings Before the Committee on Ways and Means, House of Representatives on H.R. 4120,* 559.

96. "I agree that agricultural workers and domestic service should come out. Our advisory council recommended that it be excluded also. The Cabinet committee plan included them, but we think they should be excluded. Eventually they might be brought in, but right now we would cut them out." Testimony of Marion Folsom, Eastman Kodak and CES Advisory Council, *Hearings before the Committee on Finance, United States Senate on S. 1130,* 576.

97. Testimony of Abraham Epstein, *Hearings Before the Committee on Ways and Means,* 559–560.

98. On the origin of the term *social security,* see Altmeyer, *The Formative Years of Social Security,* 2–6.

99. For example: Witte, "Organized Labor and Social Security."

100. Quoted in *Hearings before the Committee on Ways and Means, House of Representative on H.R. 4120,* 901–902.

101. According to the committee, the exclusion of agricultural and domestic workers would reduce the number of covered workers from 49 to 26 million: U.S. House of Representatives, *Report of the Committee on Ways and Means on the Social Security Bill,* H.R. 7260, 74th Cong., 1st sess., 1935, Report no. 615.

102. CES staff members originally supported the exclusion of these professional categories based on administrative considerations, but under the influence of Hopkins and Perkins, the CES report finally recommended their inclusion: Witte, *The Development of the Social Security Act,* 152.

103. Gareth Davies and Martha Derthick, "Race and Social Welfare Policy: The Social Security Act of 1935," *Political Science Quarterly* 112, no. 2 (1997): 217–236.

104. Larry DeWitt, "It Was Not about Race: The Decision to Exclude Agricultural and Domestic Workers from the U.S. Social Security Program" (unpublished paper, July 2004).

105. John B. Williamson and Fred C. Pampel, *Old-Age Security in Comparative Perspective* (New York: Oxford University Press, 1993).

106. It is worth noting that the vast majority of agrarian workers were not African American. Out of the more than 10 million workers falling under that professional category, only 2 million were African American: Robert C. Lieberman, *Shifting the Color Line: Race and the American Welfare State* (Cambridge, MA: Harvard University Press, 1998), 82.

107. Ibid.; Quadagno, *The Transformation of Old Age Security.*

108. DeWitt, "It Was Not about Race," 19.

109. Ibid., 48.

110. Witte, *The Development of the Social Security Act,* 153.

111. Mary Poole, *The Segregated Origins of Social Security: African Americans and the Welfare State* (Chapel Hill: University of North Carolina Press, 2006). Despite the criticism formulated here, one must recognize that Poole's book is a stimulating and well-researched piece of scholarship on race and social policy.

112. *Hearings before the Committee on Ways and Means, House of Representatives on H.R. 4120,* 897–911.

113. *Report of the Committee on Ways and Means on the Social Security Bill.*

114. Witte, *The Development of the Social Security Act,* 144.

115. Quadagno, *The Transformation of Old Age Security.*

116. Witte, *The Development of the Social Security Act,* 143–144.

117. Davies and Derthick, "Race and Social Welfare Policy."

118. Witte, *The Development of the Social Security Act,* 93–94.

119. This is at least the opinion of Douglas: *Social Security in the United States,* 103.

120. One of them, which was aimed at lowering the retirement age from sixty-five to sixty in order to fight unemployment, received more than 160 votes but was still defeated.

121. *Congressional Record* (April 19, 1935): 6069–6070.

122. U.S. Senate, *Report of the Senate Finance Committee,* 74th Cong., 1st sess., 1935, Report no. 628.

123. Although Graebner argued that this decision favored the generalization of retirement in American society and the final accomplishment of the managerial exclusionary logic discussed in Chapter 2, retirement would only become a nearly universal institution in the post–World War II era, after the expansion of old age insurance and the rapid development of private pensions: Graebner, *A History of Retirement,* 181–197.

124. *Congressional Record* (June 19, 1935): 9634.

125. Ibid., 9640.

126. Ibid., 9625.

127. For example, William Green from the AFL wrote a letter to the Senate to publicly condemn this amendment: Ibid., 9630.

128. Ibid., 9650.

129. Douglas, *Social Security in the United States,* 125.

130. Witte, *The Development of the Social Security Act,* 108.

131. According to Altmeyer, private firms and their political allies rapidly lost interest in that issue, knowing that the self-exclusion option would probably lead to massive federal regulation of private pension plans: Altmeyer, *The Formative Years of Social Security,* 42.

132. "Presidential Statement upon Signing the Social Security Act, August 14, 1935," in *Public Papers and Addresses of Franklin D. Roosevelt,* vol. 4, ed. Samuel I. Rosenman (New York: Random House, 1938), 326.

133. On this issue, see Tynes, *Turning Points in Social Security.*

134. Abraham Epstein, "Our Social Insecurity Act," *Harper's Magazine,* no. 172 (December 1935): 53–66.

135. Eveline Burns, *Toward Social Security: An Explanation of the Social Security Act and a Survey of the Larger Issues* (New York: Whittlesey House, 1936), 153–176.

136. The Roosevelt administration decided to temporarily push this issue aside because strong opposition from the American Medical Association could jeopardize the Social Security Act as a whole: Witte, *The Development of the Social Security Act,* 184–185.

137. Mary Anderson, cited in Mettler, *Dividing Citizens,* 81–82.

138. For example: Barbara Armstrong, *Insuring the Essentials: Minimum Wage Plus Social Insurance—A Living Wage Program* (New York: Macmillan, 1932), 45.

139. Lieberman, *Shifting the Color Line,* 82.

140. Ibid.

Chapter 4. The Politics of Expansion

1. Because federal old age insurance became known as Social Security during the period covered in this chapter, I will use this expression to refer to this program throughout the chapter and the remainder of the book.

2. Brian Balogh, "Securing Support: The Emergence of Social Security Board as a Political Actor," in *Federal Social Policy: The Historical Dimension,* ed. Ellis W. Hawley and Donald T. Critchlow (University Park: Pennsylvania State University Press, 1988), 55–78.

3. Martha Derthick, *Policymaking for Social Security* (Washington, DC: Brookings Institution, 1979), 17–37.

4. Ibid. See also Jerry R. Cates, *Insuring Inequality: Administrative Leadership in Social Security, 1935–1954* (Ann Arbor: University of Michigan Press, 1983).

5. "Text of Gov. Landon's Milwaukee Address on Economic Security," *New York Times,* August 27, 1936, 31.

6. Ibid.

7. The emergence of the Liberty League in August 1934 provides ground to this claim: Herman E. Krooss, *Executive Opinion* (New York: Doubleday, 1970), 181.

8. Charles McKinley and Robert W. Frase, *Launching Social Security: A Capture-and-Record Account, 1935–1937* (Madison: University of Wisconsin Press, 1970), 358.

9. Edward D. Berkowitz, "The First Social Security Crisis," *Prologue* 15, no. 3 (Fall 1983): 136.

10. McKinley and Frase, *Launching Social Security,* 30.

11. Ibid., 358.

12. *Congressional Record* (January 29, 1937): S 548. On this issue, see also Berkowitz, "The First Social Security Crisis," 137.

13. Cited in McKinley and Robert Frase, *Launching Social Security,* 296.

14. Ibid.

15. Theron F. Schlabach, *Edwin E. Witte: Cautious Reformer* (Madison, WI: State Historical Society, 1969), 161.

16. Ibid., 165.

17. Berkowitz, "The First Social Security Crisis," 141.

18. It is worth mentioning that the 1935 version of the program had a significant redistributive element in the form of a weighted benefit formula. According to this formula, federal old age insurance would offer higher replacement rates to lower-income workers.

19. J. Douglas Brown, *An American Philosophy of Social Security* (Princeton, NJ: Princeton University Press, 1972), 136.

20. Edward D. Berkowitz, "Family Benefits in Social Security: A Historical Commentary," in *Social Security and the Family: Addressing Unmet Needs in an Underfunded System,* ed. Melissa M. Favreault, Frank J. Sammartino, and C. Eugene Steuerle (Washington, DC: Urban Institute, 2001), 19–46.

21. Alice Kessler-Harris, "Designing Women and Old Fools: The Construction of the Social Security Amendments of 1939," in *U.S. History as Women's History,* ed. Linda K. Kerber, Alice Kessler-Harris, and Kathryn Kish Sklar (Chapel Hill: University of North Carolina Press, 1995), 87–106.

22. Brown, *An American Philosophy of Social Security,* 135.

23. Kessler-Harris, "Designing Women and Old Fools;" Suzanne Mettler, *Dividing Citizens: Gender and Federalism in New Deal Public Policy* (Ithaca, NY: Cornell University Press, 1998).

24. U.S. Advisory Council on Social Security, *Final Report* (Washington, DC: Social Security Board, 1938), 15.

25. Ibid., 109.

26. Social Security Board, *Proposed Changes in the Social Security Act* (Washington, DC: U.S. Government Printing Office, 1939).

27. "A Message Transmitting to the Congress a Report of the Social Security Board Recommending Certain Improvements in the Law," in *Public Papers and Addresses of Franklin D. Roosevelt,* vol. 8, ed. Samuel I. Rosenman (New York: Random House, 1950), 77–85.

28. In the House, Democrats dominated the 75th Congress (1937–1939): 333 Democrats, 89 Republicans, and 13 independents. The Democratic domination proved even more spectacular in the Senate: 76 Democrats, 16 Republicans, 2 Farmer-Labor, 1 Progressive, and 1 independent.

29. Leonard Baker, *Back to Back: The Duel between FDR and the Supreme Court* (New York: Macmillan, 1967).

30. In April 1938, Congress also rejected Roosevelt's ambitious administrative reform. On these issues, see Richard Polenberg, "The Decline of the New Deal, 1937–1940," in *The New Deal: The National Level,* ed. John Braeman, Robert H. Bremner, and David Brody (Columbus: Ohio State University Press, 1975), 246–265.

31. Concerning the emergence of the conservative coalition, see James T. Patterson, *Congressional Conservatism and the New Deal: The Growth of the Conservative Coalition in Congress, 1933–1939* (Lexington: University of Kentucky Press, 1969). As a result of the 1938 congressional elections, Democrats lost seven seats to the Republicans in the Senate (69 Democrats versus 23 Republicans). In the House, the gap between Republicans (169) and Democrats (262) closed. Overall, one can argue that these elections reinforced the power of southern Democrats because the president needed their support more than ever to pass his legislation.

32. Franklin D. Roosevelt, "Annual Message to the Congress, January 4, 1939," in, *Public Papers and Addresses of Franklin D. Roosevelt,* vol. 8, ed. Samuel I. Rosenman (New York: Random House, 1950), 7.

33. Concerning congressional debates about the Townsend Plan, see Abraham Holtzman, *The Townsend Movement: A Political Study* (New York: Bookman Associates, 1963), 101–124.

34. Berkowitz, "The First Social Security Crisis," 148.

35. Arthur J. Altmeyer, *The Formative Years of Social Security* (Madison: University of Wisconsin Press, 1965), 103.

36. Gareth Davies and Martha Derthick, "Race and Social Welfare Policy: The Social Security Act of 1935," *Political Science Quarterly* 112, no. 2 (1997): 217–236.

37. *Congressional Record* (June 10, 1939): H 6970–6971.

38. *Congressional Record* (July 13, 1939): S 9031.

39. Mettler, *Dividing Citizens,* 102.

40. For a discussion about this issue, see Nancy Frazer and Linda Gordon, "Contract versus Charity: Why Is There No Social Citizenship in the United States?" *Socialist Review* 22 (July 1992): 45–68, and John Myles, "Neither Rights nor Contacts: The New Means Testing in US Aging Policy," in *The Future of Age-Based Policy,* ed. Robert B. Hudson (Baltimore, MD: Johns Hopkins University Press, 1997), 46–55.

41. Berkowitz, "The First Social Security Crisis," 148.

42. For a systematic discussion on this issue, see Cates, *Insuring Inequality,* 31–38. As noted by Cates, policymakers only incorporated the language of insurance to the Social Security Act in 1939. This language was absent from the original legislation to facilitate its approval by the Supreme Court. In his book, Cates exaggerates the regressive nature of old age insurance, a program that incorporated genuine redistributive methods after 1939.

43. For a discussion concerning war-induced social and political solidarity, see Richard M. Titmuss, "War and Social Policy," in *Essays on 'The Welfare State,'* 2d ed. (Boston: Beacon Press, 1963), 75–87.

44. William Beveridge, *Social Insurance and Allied Services* (New York: Macmillan, 1942).

45. Peter Baldwin, *The Politics of Social Solidarity: Class Bases of the European Welfare States, 1875–1975* (Cambridge: Cambridge University Press, 1990).

46. In France, employers only joined the social security managerial board in 1967. Between 1945 and 1967, only labor union officials participated in the management of the French public pension scheme for private sector employees: Anne-Marie Guillemard, *Aging and the Welfare-State Crisis* (Newark: University of Delaware Press, 2000).

47. For comparative perspectives on postwar social policy development in industrialized countries, see D. A. Ashford, *The Emergence of the Welfare States* (Oxford: Blackwell, 1987); Baldwin, *The Politics of Social Solidarity;* Gøsta Esping-Andersen, *The Three Worlds of Welfare Capitalism* (Princeton, NJ: Princeton University Press, 1990); Peter Flora and Arnold J. Heidenheimer, *The Development of Welfare States in Europe and America* (New Brunswick, NJ: Transaction Books, 1981); Daniel Levine, *Poverty and Society: The Growth of the American Welfare State in International Comparison* (New Brunswick, NJ: Rutgers University Press, 1988).

48. Although formulated in the American context, the concept of credit claiming applies to other countries. Yet, one should note that in countries where labor unions participated directly in social security policymaking, these organizations claimed credit for the postwar expansion of public pensions.

49. Theda Skocpol and Edwin Amenta, "Redefining the New Deal: World War II and the Development of Social Policy in the United States," in *The Politics of Social Policy in the United States,* ed. Margaret Weir, Ann Shola Orloff, and Theda Skocpol (Princeton, NJ: Princeton University Press, 1988), 81–122.

50. Between 1940 and 1945, the GDP per capita increased dramatically while the number of unemployed dropped from 8 million to 750,000: Gilbert C. Fite and Jim E. Reese, *An Economic History of the United States,* 3rd ed. (Boston: Houghton Mifflin, 1973), 535–538. In Europe, the return to prosperity occurred more gradually than in the United States *after* the end of the war.

51. Military spending increased from only 2 percent of the U.S. GDP in 1939 to 40 percent in 1944: Francis G. Walett, *Economic History of the United States,* 2d ed. (New York: Barnes and Noble, 1963), 229. The wartime collaboration between business and government is addressed in Richard W. Polenberg, *War and Society: The United States, 1941–1945* (1972; repr., Westport, CT: Greenwood Press, 1980), 5–36, 154–183.

52. In 1942, the Democrats lost fifty seats in the House. "Because all the losses were non-Southern Democrats, the mid-war election weakened the reform element of the Democratic Party, and at a crucial point." Skocpol and Amenta, "Redefining the New Deal," 110–111. According to these authors, military defeats occurring shortly before the November election favored this electoral outcome.

53. Published in December 1942, this influential British report recommended the creation of a comprehensive safety net in the United Kingdom: Sir William Beveridge, *Social Insurance and Allied Services* [the Beveridge Report] (London: Macmillan, 1942). As Arthur Altmeyer reported, the SSB actually invited the author of the report, British scholar and former civil servant Sir William Beveridge, to the United States in order to meet with members of Congress and to keep social policy reform on the agenda: *The Formative Years of Social Security,* 144–145.

54. Committee on Long-Range Work and Relief Policies, *Security, Work, and Relief Policies* (Washington, DC: U.S. Government Printing Office, 1942).

55. Skocpol and Amenta, "Redefining the New Deal," 111. In the House, these elections closed the gap between Democrats (222) and Republicans (209). The same remark applies to the Senate, where 57 Democrats—many of them southern conservatives—faced 38 Republicans.

56. Mark H. Leff, "Speculating in Social Security Futures: The Perils of Payroll Tax Financing, 1939–1950," in *Social Security: The First Half-Century,* ed. Gerald D. Nash, Noel H. Pugach, and Richard F. Tomasson (Albuquerque: University of New Mexico Press, 1988), 243–278.

57. In 1945, for example, the Old Age and Survivors Insurance (OASI) trust fund had accumulated more than 7 billion dollars in assets, a sum more than twenty-three times higher than its annual expenditures: Carolyn L. Weaver, *The Crisis in Social Security: Economic and Political Origins* (Durham, NC: Duke Press Policy Studies, 1982), 129. On this issue, see also Sheryl R. Tynes, *Turning Points in Social Security: From "Cruel Hoax" to "Sacred Entitlement"* (Palo Alto, CA: Stanford University Press, 1996).

58. Leff, "Speculating in Social Security Futures," 244–245.

59. For an economic—and conservative—perspective on that issue, see Sylvester J. Schieber and John B. Shoven, *The Real Deal: The History and Future of Social Security* (New Haven, CT: Yale University Press, 1999).

60. Leff, "Speculating in Social Security Futures," 258.

61. Altmeyer, *The Formative Years of Social Security,* 122–123.

62. For example, the 1940 Democratic platform called for "the early realization of a minimum pension for all who have reached the age of retirement and are not gainfully employed." This text is cited in Leff, "Speculating in Social Security Futures," 261.

63. Cates, *Insuring Inequality.* As stated in Chapter 1, such a "conspiracy theory" is more or less present in other books about Social Security: Derthick, *Policymaking for Social Security;* Schieber and Shoven, *The Real Deal;* Weaver, *The Crisis in Social Security.*

64. For example, see Frank Dobbin and Terry Boychuck, "Public Policy and the Rise of Private Pension: The US Experience since 1930," in *The Privatization*

of Social Policy? Occupational Welfare and the Welfare State in America, Scandinavia and Japan, ed. Michael Shalev (London: Macmillan, 1996), 104–135.

65. Jacob S. Hacker, *The Divided Welfare State: The Battle over Public and Private Social Benefits in the United States* (Cambridge: Cambridge University Press, 2002); Jennifer Klein, *For All These Rights: Business, Labor, and the Shaping of America's Public-Private Welfare State* (Princeton, NJ: Princeton University Press, 2003); Beth Stevens, "Blurring the Boundaries: How the Federal Government Has Influenced Welfare Benefits in the Private Sector," in *The Politics of Social Policy in the United States,* ed. Margaret Weir, Ann Shola Orloff, and Theda Skocpol (Princeton, NJ: Princeton University Press, 1988), 123–148.

66. In fact, Congress rejected the administration's call for strict antidiscriminatory provisions that would have prevented employers from favoring wealthier workers at the expense of other employees. On this issue, see Hacker, *The Divided Welfare State,* 114–121.

67. Teresa Ghilarducci, *Labor's Capital: The Economics and Politics of Private Pensions* (Cambridge, MA: MIT Press, 1992), 36.

68. Hacker, *The Divided Welfare State.*

69. Klein, *For All These Rights.*

70. Hacker, *The Divided Welfare State,* 37. On this general issue, see also Michael K. Brown, "Bargaining for Social Rights: Unions and the Reemergence of Welfare Capitalism, 1945–1952," *Political Science Quarterly* 112, no. 4 (1997–1998): 645–674. The idea that the postwar pension crusade constituted a "depoliticization of labor" was formulated in Jill Quadagno, *The Transformation of Old Age Security: Class and Politics in the American Welfare State* (Chicago: University of Chicago Press, 1988).

71. For example: Steven A. Sass, *The Promise of Private Pension: The First Hundred Years* (Cambridge, MA: Harvard University Press, 1997), 126–132.

72. The decision of the National Labor Relations Board is cited in ibid., 132.

73. Ibid.

74. Quadagno, *The Transformation of Old Age Security,* 162–171.

75. Considering that many AFL members worked in small and medium-sized businesses, this organization first focused on Social Security expansion instead of fighting for the establishment of complex multi-employer plans. Witnessing the successes of the CIO in the field of collective bargaining, the AFL gradually adopted a more positive attitude toward private pensions before the great 1955 merger.

76. Organization for Economic Cooperation and Development, *Private Pensions in OECD Countries: The United States,* Special Policy Studies no.10 (Paris: Organization for Economic Cooperation and Development, 1993), 10. The majority of covered workers were union members.

77. Antonia Maioni, *Parting at the Crossroads: The Emergence of Health Insurance in the United States and Canada* (Princeton, NJ: Princeton University Press, 1998).

78. Daniel Béland, "Does Labor Matter? Institutions, Labor Unions, and Pension Reform in France and the United States," *Journal of Public Policy* 21 (2001): 153–172.

79. The following paragraph draws on Daniel Béland and Jacob S. Hacker, "Ideas, Private Institutions, and American Welfare State 'Exceptionalism': The Case of Health and Old-Age Insurance in the United States, 1915–1965," *International Journal of Social Welfare* 13, no. 1 (2004): 42–54.

80. Hacker, *The Divided Welfare State.*

81. See, for example: "Message to the Congress on the State of the Union and on the Budget for 1947" (January 14, 1946), in *Public Papers of the Presidents of the United States: Harry S. Truman, 1946* (Washington, DC: U.S. Government Printing Office, 1962), 63–64.

82. *Annual Report of the Federal Security Agency; Section V, Social Security Board, 1945* (Washington, DC: U.S. Government Printing Office, 1945), and *Annual Report of the Social Security Agency; Section VI, Social Security Board, 1946* (Washington, DC: U.S. Government Printing Office, 1946).

83. Edward D. Berkowitz, *Mr. Social Security: The Life of Wilbur J. Cohen* (Lawrence: University Press of Kansas, 1995), 57.

84. Stephen Skowronek, *The Politics Presidents Make: Leadership from John Adams to Bill Clinton* (Cambridge, MA: Harvard University Press, 1997), 41.

85. In the Senate, Democrats gained 9 seats—from 45 to 54. In the House, Democrats gained 75 seats in total—from 188 to 263. Republicans ended up with only 171 seats in 1949.

86. Derthick, *Policymaking for Social Security.*

87. Advisory Council on Social Security, *Recommendations for Social Security Legislation: The Reports of the Advisory Council on Social Security to the Senate Committee on Finance* (Washington, DC: U.S. Government Printing Office, 1949), 1.

88. Ibid., 2.

89. Edward D. Berkowitz, *America's Welfare State from Roosevelt to Reagan* (Baltimore, MD: Johns Hopkins University Press, 1991), 56.

90. Advisory Council on Social Security, *Recommendations for Social Security Legislation*, 2.

91. Ibid., 61.

92. The Advisory Council only recommended increasing the tax rate from 2 to 3 percent.

93. Schieber and Shoven, *The Real Deal.*

94. On this issue, see Hacker, *The Divided Welfare State*, 138. In President Truman's January 4, 1950, State of the Union address, he explicitly referred to the contemporary multiplication of private pension plans to justify the enactment of what would become the 1950 amendments: "The widespread movement to provide pensions in private industry dramatizes the need for improvements in the public insurance system": "Annual Message to the Congress on the State of the Union," in *Public Papers of the Presidents of the United States: Harry S. Truman, 1950* (Washington, DC: U.S. Government Printing Office, 1965), 9.

95. "Annual Message to the Congress on the State of the Union," in *Public Papers of the Presidents of the United States: Harry S. Truman, 1949* (Washington, DC: U.S. Government Printing Office, 1964), 1–7.

96. Testimony of Philip Murray in *Social Security Amendments of 1949. Hearings before the Committee on Ways and Means. Part II: Old-Age, Survivors, and*

Disability Insurance, House of Representatives, 81st Congress, 1st Session on H.R. 2893, 1949: 1728–1741.

97. Testimony of William Green in ibid., 1987–1999.

98. For example, see the testimonies of Laurence D. Luey (comptroller of Connors Steel Company) and Howard Friend (research director of the Indiana State Chamber of Commerce) reprinted in *Congressional Digest* 28, no. 12 (December 1949): 313–315, 319–320.

99. "Congressional Treatment during the '40's," *Congressional Digest* 28, no. 12 (December 1949): 297, 305.

100. Robert C. Lieberman, *Shifting the Color Line: Race and the American Welfare State* (Cambridge, MA: Harvard University Press, 1998), 109.

101. Testimony of Arthur Altmeyer in *Social Security Amendments of 1949,* 1081–1095.

102. House of Representatives, *Report no. 1300: Social Security Amendments of 1949,* 81st Cong., 1st sess., August 22, 1949. For a summary of the bill's provisions, see "What H.R. 6000 Proposes," *Congressional Digest* 28, no.12 (December 1949): 303–305.

103. For a systematic comparison between the two bills, see Altmeyer, *The Formative Years of Social Security,* 173–174.

104. "What H.R. 6000 Proposes," 303.

105. Lieberman, *Shifting the Color Line,* 110.

106. House of Representatives, *Report no. 1300,* 11.

107. Altmeyer, *The Formative Years of Social Security,* 175.

108. *Congressional Record* (October 3, 1949): H 13808–13974.

109. Dominick Pratico, *Eisenhower and Social Security: The Origins of the Disability Program* (New York: Writers Club Press, 2001).

110. *Congressional Record* (June 20, 1949): H 13808–13974.

111. For a detailed presentation of the provisions, see Wilbur J. Cohen and Robert J. Myers, "Social Security Act Amendments of 1950: A Summary and Legislative History," *Social Security Bulletin* 13, no. 10 (October 1950): 3–14.

112. Of these workers, approximately 7.5 million were covered on a compulsory basis, the others on an optional one. On this issue, see George J. Leibowitz, "Old-Age and Survivors' Insurance: Coverage under the 1950 Amendments," *Social Security Bulletin* 13, no. 12 (December 1950): 1–9.

113. Daniel S. Sanders, *The Impact of Reform Movements on Social Policy Change: The Case of Social Insurance* (Fair Lawn, NJ: R. E. Burdick, 1973), 105. On the 1950 amendments, see also Berkowitz, *Mr. Social Security.*

114. Prior to 1950, only dependent wives could receive spousal and survivor benefits.

115. In 1949, the OASI trust fund paid 961 million dollars in benefits. The year after, this amount almost doubled, reaching 1.885 billion dollars: http://www.ssa.gov/OACT/STATS/table4a5.html, accessed March 5, 2005.

116. Lieberman, *Shifting the Color Line,* 80–91.

117. Ibid., 8.

118. Ibid. Yet, the official discourse of the Social Security Administration about "earned rights" probably contributed to the positive self-image tied to the

program. The negative consequence of this discourse is that it may have reinforced the stigma traditionally associated with social assistance. In a way, this is the argument formulated by Cates in *Insuring Inequality*. But it is truly excessive to blame Social Security officials for the stigma stemming from welfare. Such a stigma existed before Social Security, and it probably would have survived if Social Security had taken a different, more explicitly redistributive, shape.

119. For a good historical survey of the AMA mobilizations, see Jonathan Engel, *Doctors and Reformers: Discussion and Debate over Health Policy, 1925–1950* (Columbia: University of South Carolina Press, 2002).

120. Colin Gordon, "Why No Health Insurance in the US? The Limits of Social Provision in War and Peace, 1941–1948," *Journal of Policy History* 9, no. 3 (1997): 277–310; Hacker, *The Divided Welfare State,* 221–337.

121. Béland and Hacker, "Ideas, Private Institutions, and American Welfare State 'Exceptionalism.'"

122. On the popularity of Social Security in the postwar era, see Charles M. Brain, *Social Security at the Crossroads: Public Opinion and Public Policy* (New York: Garland Publishing, 1991).

123. John Myles, *Old Age and the Welfare State,* 2d ed. (Lawrence: University Press of Kansas, 1989).

124. Altmeyer, *The Formative Years of Social Security,* 193.

125. Sanders, *The Impact of Reform Movements,* 107–108 In 1951, the inflation rate was as high as 8 percent, yet it dropped to only 2 percent the following year: Richard J. Carroll, *An Economic Record of Presidential Performance: From Truman to Bush* (Westport, CT: Praeger, 1995), 65.

126. "Republican Platform, 1952," in *National Party Platforms, 1840–1976,* ed. Donald Bruce Johnson and Kirk H. Porter (Urbana: University of Illinois Press, 1973), 496–505.

127. "Annual Message to the Congress on the State of the Union," in *Public Papers of the Presidents of the United States: Dwight D. Eisenhower, 1953* (Washington, DC: U.S. Government Printing Office, 1960), 12–34 (31).

128. Chamber of Commerce of the United States, *Improving Social Security* (Washington, DC: Chamber of Commerce, 1953).

129. Derthick, *Policymaking for Social Security,* 148.

130. Text cited in Sanders, *The Impact of Reform Movements,* 111.

131. Ibid., 113.

132. Consultants on Social Security, *A Report of the Secretary of Health, Education, and Welfare on the Extension of Old-Age and Survivors Insurance to Additional Groups of Current Workers* (Washington, DC: Secretary of Health, Education, and Welfare, 1953. It is worth noting that, as the staff director of the Consultants on Social Security, SSA official Robert Ball probably influenced the content of the report in a way that was consistent with his expansionist views: Edward D. Berkowitz, *Robert Ball and the Politics of Social Security* (Madison: University of Wisconsin Press, 2003), 88.

133. For an excellent discussion concerning New Republicanism, see E. J. Dionne, *Why Americans Hate Politics* (New York: Simon and Schuster, 1991),

170–208. See also Arthur Larson, *A Republican Looks at His Party* (New York: Harper and Brothers, 1956).

134. Skowronek, *The Politics Presidents Make,* 46.

135. For an original discussion concerning the application of this strategy in the field of health care reform, see Hacker, *The Divided Welfare State,* 237–243.

136. "Special Message to Congress Transmitting Proposed Changes in the Social Security Program," *Public Papers of the Presidents of the United States: Dwight D. Eisenhower, 1953* (Washington, DC: U.S. Government Printing Office, 1960), 534–536.

137. "Annual Message to the Congress on the State of the Union," in *Public Papers of the Presidents of the United States: Dwight D. Eisenhower, 1954* (U.S. Government Printing Office, 1960), 6–23 (19).

138. Sanders, *The Impact of Reform Movements,* 118.

139. Pratico, *Eisenhower and Social Security,* 26.

140. In the House, Democrats gained 19 seats, and they significantly outnumbered Republicans (232 against 203). In the Senate, Democrats gained only one seat but shifted the power balance to their advantage (48 against 47).

141. A detailed discussion concerning disability insurance is beyond the scope of this study. For historical studies on the origins of disability insurance, see Edward D. Berkowitz, *Disabled Policy: America's Programs for the Handicapped* (New York: Cambridge University Press, 1987), and Pratico, *Eisenhower and Social Security.*

142. Pratico, *Eisenhower and Social Security,* 80.

143. Most students of Social Security history have noted this incremental logic. For a rather abstract discussion about incrementalism, see Tynes, *Turning Points in Social Security.* See also Derthick, *Policymaking for Social Security,* and Berkowitz, *Mr. Social Security.*

144. For more details, see Robert J. Myers, "Old-Age, Survivors, and Disability Insurance: Financing Basis and Policy under the 1958 Amendments," *Social Security Bulletin* 21, no. 10 (October 1958): 15–21.

145. According to Carolyn Weaver, the 1960 amendments paved the way to the enactment of Medicare: *The Crisis in Social Security,* 153–154.

146. This was, for example, the logic behind the idea of Medicare, which emerged in 1951. For the proponents of this measure, health insurance tied to existing Social Security benefits could prepare the ground for universal coverage.

147. For example: Christopher Leman, "Patterns of Policy Development: Social Security in the United States and Canada," *Public Policy* 25, no. 2 (Spring 1977): 260–291. See also Tynes, *Turning Points in Social Security.*

148. Pratico, *Eisenhower and Social Security,* 102.

149. Altmeyer, *The Formative Years of Social Security,* 5–6.

150. Wilbur J. Cohen, "Social Security Amendments of 1961: Summary and Legislative History," *Social Security Bulletin* 24, no. 9 (September 1961): 3–11.

151. This trend was associated with the success of Michael Harrington's 1962 book, which fed the "problem stream" with information on the reproduction of poverty in a most prosperous nation: *The Other America* (New York: Macmillan, 1962).

152. Theodore J. Lowi, *The End of Liberalism: The Second Republic of the United States,* 2d ed. (New York: W. W. Norton, 1979). On the social experiments of the Great Society, see Gareth Davies, *From Opportunity to Entitlement: The Transformation and Decline of Great Society Liberalism* (Lawrence: University Press of Kansas, 1996).

153. On the origins of Medicare, see Peter A. Corning, *The Evolution of Medicare . . . from Idea to Law,* U.S. Department of Health, Education, and Welfare, Social Security Administration, Office of Research and Statistics, Research Report no. 29 (Washington, DC: U.S. Government Printing Office, 1969); Theodore R. Marmor, *The Politics of Medicare* (Chicago: Aldine Publishing, 1973).

154. Leonore Epstein Bixby, *Demographic and Economic Characteristics of the Aged,* Social Security Administration Report no. 45 (Washington, DC: U.S. Government Printing Office, 1965).

155. Sociologist and future Democratic senator Daniel Patrick Moynihan led what would become known as the neoconservative critique of Great Society liberalism: *Maximum Feasible Misunderstanding: Community Action in the War on Poverty* (New York: Free Press, 1969). Moynihan also served as an adviser to the president under the more conservative Nixon administration.

156. For example: Robert M. Ball, "Is Poverty Necessary?" *Social Security Bulletin* 28, no. 8 (August 1965): 18–24. On this issue, see also W. Andrew Achenbaum, *Social Security: Visions and Revisions* (Cambridge: Cambridge University Press, 1986).

157. Concerning the inclusion of the middle class in Social Security, Jill Quadagno wrote that the "integration of the middle class" with Social Security was at the foundation of its political success: "Interest-Group Politics and the Future of the U.S. Social Security," in *States, Labor Markets, and the Future of Old-Age Policy,* ed. John Myles and Jill Quadagno (Philadelphia: Temple University Press, 1991), 36–58.

158. Brain, *Social Security at the Crossroads.*

159. Henry J. Pratt, *The Gray Lobby* (Chicago: University of Chicago Press, 1976), 59–60, 107–128.

160. William Graebner, *A History of Retirement: The Meaning and the Function of an American Institution* (New Haven, CT: Yale University Press, 1980), 215–241.

161. In *How Policies Make Citizens: Senior Citizen Activism and the American Welfare State* (Princeton, NJ: Princeton University Press, 2003), Andrea Louise Campbell showed that Social Security has an especially positive effect on the political participation of low-income seniors. She also underlined the fact the Social Security has increased the interest in politics among the program's beneficiaries.

162. Wilbur J. Cohen and Robert M. Ball, "Social Security Amendments of 1965: Summary and Legislative History," *Social Security Bulletin* 28, no. 9 (September 1965): 3–21.

163. Weaver, *The Crisis in Social Security,* 158.

164. "Special Message to the Congress Proposing Programs for Older Americans," in *Public Papers of the Presidents of the United States: Lyndon B. Johnson, 1967,* vol. 1 (Washington, DC: U.S. Government Printing Office, 1968), 33.

165. Ibid.

166. Robert M. Ball, "Social Security Amendments of 1967: Summary and Legislative History," *Social Security Bulletin* 31, no. 2 (February 1968): 3–19.

167. Kevin P. Phillips, *The Emerging Republican Majority* (New Rochelle, NY: Arlington House, 1969).

168. In fact, both Eisenhower and Nixon were "preemptive leaders" who struggled to seduce elements of the dominant electoral coalition associated with the opposite political party: Skowronek, *The Politics Presidents Make.*

169. On the politics of indexation, see R. Kent Weaver, *Automatic Government: The Politics of Indexation* (Washington, DC: Brookings Institution, 1988).

170. Julian E. Zelizer, *Taxing America: Wilbur D. Mills, Congress, and the State, 1945–1975* (New York: Cambridge University Press, 1998), 312–346.

171. Within the SSA, chief actuary Robert Myers opposed Ball's stance but finally lost the battle and left the federal government in 1970. On the personal conflict between these two officials and the role of Ball during the Nixon administration, see Berkowitz, *Robert Ball and the Politics of Social Security,* 164–207; Schieber and Shoven, *The Real Deal,* 123–127, 152–157.

172. I would like to thank Larry DeWitt for his insight about this issue. The best discussion about this change in actuarial assumptions can be found in Derthick, *Policymaking for Social Security,* 349–357. As demonstrated in the next two chapters, the "politics of assumptions" has remained a key issue in Social Security reform since the 1970s.

173. Thomas Edsall, *The New Politics of Inequality* (New York: W. W. Norton, 1984), 113. See also John Myles, "Postwar Capitalism and the Extension of Social Security into a Retirement Wage," in *The Politics of Social Policy in the United States,* ed. Margaret Weir, Ann Shola Orloff, and Theda Skocpol (Princeton, NJ: Princeton University Press, 1988), 275.

174. On this issue, see Karl Hinrichs, "Elephants on the Move: Patterns of Public Pension Reform in OECD Countries," *European Review* 8, no. 3 (2000): 353–378.

175. Hacker, *The Divided Welfare State,* 145.

176. "Special Message to the Congress on Social Security," in *Public Papers of the Presidents of the United States, Richard Nixon, 1969* (Washington, DC: U.S. Government Printing Office, 1971), 740–741 (italics in original).

177. Max Orlick and Doris E. Lewis, "Adjustment of Old-Age Pensions in Foreign Programs," *Social Security Bulletin* 33, no. 5 (May 1970): 12–15.

178. For a systematic analysis, see R. Kent Weaver, *Automatic Government,* 69–74.

179. Carolyn L. Weaver, *The Crisis in Social Security,* 162.

180. For example: Testimony of William P. McHenry Jr., in U.S. House of Representatives, *Social Security and Welfare Proposals, Hearings before the Committee on Ways and Means,* 91st Cong., 1st sess. (Washington, DC: U.S. Government Printing Office, 1970) 1617–1619. McHenry represented the Chamber of Commerce.

181. On Mills and his actions during the Nixon era, see Zelizer, *Taxing America,* 312–346.

182. Social Security Administration, "Social Security Benefits Increased," *Social Security Board* 33, no. 2 (February 1970): 1.

183. "Statement on Signing the Tax Reform Act of 1969," in *Public Papers of the Presidents of the United States, Richard Nixon, 1969* (Washington, DC: U.S. Government Printing Office, 1971): 1044–1046

184. R. Kent Weaver, *Automatic Government,* 75.

185. Ibid.

186. 1971 Advisory Council on Social Security, *Report on Old Age, Survivors, and Disability Insurance and Medicare Programs* (Washington, DC: Advisory Council, 1971).

187. Pratt, *The Gray Lobby,* 158–159.

188. Carroll, *An Economic Record of Presidential Performance,* 63.

189. Robert J. Myers, *Social Security,* 4th ed. (Philadelphia: Pension Research Council/University of Pennsylvania Press, 1993), 363.

190. Carmen D. Solomon, *Major Decisions in the House and Senate Chambers on Social Security: 1935–1985* (Washington, DC: Congressional Research Service, 1986), 69.

191. R. Kent Weaver, *Automatic Government,* 76.

192. Marjorie Hunter, "Mills Asks 20% Rise in Social Security Aid," *New York Times,* February 24, 1972, 19.

193. R. Kent Weaver, *Automatic Government,* 77.

194. "Congress Raises Social Security Benefits 20 Percent," *Congressional Quarterly Almanac* 27 (1972): 399.

195. Carolyn L. Weaver, *The Crisis in Social Security,* 166.

196. "Statement on Signing a Bill Extending Temporary Ceiling on National Debt and Increasing Social Security Benefits," in *Public Papers of the Presidents of the United States, Richard Nixon, 1972* (Washington, DC: U.S. Government Printing Office, 1974), 723–724.

197. During the 1972 presidential campaign, Democratic candidate Wilbur Mills claimed credit for benefit increases enacted during and before the Nixon presidency: "In the close-to-home areas of social security, unemployment compensation and welfare, no American Congressman has done as much as Wilbur Mills to improve the standard of living and quality of life for his fellow Americans. He has been the chief sponsor of every major social security bill that has become law since the beginning of 1958. During this period, social security benefits have been increased five times, with the cumulative increase of these changes totaling 64 per cent." "Wilbur Mills for President 1972 Campaign Brochures," http://www.4president.org/brochures/wilburmills72.pdf, accessed March 5, 2005.

198. Lanelle K. Polen, "Salvaging a Safety Net: Modifying the Bar to Supplemental Security Income for Legal Aliens," *Washington University Law Quarterly* 76, no. 4 (Winter 1998): 1460.

199. In January 1974, fewer than 2 million elderly Americans received SSI benefits, more than thirteen times less than the number of OASI beneficiaries that year. Far from increasing, the number of elderly SSI beneficiaries declined after 1975 to reach approximately 1.3 million in December 2001 (as compared

to approximately 39 million OASI beneficiaries). Most SSI beneficiaries have been disabled: Social Security Administration, *Social Security Bulletin: Annual Statistical Supplement,* 2002 (Washington, DC: Social Security Administration, 2002), 277.

200. An exception to the low-profile rule was the debate surrounding SSI provisions for immigrants in the aftermath of the 1996 welfare reform: Polen, "Salvaging a Safety Net."

201. On this issue, see Theda Skocpol, "Sustainable Social Policy: Fighting Poverty without Poverty Programs," *The American Prospect,* no. 2 (Summer 1990): 58–70.

202. Myles, "Postwar Capitalism and the Extension of Social Security into a Retirement Wage," 274. Comparable developments simultaneously took place in other industrialized nations. In France, for example, the 1971 Boulin Law dramatically increased the level of public pension benefits, thus raising the replacement rate for the basic income-related public pension from 40 to 50 percent: Guillemard, *Aging and the Welfare-State Crisis.*

203. Myles, "Postwar Capitalism and the Extension of Social Security into a Retirement Wage." In 1975, for example, the average replacement rate for Social Security reached 55.9 percent, up from 33.5 percent in 1965 and 40.3 percent in 1967: Myers, *Social Security,* 363.

204. For a comparison between patterns of pension reform in postwar Canada and the United States, see Leman, "Patterns of Policy Development."

205. Brain, *Social Security at the Crossroads.*

Chapter 5. The Politics of Retrenchment

1. Giuliano Bonoli, "Two Worlds of Pension Reform in Western Europe," *Comparative Politics* 35, no. 4 (July 2003): 399–416; Sarah Brooks, "Social Protection and Economic Integration: The Politics of Pension Reform in an Era of Capital Mobility," *Comparative Political Studies* 35, no. 5 (2002): 491–525; Alan M. Jacobs, "Governing for the Long Term: Democratic Politics and Policy Investment" (Ph.D. diss., Harvard University, 2004); Karl Hinrichs, "Elephants on the Move: Patterns of Public Pension Reform in OECD Countries," *European Review* 8, no. 3 (2000): 353–378; Patrik Marier, "Institutional Structure and Policy Change, Pension Reforms in Belgium, France, Sweden, and the UK" (Ph.D. diss., University of Pittsburgh, 2002); John Myles and Paul Pierson, "The Comparative Political Economy of Pension Reform," in *The New Politics of the Welfare State,* ed. Paul Pierson (Oxford: Oxford University Press, 2001), 305–333; R. Kent Weaver, *The Politics of Public Pension Reform,* CRR Working Paper CRR WP 2003–06 (Chestnut Hill, MA: Center for Retirement Research at Boston College, 2003).

2. Avoiding protest is especially crucial in countries such as France and Italy, where labor unions play a direct role in pension politics: Daniel Béland and Patrik Marier, *The Politics of Protest Avoidance: Timing, Labor Mobilization, and Pension Reform in France,* SEDAP Research Paper 114 (Hamilton, ON: Social and Economic Dimensions of an Aging Population Programme, 2004).

3. R. Kent Weaver, "The Politics of Blame Avoidance," *Journal of Public Policy* 6, no. 4 (1986): 371–398; Paul Pierson, "The New Politics of the Welfare State," *World Politics* 48 (1996): 143–179.

4. Some programs seem more vulnerable to retrenchment efforts than others. For example, social assistance programs such as AFDC have proven more vulnerable to political attacks than Social Security because of the inferior socioeconomic status and the lower level of political organization of welfare recipients: Sylvia Bashevkin, "Rethinking Retrenchment: North American Social Policy during the Early Clinton and Chrétien Years," *Canadian Journal of Political Science* 33 (2000): 7–36. As the "welfare rights movement" declined during the 1970s, the AARP and other senior organizations emerged as prominent lobbies in the United States: Henry J. Pratt, *Gray Agendas: Interest Groups and the Public Pensions in Canada, Britain, and the United States* (Ann Arbor: University of Michigan Press, 1993). This does not mean, however, that the AARP is a monolithic and ever-powerful organization that always gets what it wants. The failure of this organization to prevent the enactment of the 1983 amendments to the Social Security Act provides ground to this claim: Paul C. Light, *Still Artful Work: The Continuing Politics of Social Security Reform* (New York: McGraw-Hill, 1995).

5. Michel Crozier, *The Trouble with America* (Berkeley: University of California Press, 1984).

6. Charles M. Brain, *Social Security at the Crossroads: Public Opinion and Public Policy* (New York: Garland Publishing, 1991).

7. John Snee and Mary Ross, "Social Security Amendments of 1977: Legislative History and Summary of Provisions," *Social Security Bulletin* 41, no. 3 (1978): 4. As early as 1973, and for the first time in the program's history, the annual report of the trustees showed a long-term actuarial imbalance in the OASDI trust funds. Between that year and 1982, all the annual reports anticipated some form of long-term actuarial imbalance: Larry DeWitt, "Key Data from Annual Trust Fund Reports," Research Note no. 14, Washington, DC, Social Security Administration, June 2001, http://www.ssa.gov/history/trustchart. html, accessed March 5, 2005.

8. Commission on the Social Security "Notch" Issue, "Final Report on the Social Security 'Notch' Issue," Washington, DC, December 31, 1994, http:// www.ssa.gov/history/notchfile1.html, accessed March 5, 2005.

9. Edward D. Berkowitz, *Robert Ball and the Politics of Social Security* (Madison: University of Wisconsin Press, 2003), 238–239.

10. In the mid-1970s, the mix of automatic indexation and high inflation did increase Social Security's replacement rate for low and average earnings beneficiaries: Robert J. Myers, "History of Replacement Rates for Various Amendments to the Social Security Act," Memorandum no. 2 (Washington, DC: National Commission on Social Security Reform, 1982).

11. Brain, *Social Security at the Crosswords.*

12. On this issue, see *Decoupling the Social Security Benefit Structure, Hearings before the Subcommittee on Social Security of the House Committee on Ways and Means,* 94th Cong., 2d sess. (Washington, DC: U.S. Government Printing Office, 1976).

13. Weaver, "The Politics of Blame Avoidance"; Paul Pierson, *Dismantling the Welfare State? Reagan, Thatcher, and the Politics of Retrenchment* (Cambridge: Cambridge University Press, 1994).

14. Before 1965, the duration of the long-range estimation period varied from one trustees' report to another. In 1957, for example, the long-range estimation period was only thirty-five years. The following year, it increased to eighty years. During the first part of the 1960s, the estimation period was sixty-five years: DeWitt, "Key Data from Annual Trust Fund Reports."

15. In Canada, for example, the time frame for actuarial projections is only sixty years. This is still a longer-term perspective than that in France, where actuarial previsions traditionally cover a forty-year period: Jean-Michel Charpin, *L'avenir de nos retraites, Rapport au Premier ministre* (Paris: La Documentation française, 1999).

16. For a general discussion about this issue, see Lawrence A. Powell, Kenneth J. Bronco, and John B. Williamson, *Senior Rights Movement: Framing the Policy Debate in America* (New York: Twayne Publishers, 1996).

17. Brain, *Social Security at the Crossroads,* 153.

18. Joseph A. Califano Jr., *Governing America: An Insider's Report from the White House and Cabinet* (New York: Simon and Schuster, 1981), 370.

19. On the emergence of the gray lobby, see Henry J. Pratt, *The Gray Lobby* (Chicago: University of Chicago Press, 1976), and Andrea Louise Campbell, *How Policies Make Citizens: Senior Citizen Activism and the American Welfare State* (Princeton, NJ: Princeton University Press, 2003).

20. For an interesting discussion concerning the elaboration of the Social Security plan within the Carter administration, see Berkowitz, *Robert Ball and the Politics of Social Security,* 240–252.

21. "Social Security System," *Public Papers of the Presidents of the United States: Jimmy Carter,* vol. 1 (Washington, DC: U.S. Government Printing Office, 1978), 837–838.

22. Jo Freeman, "The Revolution for Women in Law and Public Policy," in *Women: A Feminist Perspective,* 5th ed., ed. Jo Freeman (Mountain View, CA: Mayfield, 1995), 365–404.

23. For a detailed discussion about the support for and the opposition to the 1977 amendments, see Sheryl R. Tynes, *Turning Points in Social Security: From "Cruel Hoax" to "Sacred Entitlement"* (Stanford, CA: Stanford University Press, 1996), 162–173.

24. "Congress Clears Social Security Tax Increase," *Congressional Quarterly Almanac* 33 (1977): 161–172.

25. "Social Security Amendments of 1977," *Public Papers of the Presidents of the United States: Jimmy Carter,* vol. 1 (Washington, DC: U.S. Government Printing Office, 1978), 837–838.

26. Snee and Ross, "Social Security Amendments of 1977," 3–20.

27. Califano, *Governing America,* 382.

28. Paul Pierson and R. Kent Weaver, "Imposing Losses in Pension Policy," in *Do Institutions Matter? Government Capabilities in the United States and Abroad,* ed. R. Kent Weaver and Bert A. Rockman (Washington, DC: Brookings Institution, 1993), 117. Republicans could also accept this rationale, especially because the Ford administration had already proposed such measures the year before.

29. Pierson and Weaver, "Imposing Losses in Pension Policy," 117.

30. For a discussion on this issue, see Robert J. Myers, *Social Security,* 4th ed. (Philadelphia: Pension Research Council/University of Pennsylvania Press, 1993), 186–204. I would like to thank Larry DeWitt for his comments about this issue.

31. Snee and Ross, "Social Security Amendments of 1977," 15.

32. Califano, *Governing America,* 375.

33. Giuliano Bonoli, *The Politics of Pension Reform: Institutions and Policy Change in Western Europe* (Cambridge: Cambridge University Press, 2000); Myles and Pierson, "The Comparative Political Economy of Pension Reform."

34. Social Security Administration, "Social Security Disability Amendments of 1980: Legislative History and Summary of Provisions," *Social Security Bulletin* 44, no. 4 (1981): 14–31.

35. Califano, *Governing America,* 387–397.

36. On Cohen's crusade, see Edward D. Berkowitz, *Mr. Social Security: The Life of Wilbur J. Cohen* (Lawrence: University Press of Kansas, 1995).

37. Thomas Edsall, *The New Politics of Inequality* (New York: W. W. Norton, 1984); Andrew Rich, *Think Tanks, Public Policy, and the Politics of Expertise* (Cambridge: Cambridge University Press, 2004).

38. Pierson, *Dismantling the Welfare State?*

39. In the 97th Congress (1981–1983), Democrats (242) easily outnumbered Republicans (192). In the Senate, however, Republicans held the majority with 53 seats.

40. Pierson, *Dismantling the Welfare State?*

41. Larry M. Schwab, *The Illusion of a Conservative Revolution* (New Brunswick, NJ: Transaction Publishers, 1991).

42. Pierson, *Dismantling the Welfare State?*

43. Thomas Edsall and Mary Edsall, *Chain Reaction: The Impact of Race, Rights, and Taxes on American Politics* (New York: W. W. Norton, 1991), 191. For a good discussion about the Reagan administration and welfare reform, see Gareth Davies, "The Welfare State," in *The Reagan Presidency: Pragmatic Conservatism and Its Legacies,* ed. W. Elliot Brownlee and Hugh Davis Graham (Lawrence: University Press of Kansas, 2003): 209–232.

44. On SSI, see Jennifer L. Erkulwater, "The Forgotten Safety Net: The Expansion of Supplemental Security Income" (Ph.D. diss., Boston College, 2001).

45. For a systematic discussion of the Reagan administration's involvement in Social Security reform, see Martha Derthick and Steven M. Teles, "Riding the Third Rail: Social Security Reform," in *The Reagan Presidency: Pragmatic Conservatism and Its Legacies,* ed. W. Elliot Brownlee and Hugh Davis Graham (Lawrence: University Press of Kansas, 2003): 182–208.

46. In 1980, inflation reached 13.5 percent, which was about three times higher than expected in 1977: David Shribman, "The Social Security Crisis: Legacy of Hopeless Guesses," *New York Times,* January 5, 1983, A1, D20.

47. Pierson and Weaver, "Imposing Losses in Pension Policy," 118.

48. Eric R. Kingson, "Financing Social Security: Agenda-Setting and the Enactment of the 1983 Amendments to the Social Security Act," *Policy Studies Journal* 13, no. 1 (1984): 131–155.

49. David A. Stockman, *The Triumph of Politics: How the Reagan Revolution Failed* (New York: Harper and Row, 1986).

50. Light, *Still Artful Work,* 126.

51. "Address to the Nation on the Program for Economic Recovery," *Public Papers of the Presidents of the United States, Ronald Reagan, 1981* (Washington, DC: U.S. Government Printing Office, 1982), 831–836.

52. Kingson, "Financing Social Security."

53. To a lesser extent, this remark also applies to the 1947–1948 Advisory Council in relation to the 1950 amendments.

54. John A. Svahn, "Omnibus Reconciliation Act of 1981: Legislative History and Summary of the OASDI and Medicare Provisions," *Social Security Bulletin* 44, no. 10 (October 1981): 3–24. The regular minimum benefit would not be available for future beneficiaries: John A. Svahn and Mary Ross, "Restoration of Certain Minimum Benefits and Other OASDI Program Changes: Legislative History and Summary of Provisions," *Social Security Bulletin* 45, no. 3 (March 1982): 3–12. It is worth noting that Congress did not eliminate the special minimum benefit created in 1972 for workers who had contributed to Social Security for at least ten years. By the early 1980s, even former Social Security commissioner Robert Ball agreed that the regular minimum benefit often went to people who received another public pension and did not need that benefit: Berkowitz, *Robert Ball and the Politics of Social Security,* 283. The main problem with the provision included in the budget agreement was that it took money from *current* beneficiaries, not that it eliminated a regular minimum benefit now widely perceived as unnecessary.

55. Light, *Still Artful Work,* 130.

56. Kingson, "Financing Social Security," 145; Light, *Still Artful Work,* 163. See also Berkowitz, *Robert Ball and the Politics of Social Security.*

57. The strict timetable set by the president—and the related need for immediate political consensus—transformed the consultative and legislative process into a genuine "political sprint" that left little space for controversial solutions: Light, *Still Artful Work.*

58. Chile adopted the first modern pension privatization initiative in 1981 through a decree of the military government of Augusto Pinochet. "The Chilean pension reform supplanted the public pension system with a fundamentally private scheme managed by competing private pension fund companies." Brooks, "Social Protection and Economic Integration," 497.

59. Light, *Still Artful Work,* 96.

60. On the role of quid pro quos in European pension reform, see Bonoli, *The Politics of Pension Reform.*

61. Light, *Still Artful Work,* 98.

62. For an overview of the issue, see Dianna Granat, "Federal Workers Will Fight Social Security Coverage Plan," *Congressional Quarterly Weekly Report,* January 22, 1983, 161–162.

63. Light, *Still Artful Work,* 99.

64. Ibid., 104.

65. On this issue, see Larry DeWitt, "Taxation of Social Security Benefits,"

Research Note no. 12, Washington, DC, Social Security Administration Historian's Office, February 2001, *http://www.ssa.gov/history/taxationofbenefits.html,* accessed March 5, 2005.

66. Kingson, "Financing Social Security," 145.

67. Light, *Still Artful Work,* 182–184.

68. Berkowitz, *Robert Ball and the Politics of Social Security,* 307–316.

69. National Commission on Social Security Reform, *Report of the National Commission on Social Security Reform* (Washington, DC: U.S. Government Printing Office, 1983).

70. Ibid., 2–2.

71. Ibid., 2–8.

72. The delayed retirement credit is given for retirement *after* the normal retirement age. In 1983, that age was sixty-five.

73. Light, *Still Artful Work,* 187–188.

74. "Statement on Receiving the Recommendations of the National Commission on Social Security Reform," *Public Papers of the Presidents of the United States, Ronald Reagan, 1983* (Washington, DC: U.S. Government Printing Office, 1984), 61–62.

75. For detailed discussions about the support and the opposition to the 1983 amendments, see Light, *Still Artful Work,* and Tynes, *Turning Points in Social Security,* 173–183.

76. "Statement of James M. Pierce, National Federation of Federal Employees," *Financing Problems of the Social Security System, Hearings before the Subcommittee on Social Security of the Ways and Means Committee,* House of Representatives, 98th Cong., 1st sess. (Washington, DC: U.S. Government Printing Office, 1983), 307.

77. "Statement of Lane Kirkland, President, AFL-CIO and Member of the National Commission on Social Security Reform," *Financing Problems of the Social Security System, Hearings before the Subcommittee on Social Security of the Ways and Means Committee,* House of Representatives, 98th Cong., 1st sess. (Washington, DC: U.S. Government Printing Office, 1983), 176–189.

78. "Statement of Joseph Eichenholz, Director, Governmental and Industrial Relations, National Association of Manufacturers," *Financing Problems of the Social Security System, Hearings before the Subcommittee on Social Security of the Ways and Means Committee,* House of Representatives, 98th Cong., 1st sess. (Washington, DC: U.S. Government Printing Office, 1983), 120–124.

79. "Statement of Robert B. Thomson, Chairman of the Board, Chamber of Commerce of the United States," *Financing Problems of the Social Security System, Hearings before the Subcommittee on Social Security of the Ways and Means Committee,* House of Representatives, 98th Cong. 1st sess. (Washington, DC: U.S. Government Printing Office, 1983), 705–717.

80. "Statement of William J. Dennis, Jr., Director of Research, National Federation of Independent Business," *Financing Problems of the Social Security System, Hearings before the Subcommittee on Social Security of the Ways and Means Committee,* House of Representatives, 98th Cong., 1st sess. (Washington, DC: U.S. Government Printing Office, 1983), 125–132.

81. "Statement of Cyril F. Brickfield, Executive Director, AARP," *Financing Problems of the Social Security System, Hearings before the Subcommittee on Social Security of the Ways and Means Committee,* House of Representatives, 98th Cong., 1st sess. (Washington, DC: U.S. Government Printing Office, 1983), 184.

82. Light, *Still Artful Work,* 191.

83. *Congressional Record* (March 9, 1983): H 1945–H 2081.

84. Light, *Still Artful Work,* 200.

85. *Congressional Record* (March 23, 1983): S 2998–S 3776.

86. John A. Svahn and Mary Ross, "Social Security Amendments of 1983: Legislative History and Summary of Provisions," *Social Security Bulletin* 46, no. 7 (July 1983): 3–48.

87. "Remarks on Signing the Social Security Amendments of 1983," *Public Papers of the Presidents of the United States, Ronald Reagan, 1983* (Washington, DC: U.S. Government Printing Office, 1984), 560.

88. Kingson, "Financing Social Security," 147. On this common blame-avoidance strategy, see Weaver, "The Politics of Blame Avoidance," and Pierson, *Dismantling the Welfare State?*

89. Light, *Still Artful Work.*

90. This is especially true because it was a House Democrat (J. J. Pickle) who first proposed the amendment about retirement age.

91. Martha Derthick, *Agency under Stress: The Social Security Administration in American Government* (Washington, DC: Brookings Institution, 1990).

92. I would like to thank Larry DeWitt for his remarks concerning this issue.

93. Berkowitz, *Robert Ball and the Politics of Social Security,* 361.

94. For example, Robert Myers resigned in 1970 and Robert Ball left the SSA in 1973.

95. Daniel Béland, "Does Labor Matter? Institutions, Labor Unions, and Pension Reform in France and in the United States," *Journal of Public Policy* 21, no. 2 (May 2001): 153–172. On the role of European labor unions in contemporary Social Security politics, see David Natali and Martin Rhodes, "Trade-offs and Veto Players: Reforming Pensions in France and Italy," *French Politics* 2 (2004): 1–23, and Karen M. Anderson and Traute Meyer, "Social Democracy, Unions, and Pension Politics in Germany and Sweden," *Journal of Public Policy* 23, no. 1 (January 2003): 23–54.

96. Berkowitz, *Robert Ball and the Politics of Social Security,* 361.

97. In 1974, however, Congress failed to enact the Bolling Committee proposal, a much bolder congressional reform: Roger H. Davidson and Walter J. Oleszek, *Congress against Itself* (Bloomington: Indiana University Press, 1977).

Chapter 6. What Future for Social Security?

1. World Bank, *Averting the Old Age Crisis: Policies to Protect the Old and Promote Growth* (Washington, DC: World Bank, 1994).

2. In the case of Sweden, the development of private savings accounts within that country's social security program emerged alongside the creation of a "notional defined contribution" (NDC) plan. This plan constitutes an alternative way to calculate pension benefits designed to create a much closer link

between social security contributions and benefits. As the label implies, notional accounts exist only on paper, and the NDC plan is not fully funded but operates on a PAYGO basis. In the debate in the United States on Social Security restructuring, little attention has been paid to the NDC model, which has been implemented in several countries around the world: John B. Williamson and Matthew Williams, *The Notional Defined Contribution Model: An Assessment of the Strengths and Limitations of a New Approach to the Provision of Old Age Security,* Working Paper 2003–18 (Chestnut Hill, MA: Center for Retirement Research at Boston College, 2003).

3. Jill Quadagno, "Creating a Capital Investment Welfare State," *American Sociological Review* 64, no. 1 (1999): 1–10.

4. Daniel Béland, "Pension Reform and Financial Investment in the United States and Canada," Hamilton, SEDAP Research Paper 120, September 2004, socserv.socsci.mcmaster.ca/sedap/p/sedap120.pdf, accessed March 5, 2005.

5. On these reforms, see Patrik Marier, "Institutional Structure and Policy Change: Pension Reforms in Belgium, France, Sweden, and the UK" (Ph.D. diss., University of Pittsburgh, 2002).

6. Robin Blackburn, *Banking on Death or Investing in Life: The History and Future of Pensions* (London: Verso, 2002); Sarah Brooks, "Social Protection and Economic Integration: The Politics of Pension Reform in an Era of Capital Mobility" *Comparative Political Studies* 35, no. 5 (2002): 491–525.

7. During the 1980s and 1990s, most baby boomers were still part of the working population.

8. According to the 2004 report of the Board of Trustees, "The combined assets of the OASI and DI Trust Funds are projected to increase from $1,531 billion at the beginning of 2004, or 306 percent of annual expenditures, to $3,584 billion at the beginning of 2013, or 442 percent of annual expenditures in that year. Combined assets were projected in last year's report to rise to 309 percent of annual expenditures at the beginning of 2004, and 461 percent at the beginning of 2013. . . . Under the intermediate assumptions the combined OASI and DI Trust Funds are projected to become exhausted in 2042. For the 75-year projection period, the actuarial deficit is 1.89 percent of taxable payroll, 0.03 percentage point smaller than in last year's report." Board of Trustees, *The 2004 Annual Report of the Board of Trustees of the Federal Old-Age and Survivors Insurance and Disability Insurance Trust Funds* (Washington, DC: U.S. Government Printing Office, 2004), 2.

9. Leonid A. Gavrilov and Patrick Heuveline, "Aging of Population," in *The Encyclopedia of Population,* ed. Paul Demeny and Geoffrey McNicoll (New York: Macmillan Reference USA, 2003).

10. Yet, largely because of the decline in the fertility rate, the "consumer-to-worker support ratio" that measures the extent to which workers meet their economic needs and those of other people in society—including schoolchildren and the retired—is actually declining over time: Virginia Reno and Kathryn Olson, *Can We Afford Social Security When Baby Boomers Retire?* National Academy of Social Insurance, Social Security Brief no. 4 (Washington, DC: National Academy of Social Insurance, 1998).

11. Larry DeWitt, "Key Data from Annual Trust Fund Reports," Research Note no. 14, Washington, DC, Social Security Administration, June 2001, http://www.ssa.gov/history/trustchart.html, accessed March 5, 2005.

12. Board of Trustees, *The 2004 Annual Report of the Board of Trustees.*

13. I would like to thank Larry DeWitt for his remarks about this issue.

14. As stated above, the World Bank has contributed to the international diffusion of the financial paradigm since the early 1990s. The World Bank's *Averting the Old Age Crisis,* for example, depicted public PAYGO programs as "financially unsustainable" schemes that exacerbate intergenerational conflict as payroll taxes increase to compensate for the changing ratio of active versus inactive citizens. This organization has actively promoted pension privatization since then: François-Xavier Merrien, "The World Bank's New Social Policies: Pensions," *International Social Science Journal* 53 (2001): 537–550.

Among the numerous books propagating the financial paradigm and Social Security privatization in the United States, see Martin Feldstein, *Privatizing Social Security* (Chicago: University of Chicago Press, 1998); Peter J. Ferrara, *A New Deal for Social Security* (Washington, DC: Cato Institute National Book Network, 1998); Haeworth A. Robertson, *The Big Lie: What Every Boomer Should Know about Social Security and Medicare* (Washington, DC: Retirement Policy Institute, 1997); Michael D. Tanner, ed., *Social Security and Its Discontents: A Comprehensive Guide to Social Security Reform* (Washington, DC: Cato Institute, 2004).

15. Beyond the borders of the United States, this paradigm has enjoyed growing popularity since the 1980s, especially in Latin America and Southeast Asia: Blackburn, *Banking on Death or Investing in Life.*

16. As far as domestic issues are concerned, the American conservative movement can be divided into two main camps: libertarians and traditionalists: George H. Nash, *The Conservative Intellectual Movement in America since 1945,* 2d ed. (Wilmington, DE: Intercollegiate Studies Institute, 1996). Libertarians oppose most, if not all, forms of governmental intervention, whereas traditionalists seek to alter public policies in a way that would reinforce "traditional values." If traditionalist ideas shaped key aspects of the 1996 welfare reform, libertarians have been more active in the debate over Social Security privatization.

17. Considering the nature of Social Security financing, actuaries and other social insurance experts generally refer to "replacement rate" (proportion of the average salary being replaced) instead of "return rate" (proportion of returns on an investment). Borrowed from the financial sector, the concept of "return rate" is more common in the United States than in contemporary European debates about social insurance reform.

18. Quadagno, "Creating a Capital Investment Welfare State."

19. An exception to this pragmatism—that mixes the rhetoric of "free choice" and the idea of forced savings—is Milton Friedman's coherent yet radical stance in favor of voluntary savings as the only alternative to Social Security: "Social Security Chimeras," *New York Times,* January 11, 1999, A21.

20. By 1999, however, the support for Social Security privatization within the financial industry had already faded as concrete legislative proposals showed the administrative problems stemming from this policy alternative:

Darby Rose and Michelle Celarier, "Where's the Payoff? Wall Street Spent Millions to Promote the Privatization of Social Security—An Idea Going Increasingly Awry," *Investment Dealers Digest,* August 9, 1999, http://www.davidlanger.com/articles/misc/iddigest.8.9.99.html, accessed March 5, 2005.

21. After the Thatcher government encouraged the development of personal savings through the public pension system, approximately 2 million people lost money due to a bad financial scandal. As a consequence of mounting pressure, the government of John Major had no choice but to increase the amount of regulation. On this issue, see Steven Teles, "Pensions, Social Citizenship, and the Ubiquity of the State: The Relevance of the British Privatization Experience in the United States and Beyond," (paper presented at the workshop on Social Policy and Devolution, Brandeis University for German and European Studies, March 1999). See also Steve Idemoto, "Pension Privatization in Britain: A Boon to the Finance Industry, a Boondoggle to Workers," Economic Opportunity Institute, September 29, 2000, http://www.eoionline.org/SS-SocialInsecurityBritain.htm, accessed March 5, 2005.

22. For a personal recollection of the 1994–1996 Advisory Council, see Sylvester J. Schieber and John B. Shoven, *The Real Deal: The History and Future of Social Security* (New Haven, CT: Yale University Press, 1999).

23. Advisory Council, *Report of the 1994–1996 Advisory Council on Social Security* (Washington, DC: U.S. Government Printing Office,1997).

24. Members supporting this proposal were Robert M. Ball, Gloria T. Johnson, Thomas W. Jones, George Kourpias, and Gerald M. Shea. Moreover, Edith U. Fierst supported most provisions of the proposal.

25. The members favoring this plan were Joan T. Bok, Ann L. Combs, Sylvester J. Schieber, Fidel A. Vargas, and Carolyn L. Weaver.

26. Advisory Council, *Report of the 1994–1996 Advisory Council,* 30.

27. Robert Ball (former Social Security commissioner), interview by author, Washington, DC, May 1999. See also Robert M. Ball and Thomas N. Bethell, *Straight Talk about Social Security: An Analysis of the Issues in the Current Debate* (New York: Century Foundation/Twentieth Century Fund, 1998), 41–42.

28. The 1994–1996 Advisory Council was the last in a series initiated during the 1930s: "When the SSA was made independent of the Department of Health and Human Services in 1994, the periodical advisory councils were abolished in favor of a standing one that is not likely to have comparable significance." Martha Derthick, "The Evolving Old Politics of Social Security," in *Seeking the Center: Politics and Policymaking at the New Century,* ed. Martin A. Levin, Marc K. Landy, and Martin Shapiro (Washington, DC: Georgetown University Press, 2001), 193–214.

29. Andrew Rich and R. Kent Weaver, "Advocates and Analysts: Think Tanks and the Politicization of Expertise" in *Interest Group Politics,* 5th ed., ed. A. J. Cigler and B. A. Loomis (Washington, DC: Congressional Quarterly Press, 1998), 235–253. See also Andrew Rich, *Think Tanks, Public Policy, and the Politics of Expertise* (Cambridge: Cambridge University Press, 2004).

30. Stuart Butler and Peter Germanis, "Achieving Social Security Reform: A Leninist Strategy," *Cato Journal* 3 (1983): 547–556.

31. Steven Teles, "The Dialectics of Trust: Ideas, Finance, and Pension Privatization in the US and the UK" (paper presented at the Annual Meeting of the Association for Public Policy Analysis and Management, New York City, November 1998).

32. Daniel Béland and Alex Waddan, "From Thatcher (and Pinochet) to Clinton? Conservative Think Tanks, Foreign Models and US Pensions Reform," *Political Quarterly* 71 (2000): 202–210. One must note that the American demographic situation is relatively enviable, at least from a comparative perspective. According to the World Bank projections, the percentage of the American population over sixty will increase from 16.4 percent in 1995 to 28 percent in 2040. During the same period in Germany, for comparison, that percentage will increase from 20.6 to 37.6 percent: World Bank, *Percentage of Population over 60 Years Old (1995–2040)* (Washington, DC: World Bank, 1999).

33. John B Williamson, Diane M. Watts-Roy, and Eric R. Kingson, eds., *The Generational Equity Debate* (New York: Columbia University Press, 1999).

34. Ferrara, *A New Deal for Social Security;* Robertson, *The Big Lie.*

35. For example: Richard W. Stevenson, "Partisan Dispute over Plan to Reshape Social Security," *New York Times,* November 20, 1998, A16.

36. Although employer pension contributions have declined considerably as a share of compensation since the mid-1970s, individuals have relied more on personal savings to guarantee their future economic security: Jacob S. Hacker, "Privatizing Risk without Privatizing the Welfare State: The Hidden Politics of Social Policy Retrenchment in the United States," *American Political Science Review* 98, no. 2 (May 2004): 243–260. Fears regarding the future of Social Security have bred this financial logic: Teles, *The Dialectics of Trust.*

37. I would like to thank Eric Laursen for his insight about this issue.

38. Pension Benefit Guaranty Corporation, *Pension Insurance Data Book 2003* (Washington, DC: Pension Benefit Guaranty Corporation, 2003), 11.

39. Liberal policy experts see this trend in a different light than do conservative ones: "The precipitous decline of defined benefit pension plans and the uncertainty of 401(k)s all make Social Security's insurance provisions more important now than ever before." Marilyn Watkins, "Social Security and Public Opinion," Washington, DC, Economic Opportunity Policy Institute, March 2002, http://www.econop.org/SocialSecurity/SS-PublicOpinion2002.htm, accessed March 5, 2005.

40. Hacker, "Privatizing Risk without Privatizing the Welfare State."

41. Peter J. Ferrara and Michael D. Tanner, *Common Cents, Common Dreams: A Layman's Guide to Social Security Privatization* (Washington, DC: Cato Institute, 1998).

42. Fay Lomax Cook, Jason Barabas, and Benjamin I. Page, "Invoking Public Opinion: Policy Elites and Social Security," *Public Opinion Quarterly* 66 (2002): 235–264.

43. Paradoxically, the British experience with pension privatization and, more precisely, the Misselling Scandal demonstrated that the shift from PAYGO financing to personal accounts did not eliminate perceived governmental responsibility toward contributors and retirees: Teles, *Pensions, Social Citizenship, and the Ubiquity of the State.*

44. Ferrara and Tanner, *Common Cents, Common Dreams,* 31.

45. José Piñera, "A Real Solution to the Social Security Crisis: Testimony of José Piñera before the US House Committee on Ways and Means," Washington, DC, February 11, 1999, http://www.socialsecurity.org/pubs/testimonty/ct-jp021199.html, accessed March 5, 2005.

46. See also Béland and Waddan, "From Thatcher (and Pinochet) to Clinton?"; José Piñera, "Empowering Workers: The Privatization of Social Security in Chile," *Cato's Letter No. 10* (Washington, DC: Cato Institute, 1996). Considering major differences between U.S. Social Security and Chile's former PAYGO system, Key argued that the United States has actually little to learn from that country's not-so-positive privatization experience: Stephen J. Kay, "The Chile Con: Privatizing Social Security in South America," *American Prospect,* July-August 1997, 48–52.

47. Ferrara and Tanner, *Common Cents, Common Dreams,* 21. Two Heritage Foundation papers published in 1998 also stated that minorities such as African Americans and Hispanics should support privatization because they receive lower rates of return from Social Security: William W. Beach and Gareth G. Davis, *Social Security's Rate of Return,* Center for Data Analysis Report no. 98–01 (Washington, DC: Heritage Foundation, 1998); William W. Beach and Gareth G. Davis, *Social Security's Rate of Return for Hispanic Americans* (Washington, DC: Heritage Foundation, 1998).

48. Beach and Davis, *Social Security's Rate of Return.*

49. Ferrara and Tanner, *Common Cents, Common Dreams,* 17.

50. Ekaterina Shirley and Peter Spiegler, *The Benefits of Social Security Privatization for Women,* Project on Social Security Privatization no. 12 (Washington, DC: Cato Institute, 1998).

51. For example, see ibid; Michael Tanner, "Social Security Shortchanges African-Americans," *USA Today Magazine,* July 2001, 12–14; Tanner, *Social Security and Its Discontents.*

52. Cook, Barabas, and Page, "Invoking Public Opinion."

53. Dean Baker and Mark Weisbrot, *Social Security: The Phony Crisis* (Chicago: University of Chicago Press, 1999); Joseph White, *False Alarm* (Baltimore: Johns Hopkins University Press, 2001). Max J. Skidmore, *Social Security and Its Enemies* (Boulder, CO: Westview Press, 1999). In four 1998 and 1999 surveys, for example, "Large majorities (69, 66, 66 and 68 percent) said that Social Security would 'pay less than half of the benefits' or even 'run out of money' altogether": Cook, Barabas and Page, "Invoking Public Opinion," 249.

54. Cook, Barabas, and Page, "Invoking Public Opinion, 254–255.

55. For example: Henry J. Aaron and Robert D. Reischauer, *Countdown to Reform: The Great Social Security Debate* (New York: The Century Foundation Press, 1998); Ball and Bethell, *Straight Talk;* Peter A. Diamond and Peter R. Orszag, *Saving Social Security: A Balanced Approach* (Washington, DC: Brookings Institution Press, 2003).

56. Baker and Weisbrot, *Social Security: The Phony Crisis.*

57. For example: John R. Gist, *Social Security Reform: How Do Minorities Fare under Social Security? A Response to Two Heritage Foundation Reports* (Washington, DC: American Association of Retired Persons, 1997).

58. Ibid. In the contemporary debate on Social Security reform, labor unions support the existing PAYGO system, but their role appears relatively modest, at least compared to the situation prevailing in European countries such as France, Germany, or Sweden.

59. Christian E. Weller and Michelle Bragg, "T.I.N.A.: There Is No Alternative to Social Security," *Social Policy* 32, no. 2 (Winter 2001): 62.

60. On this issue, see Chapter 4.

61. For example: Ball and Bethell, *Straight Talk,* 61.

62. Economist Milton Friedman criticized such a cautious approach: Friedman, "Social Security Chimeras." His article illustrated the irritation of libertarian economists who seek radical reforms but perceive the reluctance of their political allies to concretely implement their financial (and individualistic) paradigm.

63. Stevenson, "Partisan Dispute." For example, Republican senator Rick Santorum embraced this rhetorical strategy during the second half of the Clinton presidency: David S. Broder, "Sharing Insights on Social Security," *Washington Post,* April 12, 1998, C07.

64. In 1994, for example, only one congressional hearing on the future of Social Security was held. Three years later, Congress held no less than ten different hearings dealing directly with that issue. After a slight decline in 1998, the number of hearings on Social Security's future increased to eighteen in 1999. The question of privatization (or partial privatization) was discussed on all occasions as well as during other hearings dealing with broader issues related to Social Security: Cook, Barabas, and Page, "Invoking Public Opinion," 244.

65. According to the official actuarial forecast of the Social Security Administration, the anticipated trust fund "exhaustion" moved farther (from 2029 in 1997 to 2034 in 1999). This situation reduced the apparent urge to fix the expected financial shortfalls of the system. R. Kent Weaver, "Public Pension Reform in the United States" in *Ageing and Pension Reform around the World,* ed. Giuliano Bonoli and Toshimitsu Shinkawa (Cheltenham, UK: Edward Elgar, 2005), 230–251.

66. Allan Sloan, "The Surplus Shell Game: How Beltway Budgeters Manipulate the Bottom Line," *Newsweek,* January 19, 1998, 28.

67. On "preemptive leadership" and the meaning of the Clinton presidency, see Stephen Skowronek, *The Politics Presidents Make: Leadership from John Adams to Bill Clinton* (Cambridge, MA: Harvard University Press, 1997).

68. Daniel Béland, Alex Waddan, and François Vergniolle de Chantal, "Third Way Social Policy: Clinton's Legacy?" *Policy and Politics* 30, no. 1 (2002): 19–30.

69. The number of presidential addresses in which Social Security is mentioned jumped from 48 in 1997 to 225 in 1998 and to 230 in 1999: Cook, Barabas, and Page, "Invoking Public Opinion," 241.

70. Richard W. Stevenson, "Lawmakers in Both Parties Are Weighing Compromise Plans to Revamp Social Security," *New York Times,* January 14, 1999, A16.

71. Derthick, "The Evolving Old Politics of Social Security," 206.

72. Ibid.

73. Right from the beginning of the 1994–1996 Advisory Council, for example, its members were told by the Clinton administration that a payroll tax

increase could not be considered as a viable reform option: Lawrence H. Thompson (principal deputy commissioner, U.S. Social Security Administration, 1993–1995), interview with author, Washington, DC, November 11, 1998.

74. Weaver, "Public Pension Reform in the United States."

75. William Clinton, "State of the Union Address" (press release, Washington, DC, White House, Office of the Press Secretary, January 19, 1999).

76. James K. Glassman, "Uncle Sam on Wall Street? No," *Washington Post,* December 8, 1998, A21.

77. As noted above, policymakers never seriously debated Social Security privatization—known at the time because of the Chilean reform enacted under the Pinochet dictatorship—in the months preceding the enactment of the 1983 amendments to the Social Security Act.

78. Derthick, "The Evolving Old Politics of Social Security," 208. During the presidential campaign, Democratic candidate Al Gore rejected partial privatization while depicting the Republican candidate's plan as a threat to Social Security's future: Kevin Sack, "Gore and Bush Trade Jabs on Pensions and Spending; Vice President Sees Threat to Future of Social Security," *New York Times,* November 2, 2000, A1. Gore's Social Security proposal was directly inspired by the "third-way" alternative that Gramlich and another member of the 1994–1996 Advisory Council had put forward.

79. The members of the commission were Daniel Patrick Moynihan (cochair), Richard Parsons (cochair), Lea Abdnor, Sam Beard, John F. Cogan, Bill Frenzel, Estelle James, Robert L. Johnson, Gwendolyn S. King, Olivia S. Mitchell, Gerald L. Parsky, Timothy J. Penny, Robert C. Pozen, Mario Rodriguez, Thomas R. Saving, and Fidel Vargas.

80. Weaver, *Public Pension Reform in the United States,* 32

81. President's Commission to Strengthen Social Security, *Strengthening Social Security and Creating Personal Wealth for All Americans* (Washington, DC: The Commission, 2001), 9.

82. Robert Kuttner, "Retirement at Risk," *American Prospect* 13, no. 17 (2002): 33.

83. George W. Bush, "State of the Union Address" (press release, Washington, DC, White House, Office of the Press Secretary, January 20, 2004).

84. Eric Laursen, "A Stealth Tax on Wages," *The Nation,* February 16, 2004 (web edition): http://www.thenation.com/doc.mhtml?i = 20040216&s = laursen.

85. Hacker, "Privatizing Risk without Privatizing the Welfare State."

86. Melissa M. Favreault, Frank J. Sammartino, and C. Eugene Steuerle, eds. *Social Security and the Family: Addressing Unmet Needs in an Underfunded System* (Washington, DC: Urban Institute, 2001).

87. Furthermore, many Democrats seem reluctant to push for benefit increases in part because they seek to avoid traditional Republican attacks about their "tax and spend" attitude. For them, *not* pushing for higher benefits represents the best possible blame avoidance strategy.

88. Congressional Budget Office, *Social Security and the Federal Budget: The Necessity of Maintaining a Comprehensive Long-Range Perspective,* Long-Range Fiscal Policy Brief no. 3 (Washington, DC: U.S. Government Printing Office, 2000).

89. Alan Greenspan, "Testimony of Chairman Alan Greenspan before the Committee on the Budget, U.S. House of Representatives," February 25, 2004, http://www.federalreserve.gov/boarddocs/testimony/2004/20040225/default.htm, accessed March 5, 2005.

90. Bush-Cheney 2004 Campaign, "A Plan for a Safer World and More Hopeful America, 2004," chapter 3, http://www.georgewbush.com/Agenda/Default.aspx, accessed March 5, 2005.

91. Commission on Presidential Debates, "The Third Bush-Kerry Presidential Debate," Temple, AZ, October 13, 2004, http://www.debates.org/pages/trans2004d.html, accessed March 5, 2005.

92. Ibid.

93. "The Third Rail," *The Economist (US Elections 2004: A Special Briefing)*, October 9–15, 2004, 18.

94. George W. Bush, "State of the Union Address" (press release, Washington, DC, White House, Office of the Press Secretary, February 2, 2005), http://www.whitehouse.gov/news/releases/2005/02/20050202-11.html, accessed on March 5, 2005.

95. For example: David Rosenbaum, "Bush Plan Poses Tough 'Safety Net' Questions," *New York Times,* January 27, 2005, A18; Tom Petruno, "Bush Plan Sharpens Retirement Investing Debate," *Los Angeles Times,* January 23, 2005, Business Desk, Pt. C; 1; Jyoti Thottam "How Would the Bush Plan Work?" *Time,* January 24, 2005, 26.

96. In the Senate after the 2004 elections, there were 55 Republicans, 44 Democrats, and one independent. In the House, there were 232 Republicans, 200 Democrats, and one independent.

97. Michael Tanner, "Election Shows that the Third Rail Is Dead," *New York Post,* November 6, 2004. For a critique of this type of argument, see Jacob S. Hacker and Paul Pierson, "Popular Fiction," *The New Republic Online,* November 8, 2004, *http://www.tnr.com/doc.mhtml?pt=wev7D5mdL8hpQdvsZw4GUB%3D%3D.*

Conclusion

1. This confirms Hacker's analysis about the role of private benefits in the United States: Jacob S. Hacker, *The Divided Welfare State: The Battle over Public and Private Social Benefits in the United States* (Cambridge: Cambridge University Press, 2002).

2. John Myles and Paul Pierson, "The Comparative Political Economy of Pension Reform," in *The New Politics of the Welfare State,* ed. Paul Pierson (Oxford: Oxford University Press, 2001), 305–333.

3. R. Kent Weaver, "Public Pension Reform in the United States" in *Ageing and Pension Reform around the World,* ed. Giuliano Boroli and Toshimitsu Shinkawa (Cheltenham, UK: Edward Elgar, 2005), 230–251.

Afterword

I would like to thank Edward D. Berkowitz, John Myles, and Jill Quadagno for their comments on this afterword.

1. George W. Bush, "Speech to Social Security Conversation in New York," Greece, NY: May 24, 2005.

2. Cited in Julie Kosterlitz, "The Ownership Society," *National Journal* 36, no. 4, (2004): 230–237 (231).

3. Jonathan Weisman, "House, Senate to Delay Action on Restructuring Social Security: Private Accounts and Solvency Remain in Limbo on Hill," *Washington Post,* July 15, 2005, A9.

4. For example: Jonathan Weisman, "GOP Agenda in Congress May Be at Risk Katrina's Costs, High Fuel Prices Working against More Tax Cuts," *Washington Post,* September 4, 2005, A2.

5. R. Kent Weaver, "Public Pension Reform in the United States" in *Ageing and Pension Reform around the World: Evidence from Eleven Countries,* ed. Giuliano Bonoli and Toshimitsu Shinkawa (Cheltenham: Edward Elgar, 2005): 230–251.

6. Board of Trustees, *2006 Annual Report of the Board of Trustees of the Federal Old-Age and Survivors Insurance and Disability Insurance Trust Funds* (Washington, DC: U.S. Government Printing Office, 2006).

7. Richard Morin and Dan Balz, "Confidence in GOP is at New Low in Poll: Democrats Favored to Address Issues," *Washington Post,* May 17, 2006, A1.

8. On recent pension reforms enacted in these countries and elsewhere see Bonoli and Shinkawa, *Ageing and Pension Reform around the World,* and John Myles and Paul Pierson, "The Comparative Political Economy of Pension Reform" in *The New Politics of the Welfare State,* ed. Paul Pierson (Oxford: Oxford University Press, 2001): 305–333. For a conservative perspective on foreign Social Security reforms see Sylvester J. Schieber, "Paying for It," *Wilson Quarterly* 30, no. 2 (2006): 57–61.

9. For example: Jill Quadagno, "Creating a Capital Investment Welfare State," *American Sociological Review,* 64, no. 1 (1999): 1–10. See also Theodore R. Marmor and Jerry L. Mashaw, "Understanding Social Insurance: Fairness, Affordability, and the 'Modernization' of Social Security and Medicare," *Health Affairs* 25, no. 3 (2006): 114–134.

10. Margaret Thatcher, *House of Commons: Hansard 80/1007-12* (London: June 13, 1985).

11. Steven Teles, "The Dialectics of Trust: Ideas, Finance, and Pension Privatization in the US and the UK" (paper presented at the annual meeting of the Association for Public Policy Analysis and Management, November 1998).

12. Ray Forrest and Alan Murie, *Selling the Welfare State: The Privatization of Public Housing* (London: Routledge, 1988).

13. Paul Pierson and R. Kent Weaver, "Imposing Losses in Pension Policy" in *Do Institutions Matter? Government Capabilities in the United States and Abroad,* ed. R. Kent Weaver and Bert A. Rockman (Washington, DC, Brookings Institution, 1993): 110–150.

14. Andrea Louise Campbell, *How Policies Make Citizens: Senior Citizen Activism and the American Welfare State* (Princeton, NJ: Princeton University Press, 2003); Paul Pierson, *Dismantling the Welfare State? Reagan, Thatcher, and the Politics of Retrenchment* (Cambridge: Cambridge University Press, 1994).

15. Pierson and Weaver, "Imposing Losses in Pension Policy," 132. Even the

British treasury opposed the plan, for which "transition costs" proved excessively high: Giuliano Bonoli, *The Politics of Pension Reform: Institutions and Policy Change in Western Europe* (Cambridge: Cambridge University Press, 2000), 72.

16. The number of SERPS participants dropped from 10.9 to 6.5 million between 1987 and 1994. At the end of that period, the number of workers who had diverted their payroll tax contributions to a personal savings account reached 5.7 million: Bonoli, *The Politics of Pension Reform,* 80.

17. On this issue see Alan Jacobs and Steven Teles, "The Perils of Market Making: The Case of British Pension Reform" in *Creating Competitive Markets,* ed. Marc K. Landy, Martin A. Levin and Martin Shapiro (Washington, DC: Brookings Institution Press, 2006). For a broad discussion about the consequences of pension privatization in Britain see John Williamson, *Social Security Privatization: Lessons from the United Kingdom* (Boston: Center for Retirement Research at Boston College, November 2000).

18. Jacob S. Hacker, "Privatizing Risk without Privatizing the Welfare State: The Hidden Politics of Social Policy Retrenchment in the United States," *American Political Science Review* 98 (2004): 243–260.

19. Ironically, the decline of defined benefit pensions in the private sector means that the federal government might have to play an even greater role in shielding the elderly population against poverty and economic insecurity.

20. John Myles, "The Social Security debate: What would the U.S. do if it were Europe?" (paper presented at the annual meeting of the American Sociological Association, Philadelphia, August 13, 2005).

21. American Political Science Association (Task Force on Inequality and American Democracy), *American Democracy in the Age of Rising Inequality* (Washington, DC: American Political Science Association, 2004).

22. In 2005, younger workers were more inclined to support the implementation of private savings accounts yet they also showed greater distrust towards President Bush and his policies: Jonathan Weisman, "Skepticism of Bush's Social Security Plan Is Growing," *Washington Post,* March 15, 2005, A1.